Conversations with M. F. K. Fisher

Literary Conversations Series
Peggy Whitman Prenshaw
General Editor

Conversations
with M. F. K. Fisher

Edited by
David Lazar

University Press of Mississippi
Jackson and London

95 94 93 92   4 3 2 1

The paper in this book meets the guidelines for permanence and durability
of the Committee on Production Guidelines for Book Longevity of the Council
on Library Resources.

Library of Congress Cataloging-in-Publication Data

Fisher, M. F. K. (Mary Frances Kennedy), 1908–1992.
    Conversations with M.F.K. Fisher / edited by David Lazar.
      p.   cm. — (Literary conversations series)
    Includes index.
    "Books by M.F.K. Fisher"—
    ISBN 0-87805-595-9 (cloth). — ISBN 0-87805-596-7 (paper)
    1. Fisher, M. F. K. (Mary Frances Kennedy), 1908–1992—Interviews.
    2. Authors, American—20th century—Interviews.   3. Food writers—
    United States—Interviews.   4. Gastronomy.   I. Lazar, David, 1945–
    II. Title.   III. Series.
    PS3511.I7428Z464   1992
    641'.092—dc20   92-28485
                                                                CIP

British Library Cataloging-in-Publication data available

Books by M. F. K. Fisher

Serve It Forth. New York: Viking, 1937; San Francisco: North Point, 1982.

Consider the Oyster. New York: Duell, Sloan & Pearce, 1941; San Francisco: North Point, 1988.

How to Cook a Wolf. New York: Duell, Sloan & Pearce, 1942; San Francisco: North Point, 1988.

The Gastronomical Me. New York: Duell, Sloan & Pearce, 1943; San Francisco: North Point, 1989.

Here Let Us Feast: A Book of Banquets. New York: Viking, 1946; San Francisco: North Point, 1989.

Not Now But Now. New York: Viking, 1947; San Francisco: North Point, 1982.

An Alphabet for Gourmets. New York: Viking, 1949; San Francisco: North Point, 1989.

The Physiology of Taste, by Jean Anthelme Brillat-Savarin. Translation. The Limited Editions Club; The Heritage Press, 1949; New York: Knopf, 1971; New York: Harcourt Brace Jovanovich, 1978.

The Art of Eating (includes *Serve It Forth, Consider the Oyster, How to Cook a Wolf, The Gastronomical Me,* and *An Alphabet for Gourmets*). Cleveland: World, 1954; New York: Vintage, 1976; New York: Collier, 1990.

A Cordiall Water: A Garland of Odd and Old Receipts to Assuage the Ills of Man and Beast. Boston: Little, Brown, 1961; San Francisco: North Point, 1981.

The Story of Wine in California. Berkeley: University of California Press, 1962.

Map of Another Town. Boston: Little, Brown, 1964.

The Cooking of Provincial France. New York: Time-Life Books, 1968.

With Bold Knife and Fork. New York: Putnam, 1969; New York Putnam, 1979.

Among Friends. New York: Knopf, 1971; San Francisco: North Point, 1983.

Not a Station But a Place (with Judith Clancy). San Francisco: Synergistic Press, 1979.

As They Were. New York: Knopf, 1982; New York: Vintage, 1984.

Two Towns in Provence: Map of Another Town and a Considerable Town. New York: Vintage, 1983.

Sister Age. New York: Knopf, 1983; New York: Vintage, 1984.

The Food Book (with Lynn Newberry). Goodheart, 1986.

Dubious Honors. San Francisco: North Point, 1988.

The Boss Dog. Covello, Ca.: Yolla Bolly Press, 1990; San Francisco, North Point, 1991.

Long Ago in France; The Years in Dijon. New York: Prentice Hall, 1991.

Contents

Introduction

The interview is one of those pseudo-literary nonfictional forms that has entered our literary discourse through a back door, quietly, unselfconsciously. Not having a sense of its place or having to answer many questions about its function, it hangs around as a kind of literary indentured servant: instrumental to the others in the house, but ultimately unrequited.

Etymologically, interview derives from "entrevue," a form of entrevoir, to have a glimpse of, as well as "s'entrevoir," to see each other. We can see early, unnamed versions of the interview in the Socratic dialogues, the conversations of Satan with God in the first chapters of Job, the imaginary interviews of Margery Kemp, but in its semantic infancy, the interview referred to a meeting of great moment, between great personages, prince to prince, king to king, a ceremonial occasion, before it degraded to person to person. By 1626, Bacon can say, in *New Atlantis,* that it has been "ordained that none doe intermarry, or contract, until a Moneth be past from their first inter-view."

In the eighteenth century, the form began to form, formally, into its modern variations, as the enlightment and the middle class informally conspired to value individual speech. We see this in the frequently fictional interviews in Defoe's *Review,* Addison and Steele's *Tatler* and *Spectator,* and we see the essence of the modern literary interview as journalist or acolyte eliciting information from an established literary figure in Boswell and Johnson. The seminal Q & A:

> **Johnson:** Why do you write down my sayings?
> **Boswell:** I write them down when they are good.

In the nineteenth century, the interview entered the exclusive province of newspapers and tabloids, notably the *Nation,* the *New York Daily News,* and the *New York Herald;* by the 1860s and 70s, the practice was ubiquitous and the interview became the object of criticism for its predictability. The invisible talking heads of politicians

and newsworthy respondents represented abuses of the form, some
felt, using the interview for political gain, spouting predictably mealy-
mouthed crowd-pleasing responses, or giving the fifteen-minutes-
famous (or infamous) too much space-time for their place on the
continuum of important contributions. In "An Encounter with an
Interviewer" in 1875, Mark Twain writes, "You know, it is the custom
now to interview any man who has become notorious."

In the twentieth century, *The New Yorker* was largely responsible
for the development of the profile—part feature story, part interview—and the literary interview was more fully and exclusively
developed by the *Paris Review* and other literary journals, sometimes
in the form of conversations: the interview between equals, the
literary equivalent of the original entrevues.

All of which leads us to the present collection of profiles, literary
interviews, oracular solicitations, and conversations. The variety
of material included here on M. F. K. Fisher mirrors the relatively
unformed place she has held in American letters. So, too, some
of the repeated questions, information, and citations (notably the
Fadiman and Auden comments) are moments in the reassertion of
Fisher's importance as woman of letters, or the constant rediscovery
of her as such. Many of the selections begin, as profiles will, by
mentioning her beauty, her house (especially her baroque bathroom), and what libations Fisher served forth. The approaches
reflected in this volume mostly fall into two camps: the treatment of
M.F.K. Fisher as a food writer, or the suggestion that such a designa-
tion is narrow and uninformed (the former seen in Nancy Scott's
profile title: "Grand Dame of Gastronomy," and the latter aptly
summarized in the title of the National Public Radio interview:
"M.F.K. Fisher Is More Than a Cookbook Author"). *Look* magazine,
in 1942, privileges Fisher's work by noting that it is not "relegated to
the women's pages," and then, as though afraid of the radical and
dire implications of Fisher's literary cross-dressing, note that "M.F. is
even more domestic than most career women."

Genre confusions and the implications of content are hardly
unprecedented in the politics of literary reputation, but as a woman
writer who has used food as a central subject and metaphor, one can
see the pigeon-hole into which Fisher has fallen, and the earnest
attempts to "rescue" her occasionally make one wish the energy

directed toward her salvation or resurrection were allowed to flow into wider channels and more interesting directions. In short, one hears Auden's sentence about Fisher's importance as American prose writer ad nauseam, and certain Fisher anecdotes and self-definitions ("I could have written about anything") more than one might like. But this is partially endemic to interview chronologies; certain stories and themes become canonized and self-canonized, and are cast and recast according to the tone, style, ideology, and aggressiveness of the interviewer. What is especially strange is that in the space of fifteen years, Fisher's reputation had progressed from relatively unknown in Nancy Scott's fine and thorough overview in 1976, to Joan Chatfield-Taylor's talk of avid fans in 1979, to Ruth Reichl's acknowledgement of Fisher as a literary star in 1981, through the spate of eighties interviews and articles which take her reputation for granted at the same they are trying to salvage her true importance.

From the time Lucius Beebe responded forlornly to the fact that M. F. K. Fisher was a woman, and not an Oxbridgian man, in the late nineteen thirties, to Jeannette Ferrary's book *Between Friends* (from which "The Fatherland" is here included), Fisher has weathered the vagaries of iconic representations. Again, some of this is endemic in the literary world, but some of this can be traced to Fisher herself, her persona on the pages she has written and on the pages where she has been transcribed. Certainly, she has staked out food as her subject matter, and despite the fact that she nearly always transcends this subject, she almost always includes it centrally. And a significant part of Fisher's career as a free-lance writer was for magazines such as *Food and Wine* and *Gourmet,* or responding to commissioned pieces with occasional premises revolving around food. But as she says in several of the interviews, as a nonacademic writer whose books sold poorly, she was under the duress of providing for the essential requirements of food and shelter, as well as exploring their spiritual and emotional resonances.

M. F. K. Fisher is mostly quite consistent in the material included here, although she will correct or complicate her sentiments mid-sentence. She is a fluid, writerly speaker. This is partly because her written voice has been so honed through prolific free-lance work, partly because her essayist's mind never stops writing. As she says to Meg McConahey, "I'm writing now in my head." In response to a Bill

Moyers' question about the loveliness of a certain paragraph, Fisher responds, "I said it to myself. Then I just put it on paper." Listening to Fisher, one is reminded of the uncanny ability of Henry James to dictate, reminded that at a certain point highly productive writers enter a relationship with language that blurs the distinction between writing and speech. Fisher's responses to questions are as elegant and poised as her essays.

Again, in Fisher's responses to oft-repeated questions, one feels the loss of spontaneity, or of fluid associations that the best interviews elicit. M. F. K. Fisher almost always speaks authoritatively. She does not, however, enter into motivational muddles when she speaks autobiographically, nor does she, when asked her opinion about moral or aesthetic questions, indulge in the rhetoric of uncertainty very much, despite the constant self-effacement of her achievements as a writer. M. F. K. Fisher speaks from a strong ego, evident in her unapologetic tone, sometimes presenting herself as so natural a writer that she doesn't need to revise laboriously, but also, as suggested above, presenting the obverse interpretation, that she isn't a writer at all.

Nevertheless, in this age to be "judgmental" is a confusingly pejorative label, Fisher, though tolerant on most questions of lifestyles, does not mute her judgements on certain central questions of life: how to distinguish self-indulgence from honest pleasure, how we might live and love more fully. She is the least pusillanimous respondent imaginable, predictable only when the questions are too prefabricated, too general for her to resist the reassertion of strongly held beliefs. One notes, in Bill Moyers' interview, for example, a cantankerous quality rising up. She is quite ill by this point, of course, with a strain of Parkinson's Disease, but one also senses a desire to avoid the broad pronouncements that are sometimes solicited.

Frequently, the aphoristic poise of Fisher's speech gives her a gnomic quality, which clearly has fascinated interviewers and readers. Her power, personally and verbally, is born of control in an age of prolixity. Fisher neither confesses, nor apologizes. She will rarely argue a point, preferring instead to respond and shut down. One could argue that, epistemologically, this bespeaks a certain skepticism, or stoicism; Fisher frequently refers to herself as "detached," and one feels that her opinions have been created out of an earlier dialectic with self and significant others. In the formal, public sense represented here, she mostly does not or has come to not believe in open-ended exchanges (again, I must tiresomely stress the con- straints of the short-form interview, however). In most cases, she converses generously, albeit strategically. Here is an anticonfessional strategy of self-revelation. I asked Ms. Fisher (all who are even mar- ginally accepted with friendship are admonished to call her Mary Frances) why she had never written of her husband Dillwyn Parrish's suicide, or her brother's. Her response was that these were private events that she never found a way to use. Bert Greene writes, "we have never discussed any truly intimate aspect of her life . . . she would simply change the subject or smile enigmatically."

There is a leitmotif or sub-theme, in Fisher's work and some of these interviews, a hidden essay on the nature of detachment. In an aside about travelling in Ted Gill's early piece, Fisher speaks of "withdrawing to the vanishing point from the consciousness of people one is with. . . ." To David Eames, she says: "Over the years, I have taught myself, and have been taught, to be a stranger. A stranger usually has the normal five senses, perhaps especially so, ready to protect and nourish him." And in my own interview, Fisher says that she has always been "something of a ghost." These images emerge most forcefully in *The Gastronomical Me,* published in 1943, in the shock of essays surrounding Dillwyn Parrish's terminal decline, and in the ugliness and horror engulfing almost everyone the couple meets on ships to and from Europe in the late thirties.

Fisher's detachment leads to projections, on occasions, or a kind of cultishness that seeks to turn Fisher into something other than an extraordinary writer: a sage, a prophet, "a white witch" in Betty Fussell's pagan-goddess Fisher-Queen profile. Fisher responds to this in annoyance on several occasions. She tells Elizabeth Hawes that, "I'm becoming marbelized," and complains to Joan Nathan that, "Some people write that I have influenced them greatly. I think I could say that about a lot of people, too. Whoever wrote the alphabet influenced me enormously." Fisher consistently tries to demystify herself and the process of writing. When Elizabeth Usher Henderson questions her about women's writing and "configurations of space," Fisher responds that she finds the abstraction "esoteric and weird." About her most common apotheosis, she tells *Publishers Weekly,*

"I get pretty peeved about being called things like 'past mistress of gastronomical pornography' and so on. I believe in living fully, as long as we seem to be meant to live at all."

Fisher also has the ability to make certain interviewers feel singled out, part of the inner circle. We see this in the interviews with Bert Greene, Jeannette Ferrary, and the editor. There is, sometimes between the lines, sometimes in them, a note of uncertainty on the interviewer/friend's part, a confusion about the combination of affective generosity and reserve. This will happen, of course, when writers with small reputations approach or are drawn in by writers later and larger in their careers, but it is hard to separate these more general or situational notes from M. F. K. Fisher's particular personality.

Questions of gender appear repeatedly. The stories of her early misidentification as a man because of her intialled identity, for example. In explaining Fisher to her friends, Nancy Scott tells us, "I say, not he. She." There is the occasional irony of an interviewer attempting a more conventionally feministic reading of Fisher than she will bear, while extolling her beauty to the readers. Comments on Fisher's allure show up from the outset. Orville Prescott comments in a 1942 *New York Times* book review that, "judging from her picture, Mrs. Fisher is one cook who has grounds to be very confident indeed without a kitchen mirror." His closing remark, no less. These never go away, and are, in fact, standard profile fodder.

Strangely, although food shows up as a subject in Fisher's work, and in questions of genre and reputation, the issue of food and eating as feminist issues do not. Perhaps one reason for this is that food is so healthy, so unchained to disorders in Fisher's own universe. In Kim Chernin's *The Hungry Self: Woman, Eating & Identity,* there is scant mention of Fisher, but it is telling. Chernin writes that Fisher is always "sensitive . . . to the culinary dimensions of existence." Whereas in the passage from *The Gastronomical Me* that Chernin discusses the relationship of women to food is autobiographically representative of earlier "turmoil," Fisher, Chernin seems to rightly suggest, is rather healthy and resolved herself in the contemporary position she wrote from, and writes from. So while her work has feminist implications for the relationship of women to food, she herself is difficult to use as any type of problematic exemplar. Perhaps it is time she were presented as exemplar of possibilities.

On other issues, Fisher emerges as a prefeminist, or protofeminist, or unconventional feminist in the interviews, depending on the review, and one's own political angle of vision. Clearly, she resists too close or formal an identification with feminism. To David Eames, she says, "I never thought of myself as part of a movement, just a liberated person." Fisher constantly resists the elimination of gender distinctions, an unresolved feminist issue. She asks Ruth Reichl, "Why not train women to recognize their own strengths," and we hear of her essay, "Why We Need a Woman's Party," in *Newsweek*. Asked about gender differences by Bill Moyers, she makes no bones about her the essential hierarchy of genders: "I like men very much. I think I would rather be with women, though, than men. I think men are less interesting than women in general. They are more limited. They don't feel the same pain. They don't have the same endurance. They don't know the same things women know." As she is wont to do, however, Fisher continues to complicate her position by asserting that "women are terrible politicians. Most women become strident, you know. They raise their voices. I don't like that." While we might wince at the old anti-feminist buzzword, we can see M. F. K. Fisher defining the measure of her powers as sensitivity, self-control, an unrestrained voicing of opinion. She has lived as she wanted, more or less, and said what she wanted. There is no mistaking the fierce power she can project, or how compellingly attractive this is, in itself, and as a paradigm of possibilities for women, for anyone.

It is much to be desired that in the years ahead, Auden's estimation of Fisher can be replaced by a more general agreement on the importance of her work, that we won't have to hear that quotation anymore, and that we will be able to listen less distractedly to Fisher herself: "One has to live, you know. You can't just die from grief or anything. You don't die. You might as well eat well, have a good glass of wine, a good tomato. Better that than no wine and a bad tomato, or no crust of bread. Since we must live, we might as well live well. Don't you think?"

       *   *   *

It is the policy of the Literary Conversations series that none of the work included be edited, other than for the correction of infrequent factual errors. The selections in this volume are chronologically skewed toward the last twenty years. The reasons for this are a combination of the time it took for Fisher's reputation to coalesce, the fact that her books were not consistently in print, and the time Fisher spent abroad in the thirties and fifties. Not a single interview is from a literary journal; to my knowledge, there are none. The bulk are from large newspapers and trade magazines, and clearly these formats determine the form of the profiles, and limit the scope of the interviews proper. But, it is hoped, they are redeemed by the voice of M. F. K. Fisher which emerges from occasional dross and gloss. It is her way of thinking, the elegance of mind behind the elegant prose, her urgency and restraint, dignity and contrariety, in short the clear connection between the form and content of life and art which speak to us. We feel, I hope, grateful for the glimpse, and wishing—even those of us who have talked with her—for the conversation to continue.

I would like to gratefully acknowledge the individuals and organizations who helped make this collection possible, specifically and generally: Nancy Shapiro and Teachers and Writers Collaborative for the generous grant that enabled me to spend a month with M. F. K. Fisher in Glen Ellen; a Baker Fund Award from Ohio University helped to complete the work for this volume expeditiously; Julie Innis, for her excellent and determined sleuthing and moral support; Phillip Lopate, Lois Parkinson Zamora, Willard Spiegelman, Cathleen Calbert; and certainly Mary Frances Kennedy Fisher for her generosity, for her work.

Chronology

1908 *July 3* Mary Frances Kennedy is born in Albion, Michigan, the first child of Rex Brenton Kennedy and Edith Oliver Holbrook.

1910 Rex Kennedy sells share of an Albion newspaper and the family moves to Whittier, California. Anne Kennedy is born (sister).

1912 Rex Kennedy becomes editor, later owner and publisher of *The Whittier News*.

1914–25 MFKF attends public school in Whittier.

1917 Norah Kennedy is born (sister).

1919 David Kennedy is born (brother).

1925–27 MFKF attends the Bishop's School, a prepatory boarding school.

1927–28 MFKF attends Illinois College in Jacksonville; and Whittier College.

1928–29 MFKF studies at Occidental College and the University of California, where she meets Alfred Young Fisher.

1929 MFKF marries Alfred Young Fisher. They move to Dijon, Aix-en-Provence, where Al Fisher begins doctoral studies at the University of Dijon. MFKF also attends.

1931 MFKF receives the baccalaureate from the University of Dijon.

1932   After Al Fisher receives his doctorate, he and MFKF
        return to the United States. Al Fisher begins teaching at
        Occidental College, and MFKF works in a picture-framing
        shop. She begins to write essays on cooking and food,
        inspired by reading cookbooks in the Los Angeles Public
        Library. MFKF meets Dillwyn Parrish.

1934   MFKF's first paid publication, "Pacific Village," a descrip-
        tion of the development of Laguna Beach, is published in
        Westways.

1936   Separation from Al Fisher; MFKF, Dillwyn Parrish, and
        Parrish's mother sail to Europe.

1937   *Serve It Forth* published by Viking; MFKF divorces Fisher.

1938   MFKF marries Dillwyn Parrish. MFKF and Parrish buy a
        home and live in Vevey, Switzerland.

1939   MFKF, writing as Victoria Berne, and Parrish collaborate
        on a novel, *Touch and Go,* published by Harper. MFKF
        and Parrish return to U. S. and live in Hemet, Ca. Parrish
        is diagnosed as terminally ill with Buerger's Disease, a
        circulatory ailment, and has to have his leg amputated.

1940   MFKF and Parrish make their last trip to Europe, going to
        Switzerland to obtain medication for Parrish and close up
        their house with war approaching; she writes about this in
        the chapter "The Flaw" in *The Gastronomical Me.*

1941   Dillwyn Parrish dies, a suicide, after struggling for years
        with terminal cancer. *Consider the Oyster* is published by
        Duell, Sloan & Pearce.

1942   MFKF lives in Guadalajara, Mexico, with her sister Norah,
        her brother David, and David's newly-wed wife Sarah,
        who is pregnant. Returning to the U. S., David commits

suicide, the day before he is to report to the army. *How to Cook a Wolf* is published by Duell, Sloan & Pearce.

1942–43   MFKF works as a screenwriter at Paramount.

1943   *The Gastronomical Me* is published by Duell, Sloan & Pearce. MFKF gives birth to first child, Anne.

1945   MFKF meets and marries Donald Friede, whom she has met in New York. They live in Hemet.

1946   *Here Let Us Feast: A Book of Banquets* is published by Viking. MFKF and Friede move to St. Helena, Ca., in wine country. MFKF gives birth to second daughter, Mary (Kennedy).

1947   *Not Now But Now* is published by Viking.

1947–49   Work on translation of Brillat-Savarin's *Physiology of Taste*

1949   *An Alphabet for Gourmets* is published by Viking. Translation of *The Physiology of Taste*, by Jean Anthelme Brillat-Savarin is published by Limited Editions Club and Heritage Press.

1951   MFKF and Donald Friede divorce.

1953   Rex Kennedy dies. MFKF moves to St. Helena, Ca.

1954   *The Art of Eating* (including *Serve It Forth, Consider the Oyster, How to Cook a Wolf, The Gastronomical Me,* and *An Alphabet for Gourmets*) is published by World. MFKF is in Provence for almost a year with daughters.

1961   *A Cordiall Water: A Garland of Odd and Old Receipts to Assuage the Ills of Man and Beast* is published by Little,

Brown. MFKF is in France to research *The Cooking of Provincial France* for Time-Life.

1962   *The Story of Wine in California* is published by University of California Press.

1964   *Map of Another Town* is published by Little Brown. MFKF spends six months in Piney Woods, Mississippi, teaching black children.

1965   MFKF's sister Anne dies of cancer. MFKF travels to Paris.

1968   *The Cooking of Provincial France* is published by Time-Life Books.

1968–69   "Gastronomy Recalled," MFKF's column in *The New Yorker.*

1969   *With Bold Knife and Fork* is published by Putnam.

1970   MFKF sells her house in St. Helena, travels to France with Norah. Moves to house she has designed and built on the land of her friend David Bouverie, in Glen Ellen, Ca.

1971   *Among Friends* published by Knopf; *The Physiology of Taste* republished by Knopf.

1973   MFKF and Norah travel to Provence and Marseilles.

1976   *The Art of Eating* is republished by Vintage. MFKF and Norah travel to Aix-en-Provence.

1978   MFKF honored by the Dames d'Escoffier in New York. She and Norah visit Japan, return to Aix. *The Physiology of Taste* is republished by Harcourt Brace.

1979   *Not a Station But a Place* (with Judith Clancy) is published by Synergistic Press.

1981–89   *Consider the Oyster, How to Cook a Wolf, The Gas-*
           tronomical Me, Here Let Us Feast, Not Now But Now,
           Among Friends, and *A Cordiall Water* are individually
           republished by North Point.

1982   *As They Were* is published by Knopf.

1983   *Two Towns in Provence: Map of Another Town and a*
           Considerable Town is published by Vintage. *Sister Age* is
           published by Knopf. MFKF is given Robert Kirsch Award
           by *Los Angeles Times.*

1984   *As They Were* and *Sister Age* are published by Vintage.

1986   *The Food Book* (with Lynn Newberry) is published by
           Goodheart.

1988   *Dubious Honors* is published by North Point.

1990   *The Art of Eating* is republished by Collier.

1991   *The Boss Dog* is published by North Point. *Long Ago in*
           France; The Years in Dijon is published by Prentice Hall.
           MFKF is elected to American Academy and National
           Institute of Arts and Letters.

1992   MFKF dies on 22 June.

Conversations with M. F. K. Fisher

Career Woman—1942 Style

Look Magazine/1942

From *Look* magazine, 28 July, 1942, vol. 6, pp. 24 +.

When Mary Frances Kennedy Fisher published a sharp-witted book on food called *How to Cook a Wolf* (the wolf at your door) extraordinary things began to happen.

The book was reviewed in literary columns, instead of being relegated to the women's pages. It provoked learned Clifton Fadiman, star of "Information Please" and literary critic of the *New Yorker,* to say: "M. F. K. Fisher writes about food as others do about love, only rather better." And Paramount Studios, to which she is currently attached as a writer, so admired a picture of her that they sent a talent scout to hire her as an actress.

The talent-scout episode was the most flattering of all these developments, for M. F. (as friends call her) makes no pretense of being a glamour girl. She is a career woman and she likes being one. Beside *How to Cook a Wolf,* she has written two other food books— *Consider the Oyster* and *Serve it Forth.* She has done articles on food for magazines, as well as short stories and a romantic novel. But she is typical of the new-era career woman because she believes that, the more charm and femininity a woman has, the better her chances for success.

Like more than half America's career women, in business, professions or the arts, M. F. has been married. Her husband was the late Dillwyn Parrish, painter and novelist. Like 76 per cent of America's outstanding women, she achieved success in one of five fields— writing, education, art, social work, music. Unlike more than half of America's married career women, who average 2.5 children apiece, she has none. But she thinks women with children are the happiest and feels career women make excellent mothers because they keep mentally alive and young.

M. F. is even more domestic than most career women, 60 per cent of whom do their own housekeeping. She loves to cook for friends at her 90-acre ranch, 100 miles east of Los Angeles. (Like 63 per cent of married career women, she owns her own home.) She has an herb garden and a vineyard and works hard in them. And the low California ranch house vividly reflects her warm personality and home-making talents.

M. F. was born in Albion, Mich., in 1908, and cooked from the time she was old enough to hold a mixing spoon. But, when she was 20, she spent a year in Dijon, France, a little fishing village where everybody cooked, from the street sweeper to the mayor. M. F. watched, listened—and ate. Right there was born her special enthusiasm.

There's only one trouble with being a food authority. M. F. gets scores of fan letters, many from celebrities. They usually end, "We'd love to have you come to dinner but we wouldn't dare ask you." "So," says M. F. wistfully, "they don't. And I eat a lonely rye crisp at home."

That Wolf at Your Front Door

Ted Gill/1942

From *The San Francisco Chronicle,* 17 August, 1942. © 1942
Associated Press. Reprinted by permission.

LOS ANGELES, Aug. 16 (Wide World)—If and when hard times
come a-knocking at your door, you may want M. F. K. Fisher's
choice recipes on "How to Cook a Wolf!"

You'll find them published in her book of that title—highly entertaining and filled with gastronomical delights the likes of which
you've probably never sampled.

Although sprinkled intermittently with unusual and ritzy recipes,
such as "fruits aux sept" with ten kinds of fruits and seven kinds of
liqueurs, her book mostly treats with balanced menus so economical
that one, which she calls a whole-grain sludge or mush, is designed
to keep you alive and hearty on 50 cents a week.

A firm believer of menus balanced by the day and not for each
meal of the day, Mrs. Fisher, who has studied and dined with some of
the most famous gourmets, takes loud exception to many of the
nation's food editors who recommend elaborate, multi-dish menus
for each meal in order that each should contain a properly balanced
diet.

"In the first place, not all people need or want three meals a day.
Many of them feel better with two, one and one-half, or five.

"Next, 'balance' is something that depends entirely on the individual.

"One man, because of his chemical set-up, may need many pro-
teins. Another may have to live with what grace he can on salads and
cooked squash.

"Of course, where countless humans are herded together, as in
military camps or schools or prisons, it is necessary to strike what is
ironically called the happy medium.

"In this case, what kills the least number with the most ease is the
chosen way."

Mrs. Fisher firmly recommends that instead of combining a lot of dull and sometimes actively hostile foods into one routine meal after another, three times a day, year after year—try the simple plan of balancing the day, not each meal in the day.

"Your plan," she says, "includes the meal of starches, one of vegetables, or fruits, and one of meat.

"For breakfast, for instance, eat piles of toast, generously buttered, and a bowl of honey or jam, and a drink. And on cold mornings you can have all you want of hot cereal, possibly with maple syrup and melted butter instead of milk and sugar. Or put some raisins or chopped dates in it.

"For lunch, make an enormous salad, in the summer, or a casserole of vegetables, or a heartening and ample soup. That is all you need, if there is enough of it.

"And for dinner, have a cheese souffle and a light salad or a broiled rare steak and a beautiful platter of sliced herb-besprinkled ripe tomatoes.

"That with some red wine or ale if you like it, and good coffee afterward, is a meal that may startle your company at first with its simplicity, but will satisfy their hunger and their sense of fitness and of balance, all at once.

"And later, when they begin to think of the automatic extravagance of most of our menus, and above all of the ghastly stupid monotony of them, they, too, will cast off many of their habits and begin, like you, to eat the way they want to, instead of the way their parents and grandparents taught them."

Mrs. Fisher believes that "when we get too deeply into the subjects of vitamins and calories and a lot of other high-sounding terms, we sometimes go off the deep end."

Born Mary Francis Kennedy in Albion, Mich., the twice-married but now widowed author moved as a child to California where her father became a newspaper publisher at Whittier. She early took a decided liking to culinary arts, but didn't make an intensive study of them until a lengthy sojourn to Europe, which ended just before the war's outbreak.

Then she decided to write her first book. She called it *Serve It Forth,* a history of gastronomy. It also included some ancient if fantastic concoctions such as a mixture of coffee, mustard, and champagne liked by Frederick the Great. Then followed *Consider the Oyster,* a book on how and why and when to eat the succulent bi-valves.

In *How to Cook a Wolf,* her current success, striking Mrs. Fisher, who has a figure that protests her interest in food, also tells the reader under these chapter headings: "How to Catch the Wolf," "How to Boil Water," "How Not to Boil an Egg," "How to Drink the Wolf."

Sandwiched into the conversational lines of her text that are as flip as the chapter headings, are very sound and appetite-stimulating recipes.

Now that war has curbed her world travels, Mrs. Fisher currently has ambitions to become a movie scenario writer. She jokingly remarks that her next book probably will be light fiction—"Perhaps on 'How to Cook a Producer'."

In Provence, That Land of Brittle Languors
Charles Poore/1964

From *The New York Times*, 4 April 1964, sec. A, p. 25. Copyright
© 1964 by The New York Times Company. Reprinted by permission.

The flaws in the idea of expatriation is that the expatriate must take
himself along. Yet that very flaw can also be an immense advantage
to the imaginative, as M. F. K. Fisher shows us in this glowing memoir
of Provence.

At long intervals in the prewar days, in the 1950s, and at the turn
of the present decade, Mrs. Fisher lived in France. Particularly in
Southern France, that land of brittle languors. She loves the place, its
darkly glorious historical associations, its provincial separateness and
well-worn elegance. Above all, she loves Aix-en-Provence, where,
with her two young daughters, Anne and Mary, she spent, all told,
about four years. The experiences of that time are sketched in her
book with lucid candor.

Since Mrs. Fisher is a noted gastronome, an epicure of the loftiest
cuisine, she naturally avoids the sticky meringues of alarmingly
enthusiastic travel literature.

Look out, she seems to be saying: the privacy you violate may be
your own. Which, I think, is a good warning to all of us who come
home (whistling back by jet) to say we've discovered some faraway
enclave bursting with solitude.

This is one of the best travel books you will find this year. Its
excellence does not lie in lists of restaurant prices, train and plane
schedules, or what a friend of mine calls the forlorn rituals of hotel-
smartness.

Mrs. Fisher went to Aix to stay—but how long she would or could
stay without breaking the patterns of expatriation by returns to
America she could never foretell. In any case, her homecomings
were not precipitate. Thus, when she thought it was time to see her
native California again she chose a slow freighter that permitted

weeks of voyage. The course was through the Panama Canal. No doubt Mrs. Fisher and her lively brood might have preferred to go around Cape Horn.

At sea or on land, Mrs. Fisher practices at will a useful kind of personal retreat. In action her technique must resemble the effect we produce when we realize that we are telling a familiar story to someone who has heard it a trifle too often.

In Mrs. Fisher's case, "it is mainly a question of withdrawing to the vanishing point from the consciousness of people one is with, before one actually leaves. It is invaluable at parties, testimonial dinners, discussions of evacuation routes in California towns, and coffee-breaks held for electioneering congressmen. . . ."

And, of course, it was useful at Aix-en-Provence, where Mrs. Fisher was trying to enjoy festivals that sometimes grew raucous, longing to return to her beloved walks among the many fountains, thinking of mundane bills and other obligations, hoping to see the Arrowsmith-dedicated doctor before he became a pill-for-every-ill practitioner.

The turbulence of the recent time when the war over Algeria threatened to throw all France into a colossal smashup is reflected vividly here. But far more space is devoted to the architecture of buildings that have survived so much French warfare and the Roman ruins that in Europe remind the current populations that their ancestors were once colonials of a distant power.

Inescapably, Mrs. Fisher goes at great length into the quaint rigors of acquiring an acceptable French accent. It is really an odd fixation when you come to think about it, isn't it? Why can't every nationality take a suave leaf from French manners, do as the French do abroad, sturdily let their accents show ("Eees zees 'ow you call eeet?") and go blandly everywhere?

As a matter of courtesy, Americans can afford to be generous about letting foreigners cherish their greatest and perhaps last illusions about us: the theories that we are terribly naive, awesomely rich if not immoderately couth, and all that. Yet in describing the pains an Aix friend took to be ruthlessly helpful, Mrs. Fisher sums up a type that every tourist or expatriate has encountered: "She explained to me things I had known for decades."

The Art of Eating, the Art of Living
Publishers Weekly/1971

From *Publishers Weekly,* 29 March 1971, vol. 199, pp. 17–18.
Reprinted by permission of *Publishers Weekly,* published by
R. R. Bowker Company, a Xerox Company. Copyright © 1971
by Xerox Corporation.

M. F. K. Fisher is one of the most distinguished writers on
food in America today, the author and editor of numerous
books on the subject. Five of her most highly regarded
works—*Serve It Forth, Consider the Oyster, How to Cook
a Wolf, The Gastronomical Me,* and *An Alphabet for Gourmets*—have just been brought out in a handsome new
one-volume edition of *The Art of Eating,* published by
Macmillan. In his introduction to *The Art of Eating,* written
originally in 1954, Clifton Fadiman says of Mrs. Fisher: "Of
all writers on food now using our English tongue she
seems to me to approach most nearly, in range, depth, and
perception, the attitude of Brillat-Savarin himself."

There is another side to Mrs. Fisher's writing, however,
and one that we are about to see more of. She is at work on
an as-yet-untitled book for Knopf about her experiences
growing up in Whittier, California, as a non-Quaker in this
largely Quaker community, which happens also to have
been the birthplace of Jessamyn West and her first cousin,
Richard M. Nixon. Portions of the book have run in the
New Yorker.

Mrs. Fisher's own comments on cookbooks, on writing about food,
and on her forthcoming family memoir are given here in response to
some questions posed by *PW.*

Question: Mrs. Fisher, you have a great deal to say in your books
about the art of eating "with both grace and gusto." Is there any
further comment you would like to make on the subject, as of 1971?
Do more people today eat "with both grace and gusto?"

Answer: "Yes, I think more and more people today eat 'with grace
and gusto.' The reasons for this may not be propitious, but they exist:

as we grow aware of outward insecurities we turn to the private pleasures, the shared sensuous delights. One of the pleasantest ways to commune with trusted people is to break bread and drink wine together. Then problems seem to grow less complex, and their solutions more attainable. That is why, here in America and perhaps in other countries, the art of eating is of an increasing interest.

"Of course, it often turns into pompous snobbism. There will always be snobs, just as there will be dullards, and that is why there are so many worthless cookbooks. I look at most of them, and I remain cheered by my conviction that in even the dullest or most snobbish there will be one jewel, one precious tip or tidbit worth all the paper the rest of the nonsense has been printed on."

Q: What would you say are the most *unhelpful* kinds of cookbooks? What do you object to most in some of the writing about food that is being done today?

A: "Run-of-the-mill cookbooks in this current frenzy for publishing are usually based on what are somewhat ironically called 'ideas': 'Sandwiches, Anyone' 'Soups for the Seventeeners,' 'Caviar in My Former Castles' . . . Such unhelpful publications cost a lot of money. They are hopelessly superficial. For their one or two good recipes they are fobbed off on eager hopeful people as authoritative 'guides.' I hate to have potential gastronomers (and even plain nice people!) cheated. Often, in fact more often than not, the recipes they try to follow have been written carelessly, without proper sequence in the ingredients and then in the methods. Almost as often, the recipes have not been honestly tested or verified. Well-meaning amateur cooks have been bamboozled, often embarrassed, by following the slapdash directions in nine out of ten of the cookbooks now being printed. This angers and hurts me."

Q: In terms of the current economic picture your money-saving *How to Cook a Wolf* seems a particularly appropriate reissue, doesn't it?

A: "I am truly astounded, and of course pleased, that people still read *How to Cook a Wolf*. It is heart-warming that young people still consult it for culinary encouragement in their unaffluent days, when they want to eat together. I did not know the word *macrobiotic* when I wrote about *sludge* but there is apparently some relationship there!"

Q: How do you feel, Mrs. Fisher, about the reputation you seem to have acquired as a "sensuous" writer about food?

A: "I get pretty peeved about being called things like 'past mistress of gastronomical pornography' and so on. I believe in living fully, as long as we seem to be meant to live at all. This implies the deliberate use of all our senses. We must eat, just as we must breathe, in order to exist. Eating demands the use of several of our senses in order to attain plain physiological success: taste, touch, smell, and so on. But I think it is Puritanical rubbish to say that the enjoyment of freshly picked green peas cooked over hot coals on a hillside is 'porno-graphic.' I really do not understand this seeming confusion of lasciv-ious sensuality and real innocence. I think we should enjoy what our senses can give us, and not twist and hide that enjoyment—and one of the best ways we can do it is to eat good food with good people."

Q: We would be delighted to hear something about your child-hood in Whittier, California—a kind of preview of the new book you are writing.

A: "As a child in Whittier, I was undoubtedly shaped, gastronomi-cally, by the fact that my maternal grandmother, who was an impor-tant part of our household, had what was discreetly called a Nervous Stomach. When she was in residence we ate a bland cuisine dictated by her dieticians in Battle Creek. When she was in Battle Creek, herself, which was blessedly often, we uproared through rare steaks, vinaigrette dressing on wild watercress, rich pastries, Green pastures!

"Socially, we lived apart from the quiet Quakers in Whittier. There was absolutely no suspicion, no bitterness, about this tacit *apartheid.* As long as we behaved ourselves we were welcome to stay in the little town, founded by and for members of the Society of Friends: we were white, of Anglo-Saxon descent, and Episcopalians (agreed to be a Protestant if overly Romish branch of the Faith). I lived what seems to me to have been a wonderful childhood, in an unspoiled and gentle community. Most of my peers were 'Friends.' We all lived our own lives at home and in our Sunday Schools, and for the rest of the time we were a corporate body, far beyond religious or racial strictures. We roistered like healthy puppies between school and home, and led a fine life with our teachers. Once classes were out, we went our separate ways, unquestioningly, and seldom played together. This may seem strange in today's patterns, but that is the way it was in 1912–20, in Whittier.

"I think this way of life was a good introduction to the powers and also the weaknesses of human prejudice, if not of love itself. It taught me a lot about why people must turn other people off. They seem to press an invisible button that says 'NO,' or 'JEWISH' or 'GARLIC,' and something mystical goes dead. Well, with children all the buttons can be pressed, but if the little human beings are healthy in their spirits, the life flows on, innocently, irreversibly. It did with me, and I'm thankful for this plain fact."

The Grand Dame of Gastronomy

Nancy Scott/1977

From *The San Francisco Sunday Chronicle-Examiner,* 22 May 1977, pp. 22 +. Reprinted with permission from the San Francisco Examiner. © 1992 San Francisco Examiner.

When this was first begun I thought, in my innocent enthusiasm, that everyone had heard of M. F. K. Fisher. Not so. People say, M. F. K. who? Who's he?

I say, not he. She. She is one of the finest writers in northern California, maybe North America. So, they ask, what does she write about? Mainly food. Ah, cookbooks. No. She writes about . . . let me explain in this way:

You are sitting at a table in a ranch house in Sonoma County. There is the melon in front of you; there is the luxurious pink prosciutto on top. Wonderful melon, you say. The cook's eye gleams.

"Let me tell you about that melon," she says. "It comes from south of here and it's called a Parson's melon."

It's a hybrid melon, she explains, sold from the Parson family melon patch. When one goes to buy a melon, she says, one finds the oldest son of the family sitting outside the barn in a director's chair. He wears a yachting cap and, under the delusion he is a captain, issues orders to the younger son in a voice more suited to the open sea than a dusty melon patch. The younger son is a dwarf, which is perhaps practical for one who must creep among the melons, but is also, she thinks, like an imitation of Carson McCullers; it is strange and disturbing.

Old man Parson had better luck with his melons than his boys, she says.

By now this singular fruit has acquired a flavor unlike any in the world. It began as a slice of innocent melon; as the cook tells the story, it becomes exquisitely ripe, perversely delicate and sharp to the teeth. It is the world's only mordant melon, a perfect hybrid, grown by a madman and a dwarf.

Later you think, was that melon really so special? Probably not. It was the cook who made it special because no other cook but M. F. K. Fisher could turn an innocent melon into a gothic anecdote. And I'm sorry if you've not heard of her, but not surprised. Her books have been out of print until this past year, which is a puzzle (into which I shall look in a moment) and a pity because I believe she knows more about food, drink and eating than anybody. In fact, calling Fisher a cook is like calling Moses a travel guide. Still, it's an honorable title and it's how I first met her.

I met her because I was invited to lunch; she cooked. If that doesn't sound exciting to you—because you never heard of her— then, how would you feel if Julia Child asked you to a meal? Or Mrs. Rombauer? Or James Beard? If you have read Fisher's books, you will know that an invitation from her is comparable to an invitation from Laurence Olivier or Beverly Sills or a night at the fights with Muhammad Ali. Never mind your Rombauers or your Childs. Fisher is the greatest.

Why?

I could write, solemnly, that Fisher is the greatest because she is the most distinguished authority on gastronomy in the country; that she has written a translation of Brillat-Savarin's *The Physiology of Taste* that is conceded to be the most scholarly ever published.

That's impressive, but not helpful.

I could say that she writes elegant prose; I could quote Clifton Fadiman, who calls her "the most interesting philosopher of food now practicing in our country."

That's better. Still, let me try it this way. Each of the great cooks, past and present, is indispensible for one or another reason. Julia Child is the finest technical writer in the U.S.; she has made haute cuisine accessible to anyone willing to follow her precise instructions. Mrs. Rombauer's *Joy of Cooking* is the ultimate encyclopedia for American readers.

Fannie Farmer reminds us that simplicity is useful. Escoffier teaches opinionated chemistry. And, then, there is the clutter of casserole cookbooks, ethnic cookbooks, soup, dessert . . . each with the one recipe that you can't find any place else. Indispensable, all; yet none, in its pigeonhole, seems to have much to do with the others, nor do they always have much to do with our own lives in our own kitchens.

Fisher has everything to do with all of them and with us. She writes
recipes, certainly, sometimes whole books of recipes, but they are not
cookbooks. They are books about the complicated connection between cooking and eating and living and loving (or hating). They are
about "an art which may be one of our last firm grasps on reality, that
of eating and drinking with intelligence and grace in evil days . . ."

The book in which this remark appears (*With Bold Knife and Fork*)
is still out of print; so are all but five of her twelve books. Last year
those five were published in one fat paperback called *The Art of
Eating* (Vintage Books, Random House). They are: *How to Cook a
Wolf; Consider the Oyster; Serve It Forth; The Gastronomical Me;*
and *An Alphabet for Gourmets.*

The first of these was published in 1937, the last in 1954, and I
don't know why they were not re-issued sooner. But I suspect that
now, finally, there is a new and larger market for Fisher's work.
Cookery appears to have become more than a fad; it's an obsession.
Men who used to talk chiefly of the relative merits of the Porsche
versus the Alfa Romeo now tell you confidingly of their recipe for
pâté de canard en croute. The healthy adolescent who ate the entire
Sunday roast last week eats two pounds of salad this week and
lectures earnestly on the virtues of organic alfalfa sprouts. Young
women who once made nothing more elaborate than chocolate chip
cookies are into puff paste.

And I think it's all a very good thing, for cooking and eating should
be taken seriously. Yet, there are some old pitfalls facing the new
enthusiasts and I can think of no one, save Fisher, who can so
capably come to the rescue. Fisher provokes, first of all, the question:
why do we cook what we cook? For efficiency, for health, out of
poverty or ostentation? It's rarely so simple as plain hunger. We are
poor; or we are not poor, and we want to bolster our egos or our
social standing and thus need an infallible guide to the latest recipe
from the mysterious East . . . we need more vitamin A (B,C) . . . we
think oysters are an aphrodisiac.

Whatever the reason, there is always some kind of anxiety lurking
underneath. I think most books about food exacerbate this anxiety.
They don't cause it, not the family fights, the love affairs, the poverty
or politics. But, consider, there you are 'in the kitchen, worrying
about your job (or your man, woman or child) and there is the book

with its narrow admonitions, its absolute rules and its endless, diddly list of ingredients and you say the hell with it and open a can instead. And, once again, you've opted for survival rations instead of *boeuf bourguignon*. And you feel bad.

Or, maybe, you *do* spend the afternoon making *boeuf bourguignon* when you should be working on your taxes . . . or writing your thesis . . . or visiting your old aunt. And you feel bad.

What to do? I can't give you a formula nor will Fisher. I can only say that a leisurely reading of her work will help you decide where and how cooking and eating fit into your life.

For instance: you are forty-five years old and you have left your husband after three kids and twenty-five years. You have never lived by yourself; now, in a one-room apartment, you are eating alone. Still 90 percent wife and mother, you are reluctant to buy special goodies for yourself or to cook them with the care you once lavished on your family. Going out to dinner alone is an uneasy proposition. You discover *An Alphabet for Gourmets* and read "A is for Dining Alone." Good. Here is Fisher, a woman of entertaining sophistication, and even she has reservations about eating alone in public or in private.

Fisher dealt with the problem in her own way; her answers may not suit your precise situation but within each answer is the kind of wit and self-respect that sustains your own self-respect, that can sustain anyone cast suddenly loose and alone.

Whatever your situation, you can learn from Fisher to take care of yourself—which means taking yourself seriously. Fisher has a fine humor but she takes her craft seriously; she takes herself seriously as a woman and, because she does, I think her books have a special importance for women. Many of us have decided to hell with the joy of cooking; it's just another unpaid female chore. We sneer at the woman who spends hours on the ladies' club cupcakes; we cast a cynical eye on the man who takes up cooking as a weekend diversion, and we are infuriated when his wife says, "Oh, George is a much better cook than I am." Sure he is. He has lots of time, energy and self-importance. Furthermore, his wife cleans up after him.

We're trapped between male ego and female obligation and we're still hungry for a good meal. It's possible to spring the trap—with Fisher's help—and to begin cooking with the knowledge that, if we are to cook at all, we have every right to cook well, with care for ourselves and love for our families and friends. Otherwise, let George do it.

I can't be sure, after one brief visit, that Fisher lives as she writes; no doubt there are dark corners and inconsistencies (to which she is entitled), but the Fisher I met is the Fisher I have read. Her manner, her style, the very house she lives in seem to be of a piece with her prose. The house is elegant and eccentric; it sits by itself on a ranch where vines and cows are raised simultaneously and it looks, at first glance, Spanish/Californian.

There are the appropriate tiles and arches, the thick outside walls and, on the porch, geraniums tall enough to be honored as trees, not plants. The ceiling, however, has a distinct Norman arch and the tiles are a strange and lovely black grass. Not Californian; perhaps a mix of French farm house and mad Moorish millionaire? The main room serves as living room, library, work room and kitchen and it is clearly the room of one who lives well and works hard. One wants to say, my, you have a lot of lovely things, but with the writer's desk dominating the room, it would sound silly. Nothing is for show; no one lovely thing asserts itself smugly; it is whole and comfortable, suited to a skilled, scholarly, beautiful woman.

Fisher is in her sixties now and one can see that she has always had the kind of beauty that confuses those who don't believe a good mind can co-exist with a tip-turned nose and fine Irish blue eyes. Her manner is generous and kindly but her smile is small and ironic, a combination which is largely true of her prose. She has written fiction (a novel, a number of fine short stories) and a gem of a memoir called *Among Friends* about her childhood in the Quaker town of Whittier. Her wit can be wicked and her perception is delicate but that is only the half of it. She can also be robustly critical and, when she writes of food and drink, watch out.

She writes of them with such indulgent gusto, such cultivated sensuality that her books would be kept on the library's locked shelf if she were writing about sex. One feels confident she could write as compellingly about sex if she chose; the result would be . . . interesting.

There is, for instance, the three-page essay on gin. Read it at five in the evening; not, as I did, at ten a.m. There is the elegaic discourse on tiny green peas, eaten fresh from the vine in a Swiss garden. She can even make a greasy fried egg sandwich sound desirable (for an insane moment or two) when she writes of how much she loved them as a child.

I would be irresponsible, however, if I did not warn you that it would be wise to save certain chapters—if you like to read as you eat—for late-night reading. You will likely lose your lunch if you happen on "Garum," an essay (in *Serve It Forth*) which describes the ancient Roman's idea of haute cuisine and includes the recipe for *garum* itself, a ghastly mess made chiefly of decaying fish gut. Fisher writes of decadent tastes (or just plain bad food) as precisely as she writes of good food, on the theory, I assume, that you can't decide what's good until you have analyzed what's bad.

I asked her, pursuing this theory, if she had ever eaten my idea of the world's worst food: a McDonald's hamburger.

"Yes," she said. "It was bilgewater."

She had been, she said, out with her daughter and her grandchild. They were twenty-eight miles from home and hungry; they bought three hamburgers, each took a bite or two and decided they were not hungry. Fisher stowed the remains in a paper sack and they began the drive home.

She said, "I noticed a funny smell but I thought it was something wrong with the car. When we got home, I said to my daughter, 'Don't you want me to warm up your hamburger? You must be hungry.' I warmed it up and then I knew why the car smelled funny."

Her advice: if you must eat fast, plastic food, eat it fast. Otherwise it will decompose into its original ingredients.

"Which are?"

"Bilgewater," she repeated.

All right, so much for plastic food; how about "natural" foods? I asked; how about the organic food enthusiasts?; the young people who grow their own vegetables and grind their own flour?

Fisher said she had lived for a time near a commune and bought staples in the same store where the young people shopped. Apparently they were so busy re-inventing the wheel, it didn't occur to them that this civilized lady knew all about natural food.

"They were astonished," she said, "that I bought raw sugar, stone ground flour and sweet butter."

She added, with what I took to be mild indignation, that they were also astonished to discover she knew so much about women's liberation.

"I love the young people," she said, "but I abhor their loaves of bread (like little rocks) and their nubbly, grubby, wormy little vegetables.

"Furthermore," she said cheerfully (adding another couple of miles to the generation gap), "young people are prudes. You need to be mature to be civilized about food."

In that case, I asked, how do you feel about the boom in expensive gourmet cooking schools?

"I love it," she says, her eyes glinting, "when James Beard says, 'Take off your rings, girls, get into the dough, scrape the egg from the shell with your fingernails.'

"I have no objection," she added benignly, "to the rich spending their money this way."

She shifted—as she often does in prose—to a grave and courteous generality:

"Actually, I believe very strongly that the young people have been and are a blessed influence in current American eating habits. Sometimes their vegetables are pathetic and their stoneground loaves are pretty gritty, but in general I'm a thousand percent for them."

She said she thought the new interest in food—gourmet or organic—was bound to be a very good thing.

"It will beat out plastic food and synthetic cooking," she said, "and I am optimistic about American cooking."

Fisher knows in her bones about American cooking. Her erudition and her sensibilities are European but the eye which notes every culinary detail in France's most exquisite restaurant still belongs to the Irish kid from Whittier whose grandmother thought garden salads and foreign sauces were immoral. Fisher knows that many of us had grandmothers who were determined we should not enjoy food (much less sex), but somehow she escaped the puritan chill with a warm recollection of how much she enjoyed food as a child. She translates that into a mature enjoyment which we may, if we are willing, share.

I felt she enjoyed making lunch and I felt welcome in her house. It was all of a piece: the food, her timing, her courtesy. The timing was almost theatrical in its precision (I don't mean dramatic, I mean well understood and well practiced). Lunch was not elaborate; I know several good cooks who could have done one or another dish. I know of no other who could put it all together with such grace.

Oh, yes, what did we eat? All right, first, a drink (gin). One drink and some unnamed goodies made of "ordinary" (her word) pastry, cut into rounds and triangles and toasted with anchovy butter. Then the Parson's melon. Then "green" shrimp and baked tomatoes stuffed with crumbs and garlic and herbs. She sauteed the shrimp briefly and put them on top of the tomatoes. The shrimp crunched; the tomatoes were hot and firm. Also, Sonoma County sourdough (which is very sour, creamy inside and brittle outside as it should be but almost never is), and a good California white wine.

That's all. And it was marvelous.

fwd

A Simple Country Lunch with M. F. K. Fisher
James Villas/1978

She is now in her seventies and a strikingly beautiful woman, with knowing blue eyes, impeccable skin, and silver hair drawn back sleekly over the ears. Her voice is soft and she speaks slowly, but as one might suspect, every word is weighed and every thought carefully composed. She is polite, often tender, but when confronted with examples of human mediocrity, pretension, and hypocrisy she can be brutally critical. In another age she would have been stamped a libertine; today she is respected as one of the world's finest food writers and, in the eyes of many, the grande dame of gastronomy.

None other than W. H. Auden once said of M. F. K. Fisher, "I do not know of anyone in the United States who writes better prose." That some people in the present generation either have never heard of this distinguished lady or, if so, believe her to be a man, is most probably due to the lamentable fact that until recently, when five of her books were republished under a single title, *The Art of Eating*, most of her work has remained out of print. "Back in 1936," she recalls, "my first publisher was stunned when he eventually discovered I was female, and I still get letters that begin 'Dear Mr. Fisher.'" But for those of us who've been lucky enough over the last three decades to happen upon her volumes, M. F. K. Fisher has remained our guiding light, the source of infinite gastronomic and philosophic wisdom, the model of what a truly refined food writer should strive for.

Often considered a rebel and eccentric, she didn't write cookbooks or publish restaurant reviews or dwell on endless numbers of uninteresting recipes. Rather, she has always devoted her exceptional talents to explaining and illustrating a very simple principle that is as valid today as fifty years ago: Since we must eat to live, let's learn to do it intelligently and gracefully, and let's try to understand its relationship with the other hungers of the world.

With the maxim fixed in our brains, we followed Mrs. Fisher across oceans and continents, we admired her wit, intelligence, and fierce independence, and no doubt we discovered through her experience that "there is a communion of much more than our bodies when bread is broken and wine drunk." In her first book, *Serve It Forth,* we read about the art of dining alone, we were challenged to eat bananas with Limburger, and we studied carefully the components of the ideal kitchen. In *Consider the Oyster,* we tested a recipe for oyster catsup, while in *How to Cook a Wolf,* we learned how to prepare tasty dishes even under the shadow of war rationing and poverty.

We laughed at Mrs. Fisher while she strove to get her fill of caviar in *The Gastronomical Me,* but we shared her pain and heartbreak when she and the dying man she loved sipped champagne and talked slowly on the final voyage of the *Normandie. An Alphabet for Gourmets* taught us how to train a child's palate correctly, why salad should indeed be eaten before the main course, what the perfect meal should involve, how to drink Martinis, and so much more.

We admired her brilliant translation of Brillat-Savarin's *La Physiologie du Goût,* and how proud we all felt in the late sixties when this great American lady was chosen to write *The Cooking of Provincial France* for the Time-Life food series.

Today M. F. K. Fisher lives alone on a ranch in Sonoma County, California, one of the greatest wine-producing areas of the world. Having been invited to lunch, I ignored the sign warning that trespassers would be prosecuted, proceeded to drive through lush green countryside redolent of eucalyptus, and eventually arrived at exactly the type of unconventional but stylish home in which you would expect to find Mary Frances Kennedy Fisher.

Outside is a small porch filled with wine bottles, baskets of fruit ripening, pots of flowers, boxes of books and papers, and various bric-a-brac awaiting delivery to neighbors. Inside is a large bathroom with paintings and mementos covering the walls, a larger second room that doubles as bedroom and study, and a magnificent redwood-beamed third room that serves as kitchen, dining room, library, workroom, or simply an area where one could sit for hours in undisturbed tranquillity before an open fire and gaze out at the pastoral setting. There is no television set, only a 1940s-vintage record player perched atop a well-stocked liquor cabinet, and a slim cat named Charlie whose beckonings always draw Mrs. Fisher's undivided attention.

The kitchen is practical, but nowhere in sight is there a food processor or wok or any other fashionable equipment now considered essential to an up-to-date kitchen. What you see instead on the counters are a few time-proved cooking vessels and utensils, bowls of ripe fruit, fresh vegetables, a bin of homemade cookies, loaves of fresh Sonoma sourdough bread, and a few bottles of wine. The house is livable and comfortable, and above all, it seems right.

After preparing a gin and tonic for me and a white vermouth for herself, Mrs. Fisher sank down in the corner of a deep old sofa, took Charlie into her lap, and, looking every bit the sensuous individual she is, began discussing her fascinating life and her views on food. From time to time she'd move over to the kitchen to work on lunch, and at one point she stopped to answer the phone and give a neighbor a little heated advice on what to do with kumquats. Her attitude was generous and her interest clearly genuine.

And the lunch? Oh, nothing really fancy: a few large Mexican prawns marinated in oyster sauce, baked quickly and served on a bed of duxelles; sliced plum tomatoes and zucchini topped with mild chilies; fresh sourdough bread with individual crocks of the sweetest butter; baked pears with fresh cream; and a carafe of Chablis from a local winery. No, nothing fancy, just one of the best-prepared and most-memorable meals of my life.

Since M. F. K. Fisher's life and career have always involved radical and complex changes, it's not that easy to draw out of her definitive responses to subjects that today might require a totally different approach than they would have thirty or forty years ago. Throughout our conversation, I was constantly reminded that her present opinions on certain topics might be totally contradictory to what she once said or believed or wrote, but, she emphasized, "that's what learning is all about, and I've never stopped learning." I suppose what is so interesting is that, although many of the questions I asked were inspired by what I'd read in Mrs. Fisher's books, never once was

I able to anticipate a certain answer, and at times I was completely surprised by what she had to say.

J. V.: When did you develop such an intense interest in food?

M. F. K. F.: I'd guess I first became interested in the relationship between digestion and emotions in about 1914—when I was five or six years old. As a child I was always exposed to and aware of good food in the family. We never ate anything but homemade breads, the freshest vegetables, and real butter. Of course my grandmother was totally dedicated to gastric interests, and although she always considered things like French sauces immoral, she had a great influence on me.

[As the author talked, I couldn't help recalling from *The Gastronomical Me* how her grandmother would discourse at table on the virtues of "plain good food," then proceed to belch voluptuously in reaction to Ora's (the cook's) inventive dishes. What she said of her childhood also reminded me of something else important she'd once written: "I was very young, but I can remember observing, privately of course, that meat hashed with a knife is better than meat mauled in a food chopper; that freshly minced herbs make almost any good things better; that chopped celery tastes different from celery in the stalk, just as carrots in thin curls and toast in crescents are infinitely more appetizing than in thick chunks and squares."]

J. V.: How did you begin to write about food?

M. F. K. F.: It all came very naturally since, after all, I really didn't have anything else to write about. But, specifically, I suppose it happened one day in Los Angeles when, while awaiting my first husband, Al Fisher, to finish his teaching day, I went to the public library and was fascinated by the smell of an old book of Elizabethan recipes a man was reading. Well, when he left the book on the table, I began to absorb every page. Later I wrote about those recipes simply to amuse my husband and our friends, just as to this day I write books for myself. Actually I've never written with the idea of publishing. I produce a book simply because I want to.

[And, indeed, there is almost no cuisine, be it Elizabethan, Byzantine, or Ancient Roman, that M. F. K. Fisher has not investigated with the same keen interest that others express only in something like

French cooking. Who, for example, but this extraordinary lady would not only have written with honest curiosity about an unsavory Roman seasoning called *garum* but actually produced a recipe: "Place in a vessel all the insides of fish, both large fish and small. Salt them well. Expose them to the air until they are completely putrid. In a short time a liquid is produced. Drain this off." Unappetizing? Perhaps so, but Fisher always had her reasons: "Romans used *garum* not as a condiment in itself but combined with a startling variety of spices. . . . Almost every known savour except parsley, which they wore in garlands on their heads, made the simplest banquet dish a mess of inextricable flavours."]

J. V.: How do you feel about being referred to as the grande dame of gastronomy?

M. F. K. F.: I haven't the faintest idea why anyone would call me that. I haven't said anything about food that hasn't been said a dozen times before. I guess since I didn't split infinitives people thought I just wrote better than others.

J. V.: You have said you don't write cookbooks, only books about food. Yet certainly you know food and cook it well, and readers cook from your recipes. How exactly do you make that distinction?

M. F. K. F.: For me there's always been so much more to food and cooking than just recipes or specific ways of preparing certain dishes. No doubt a good cookbook has its place in any kitchen, but I feel that if what I cook and eat doesn't relate somehow to my emotional and intellectual life, then something's wrong. When I compose a recipe, there's always some reason why, some personal inspiration that causes me to want to pass along a dish I enjoyed. If others care to try it, fine.

J. V.: What do you consider five basic cookbooks?

M. F. K. F.: Certainly *Fannie Farmer* and Mrs. Rombauer's *Joy of Cooking*—which I still consider my bible. Then I'd have to say Julia Child, the *Larousse Gastronomique,* and always Escoffier.

[Quickly I glanced over at a small book shelf in the kitchen. Mrs. Fisher must have hundreds and hundreds of cookbooks amidst the large library that covers much of the wall space in both rooms, but sure enough, within easy reaching distance in the kitchen are the titles she mentioned, plus, of course, a handsome leather-bound edition of *The Art of Eating.*]

J. V.: You once wrote that gastronomical precepts are perhaps among the most delicate ones in the modern arts. They must, in the main, be followed before they can be broken. Can you expand on that statement?

M. F. K. F.: It's very simple. We must respect the work of those innovators who spent their lives analyzing and interpreting the subtleties of preparing food. Sure, it's fine to experiment and create, but there are certain basics which must always serve as a foundation for new methods and ideas. Take, for example, the *nouvelle cuisine française*. The entire trend toward lightness and simplicity is no more than an extension of a few basic principles established by Escoffier more than a half-century ago.

J. V.: Your book *A Considerable Town* revolves around Marseille. Where in the world would you most like to be living now? Is it here in Sonoma?

M. F. K. F.: No. If I were able I'd like to live in Aix-en-Provence, which is near Marseille. I first went there in 1929 and have loved it ever since, most likely because it is so close to that dirty, mysterious port town. I wrote a book on Marseille in an attempt to explain to myself this inordinate attraction I've always had to the place.

[Suddenly M. F. K. Fisher's blue eyes became fixed on the flames quietly lapping the small logs in the fireplace, and I tried to imagine to just what point in the far distant past my question had forced her to retreat momentarily. Perhaps she was thinking about the time she, Al, and her sister Norah (who now lives down the road and is still one of her closest companions) sat in a small restaurant overlooking the Old Port in Marseille, played an accordion, and shared a steaming bouillabaisse. Or maybe the vision went back further, to the whorehouse in Marseille where she and Al innocently booked a room and spent the evening eating fresh cherries. Or, who knows, she could have been remembering the old butcher, César, whom every woman in town thought to be the devil himself but who once prepared the best steak she'd ever eaten.]

J. V.: How is your health?

M. F. K. F.: Pretty good, I suppose. Of course I have a horrible liver, but I really can't help that and have no intention of doing anything about it.

J. V.: Do you diet?

M. F. K. F.: No, never. I eat and drink exactly what I like.

J. V.: What do you prepare at home for breakfast, and how do you feel about breakfast?

M. F. K. F.: I don't eat breakfast, never have ever since as a child I was forced to eat my grandmother's boiled oatmeal every single morning. But even though I personally don't like this meal, I can't help but feel it's good for most people.

J. V.: How do you feel about drinking cocktails before a fine meal? Would you frown upon a good Martini or Manhattan?

M. F. K. F.: Of course not. Who's to tell anybody he or she shouldn't take a drink? I love a good Martini or Gibson before a meal, though I should say that I personally never mix gin and red wine. But if a well-prepared cocktail makes you feel good and stimulates the appetite, well, why not?

[When my hostess asked if I'd like my gin and tonic freshened, I was almost tempted to say that what I'd really like is a Martini prepared by this sybarite, who once wrote that "a well-made dry Martini or Gibson, correctly chilled and nicely served, has been more often my true friend than any two-legged creature." But I held back since it was the middle of the day, once again chuckling to myself when I thought what today's mineral-water apéritif purists might say to Mrs. Fisher's very sensible reasons for loving and respecting this sinful libation: "It is as warming as a hearthfire in December, as stimulating as a good review by my favorite critic of a book I have published into a seeming void, as exciting as a thorough buss I have yearned for from a man I didn't even suspect *suspected* me."]

J. V.: What do you drink with your meals?

M. F. K. F.: Generally wine. I love beer with food, but the wine here in the valley is now so superb I'm in the habit of drinking it most of the time. As for the fashionable vogue of drinking mineral water with meals, it's not for me. Before or after a meal, but not during.

J. V.: Have you ever had your fill of caviar?

M. F. K. F.: Never!

J. V.: Do you enjoy a good hamburger as much as a well-made steak tartare?

M. F. K. F.: I certainly do. And a good hamburger is hard to find these days.

[M. F. K. Fisher's recipe? Here it is with her typical concern for detail and, believe me, the burger's great—the very antithesis of those concoctions called "Rite-Spot Specials" she ate as a child and which now "make me gag":

> 1½ to 2 pounds best sirloin, trimmed of fat and coarsely
>   chopped
> 1 cup red table wine
> 3 or 4 tablespoons butter
> 1 cup mixed chopped onion, parsley, green pepper, herbs,
>   each according to taste
> ¼ cup oyster sauce

Shape the meat firmly into four round patties at least 1½ inches thick. Have the skillet very hot. Sear the meat (very smoky procedure) on both sides and remove at once to a hot buttered platter, where the meat will continue to heat through. (Extend the searing time if rare meat is not wanted.) Remove the skillet from the fire. When it is slightly cooled, put the wine and butter in and swirl, to collect what Brillat-Savarin would have called the "osmazone." Return to the heat and toss in the chopped ingredients, and cover closely. Turn off the heat as soon as these begin to hiss. Remove from the stove, take off the cover, add oyster sauce, swirl once more, and pour over the hot meat. Serve at once, since the heat contained in the sauce and the patties continues the cooking process.]

J. V.: Do you follow the seasons when planning your menus?

M. F. K. F.: Yes, I try, but I must say that "following the seasons" doesn't mean today what it once meant. Now so much is picked green, put into controlled rooms with all these mirrors and lights, injected with chemicals and colorings, and sprayed with God knows what-all. It's horrible. And I don't see much hope for improvement. But those willing to make the effort can still find naturally grown vegetables and fruits, picked in the morning, purchased at noon, and eaten in the evening.

J. V.: Have you ever needed to use canned or frozen foods?

M. F. K. F.: Sure, and my freezer and "emergency shelf" are full of them. Some of the frozen products are quite good. As for the canned, I use them only when forced by necessity, and, of course, I'd never serve something like canned peas to guests.

J. V.: What are your favorite time-saving machines in the kitchen?

M. F. K. F.: I have two machines in this house: a blender and a toaster that doesn't work. People are always surprised that I don't own a food processor. Well, I don't and have no desire to get one. Don't get me wrong. We live in a machine age, and if a food processor can serve to inspire people to cook, fine. But I personally don't want to have to push another button; I love cooking too much.

J. V.: What is the biggest cooking emergency you ever had, and how did you solve it?

M. F. K. F.: Probably when the electricity here went off for eight straight days and nights. But I had my "emergency shelf" full of canned goods and homemade pickles and preserves, and I wouldn't be caught dead without a chafing dish in the house.

J. V.: Is there any food that you hate?

M. F. K. F.: No, though there are some I don't like particularly: parsnips, turnips, even broccoli.

[I didn't have the nerve to ask Mrs. Fisher if, as she suggested in *An Alphabet for Gourmets,* she still had the desire to taste elephant meat, crocodile, white termites, and roasted locusts basted in camel butter. Knowing her, however, she probably sampled each and every one of those delicacies somewhere along the way and savored them with the same curiosity she had when she ate her first oyster and fillet of wild boar. "I have always believed," she wrote, "that I would like to taste everything once, never from such hunger as made friends of mine in France in 1942 eat guinea-pig ragout, but from pure gourmandism."]

J. V.: Can anyone learn to cook? Where does a novice begin?

M. F. K. F.: I hate to say this, but some people will simply never learn even how to put a pat of butter in a skillet, no matter how hard they try. Cooking involves an instinct based on some complex communication between the brain and the body, and as with any fine art it's not something you can master automatically. Just recently, for instance, I was talking with Jim Beard, who told me that out of a class of thirty students, he had exactly one who showed great promise.

J. V.: You have aired your disdain for the trend toward posh cooking courses. What should a student looking for a cooking class use as a criterion for selection?

M. F. K. F.: Generally I don't have much faith in cooking classes. I never took any myself. Essentially, if you really want to cook, just get a good cookbook like *Joy of Cooking* and start.

J. V.: How do you feel about women professional chefs? Do you think they are progressing?

M. F. K. F.: Yes, indeed they are. And with encouragement from societies like the Dames d'Escoffier in New York, things will get better and better. The idea that no woman can stand the heat and weight on her feet is absurd. If she can't, she'll drop out, just as a man would in those circumstances.

J. V.: What do you think of restaurant cooking in the U.S.? Of restaurants in general, as opposed to those in, say, France?

M. F. K. F.: I take a pretty dim view, for the overall situation seems to be deteriorating. First, there seems to be more and more pre-cooked food being served, even in the finest restaurants. Second, neither chefs nor waiters have much training now, much less pride in their work. Very few have the faintest conception of what their counterparts in Europe go through. It's really two different worlds.

J. V.: Is there much hope for improvement in this country?

M. F. K. F.: Not in the sense you're referring to. We have regional cooking—often superb. We do not, and perhaps *cannot,* have "American" cuisine because of the country's size. We are just too big, too vast and stretched-out, to enable a cuisine such as the one in France to develop. A chef in New Mexico, for example, who tries to satisfy the demands of a man from Minnesota is up against a real challenge. And how do you think the manners and dress of someone from Texas are going to go over in a posh Manhattan restaurant? These things create terrible emotional friction among human beings, and this all has some bearing on the development of our cookery and eating habits. Within the various regions of the U.S., however, there is tremendous room for improvement, and I definitely think there are exciting things happening with our regional cuisines.

[Never letting up for air while giving me examples of what all she felt could be accomplished in the way of regional American cookery. M. F. K. Fisher moved into the kitchen and signaled me to join her. "Lovely, aren't they?" she said with a smile, lifting a large prawn from its bath of oyster sauce. She then gingerly spread out a layer of duxelles on the bottom of a baking dish, artistically arranged the prawns on top, and placed the already seasoned dish in the oven. "If

they overcook," she said, "it's your fault since you've got me talking
so!"]

J. V.: Who are the most influential food persons in the world today?

M. F. K. F.: Bocuse, Guérard, and the whole school of *la nouvelle
cuisine française* are of course having a tremendous impact on food
and cooking everywhere, and I'm all for what they're trying to
accomplish. In this country, though, I'd have to say Julia Child and
James Beard, mainly because they've created such a widespread
interest in food and shown people how to deal with the subject
intelligently. As for most food writers I read in magazines, they don't
seem to have too much of importance to say.

J. V.: Do you see anything redeeming in today's fast foods?

M. F. K. F.: Nothing, absolutely nothing.

J. V.: Recently I heard a prediction that by the year 2000 there
would be no home cooking. Do you think home cooking could
disappear?

M. F. K. F.: No doubt with the power of Big Mac and Colonel
Sanders and Roy Rogers the odds are pretty rough, but I refuse to
believe the situation is hopeless. Out there in America there *are*
mothers who still care and youngsters who are eating properly. Here
in the Sonoma Valley I see young people growing their own food and
making their own bread. And, of course, the American people seem
to be demanding so much more and, with exposure, choosing more
wisely what they put in their stomachs. No, I refuse to despair.

J. V.: When all is said and done, how important is fine food in the
great scheme of life? What does a preoccupation with food contribute
to the creative experience?

M. F. K. F.: I can only repeat what I've said for many years: Since
we're forced to nourish ourselves, why not do it with all possible skill,
delicacy, and ever-increasing enjoyment? I just can't help but feel that
a sensible approach to how we satisfy the hunger of the stomach has
a direct connection with those other two important needs: security
and love. The three are so related we can't think of one without the
others, and not until we acknowledge this fact can we possibly begin
to understand something about what can be accomplished in this life.

Driving back to San Francisco, I had a strong feeling that M. F. K.
Fisher is indeed a person who has managed, through her generosity,

truthfulness, and hard work, not only to satisfy many hungers but also to accomplish a good deal more than most of us can ever hope for. Just as I was leaving the small ranch house, she informed me that after attending a dinner in New York given in her honor by the Dames d'Escoffier, she and her sister Norah would continue straight on to Aix-en-Provence. No doubt the first evening these two headed for Marseille—most certainly to find an unpretentious restaurant overlooking the Old Port, and order a steaming bouillabaisse like the one they shared with Al back in '32. I'd like to think they toasted their survival with glasses of fresh local wine.

Postscript
I'm very proud of this profile, not only because I consider M. F. K. Fisher the most important and relevant American food writer of this century but also because this was the first interview she had granted for many years. Although now well into her twilight years, Mary Frances is still as astute, original, and trenchant as ever, a true professional whose ideas and refined style of expression represent standards every food journalist would do well to emulate. After disgracefully being out of print for so long, most of her classic works are now once again available, providing intelligent and refreshing counterpoint to the embarrassing number of shoddy cookbooks and illiterate food articles that plague today's market. James Beard is gone, and when M. F. K. Fisher follows to join her old friend at that celestial banquet table, a void will exist in the food world that we can only pray may one day be filled.

Dawdling in Marseilles

Charles Michener/1978

From *Newsweek*, 15 May 1978, vol. 91, pp. 99+. © 1983 Newsweek, Inc.

Travel writers, for the most part, are lousy companions. Because they don't take trips like the rest of us—that is, without benefit of special courtesies—their accounts of far-away pleasures tend to be over-stated. M. F. K. Fisher is a terrific exception. She travels on her own and likes, she says, "to dawdle and watch." Her new book provides a great opportunity to do just that in a city usually shunned by conventional travelers as dangerous and dirty—the French port, Marseilles.

Mrs. Fisher has long been the preeminent essayist in English about food; her culinary books, collected in *The Art of Eating,* are classics. But her vision is as sharp as her palate. "I keep an eye on things, like what wars do to little shops," she notes, but that is only half the story. During one of her many stays in Marseilles—she has been returning "helplessly" there since 1929—she told a local typewriter repairman why she wanted to write about his city: "I don't want to explain Marseilles. I want to try to tell what it does about explaining myself." It is her need for self-discovery that brings her observations to such vivid life.

Like all good travelers, she is fascinated most by people. She is marvelous on the "short and trimly wide" women of the city: "when they walk down a street they cleave its air like small solid wooden ships driven by a mysterious inner combustion. Their men walk close alongside, often with an arm around the woman's waist or over her broad solid shoulders, pilot fish escorting a trusted shark." To her, middle-class men at lunch look like "affable stone."

She makes friends sparingly but keenly: an ancient little Virgin sitting in the catacombs of a church; a garrulous doctor whose brilliant career as a surgeon was cut short because of an allergy to wearing rubber gloves. She has dawdled most in the city's Old Port section, where she puzzles over the youths who swarm the pinball tables in the espresso joints, noticing that "when they spit out or drop their cigarette butts, they never step on them, as if that were a kind of code or password, a *proof* of something." She is drawn to the "she-wolves," the female barkers who try to lure passers-by into the fishhouses along the Rive Neuve; she admits to "being cowed by them at times" but is still able "to feed on an intrinsic courage that emanated from them."

Accidents sharpen her senses. After a fall in the street, she is taken to an emergency room. While a "ferocious little nurse" closes a gash in her forehead, she overhears a doctor murmuring, "superb, magnificent!" "I felt happy," she recalls, "that they might sleep together later." An account of the port's past as a center for galley slaves leads to this insight: "a mysterious thing about Marseilles . . . is that its collective evil is balanced by a wonderful healthiness." It is a balance maintained, she suggests, by the city's deep religiosity, its need for "something to shout to and dance around, to curse and to beseech."

By now it should be clear that M. F. K. Fisher deserves the praise W. H. Auden once bestowed on her: "I do not know of anyone in the United States today who writes better prose." The climax of this stirring book comes at Mrs. Fisher's favorite hotel, the Beauveau, where she and her two daughters, then small, once celebrated Christmas. Instead of trimming a proper tree, they made do with an old Victorian hatrack. Instead of the usual Christmas feast, they consumed—at breakfast—caviar on hot rolls, big cups of *café au lait,* wine for the mother and a chocolate log filled with whipped cream and sponge cake. M. F. K. Fisher calls herself "a professional ghost." Like all good traveling ghosts, she knows how to be at home far away from home.

Mary Frances Kennedy Fisher was raised a "heathen" in the Quaker community of Whittier, Calif.—an experience she wittily chronicled in her last book, *Among Friends*—and she finds herself a living "dichotomy." Home is a house on a ranch in northern California, but her favorite country is France. "Actually," she says, "Aix-en-Provence, not Marseilles, is really my favorite town. When I'm there, I'm always in a dilemma. Should I could home or should I stay? It's hard to live in a country that has a President with that born-again

smile. I feel fastidious about it. But I'm an American and I don't want
to be an expatriate. I'll go to my grave feeling split."

Does she travel with a camera? "No," she says firmly. "My last
husband was a camera buff [she has outlived three husbands] and
although I'd always had a good instinctive eye for taking pictures,
I completely lost interest in it because of all the technical books on
photography he encouraged me to read. He also got me a lot of
books about cats, and after I started reading them, our cats began to
die or have nervous breakdowns. It was because I knew too much."
Nearly 70, a tall, bright-eyed woman with a girlish voice, she was
recently lodged at a Manhattan hotel en route to the south of France
with her younger sister, Norah. She is suffering from cataracts and
arthritis, but they are "only handicaps of the moment." Indeed,
although she complains of "fluctuating focus," she is sufficiently
keen-eyed to have noted some strange scars on the tile walls of her
hotel bathroom. "I've been thinking about them" she says. "and
wondering who threw what." She is also perceptive enough to know
why she no longer much likes New York City. "People don't walk
happily here any more," laments M. F. K. Fisher. "They scuttle."

Romancing People, Places and Food

Joan Chatfield-Taylor/1979

From *The San Francisco Chronicle*, 21 September 1979. © *San Francisco Chronicle*. Reprinted by permission.

Most of us take water for granted. It's that clear stuff that flows obediently from the tap, useful to boil things in but hardly something to offer as a special treat to guests.

M. F. K. Fisher does not regard it so casually. She offers a glass of water from the tap of her Sonoma cottage as if it were something extraordinary, describing it as "very good water" and "my vintage water."

It is quintessential Fisher to turn the most banal detail into an adventure. Her fans would recognize it immediately; it's the same thing she does in her writing. In Fisher's hands, even a ham and cheese sandwich, cellophane-wrapped for airplane consumption, can be a subject for intense consideration.

And then there's her story of Ora, the only good cook of her childhood, which starts out as a quiet description of some good meals and suddenly turns into a Gothic horror tale when Ora murders her mother and herself with her treasured French carving knife.

Many people consider M. F. K. (the initials stand for Mary Frances Kennedy, her maiden name) Fisher one of the finest writers in America. W. H. Auden said, "I do not know of anyone in the United States today who writes better prose."

Her books have always been difficult to categorize; when Vintage Press reissued five of her early books in a paperback called, *The Art of Eating,* they labeled it rather vaguely "Belles Lettres and Cooking."

Perhaps some make the mistake of thinking of her as a cookbook writer simply because she often writes about food.

She said recently, "My books have never sold well, although there was always kind of an elite group that liked them. Once I wrote a novel and there were many copies returned by people who were disappointed that there were no recipes."

Recipes appear in some Fisher books, like *How to Cook a Wolf,*
The Gastronomical Me and *Serve It Forth,* but they're like truffles,
flavorful morsels that intensify the perfume of a pate of places and
travels and experiences and people.

While she clearly revels in good food, she takes equal pleasure in
describing singularly bad food. A fond remembrance of a next door
neighbor is given a special kind of reality by the addition of the recipe
for the greasy fried-egg sandwiches she used to make for the children
of the neighborhood.

Lovers, Fisher style, do not merely stop somewhere for lunch;
instead, they dine on something quite specific that becomes part of
the romance.

In her hands, a meal becomes something passionate and sexy. For
those who read cookbooks the way others read dirty books, Fisher is
the ultimate pornographer.

Food is often a metaphor for her own experiences. When she was
growing up in Whittier, food was a forbidden pleasure. Her grandmother, who ran the house, believed that too much enjoyment of
food was both sinful and impolite. Her idea of respectable food
included steamed soda crackers in milk and another soggy blend of
tomatoes stewed with spongy lumps of bread.

When she was 20, she went to France with her first husband, a
dashing professor named Alfred Fisher, and, in the bloom of young
love, was seduced by French food.

She started writing about these things during the Depression,
when she and Al Fisher returned from Europe to Southern California, where he had a job at Occidental College.

"I had a part-time job in a filthy postcard shop. I was the front,
because I looked so respectable," she said. "And every day I went to
the Los Angeles Municipal Library. A man next to me in the reading
room kept leaving books about Elizabethan cookery, and so I started
writing pieces about it for my husband.

"I wanted to amuse him. I think you must write toward somebody,
toward a loved object. If you write toward the great dollar bill or
toward an editor you want to please, it doesn't come out as well."

Nevertheless, Fisher has had plenty of experience in writing for
money, particularly in the 1940s when, divorced from her third
husband, she was bringing up her two daughters in St. Helena.

"I never believed in alimony, so I earned my living when I really needed to. There were times when I had contracts with three or four magazines. I wrote things like 'a bride's lunch for June.' They wanted pretentious food, not a great recipe for potato soup. In those days, food still showed the effects of 1890s pretentiousness."

She believes that American food has improved since then, as people live more simply. French food, on the other hand, is "much worse" than it used to be.

"I blame it on the Common Market. Last time I was in Marseille, there were half-frozen oranges from Morocco, half-frozen peas from Portugal."

Fisher says that the first and only review she ever read was by Senator Sam Hayakawa, who was then writing book reviews for some minor Chicago paper.

"It was a good review, the kind I wanted to read, and I never read another," she said.

Today, she is a sweet-faced woman, now rounded and grayed by her 70 years, but still beautiful. She speaks softly, in an almost child-like, gentle voice, choosing her words carefully, telling stories that, like her prose, start out on the most ordinary level and suddenly blossom into amazing dramas.

She recalled spending almost a year teaching at a black school in Mississippi in the early 1960s.

"I wanted to find out if the South was as awful as I thought it was," she said. Apparently it was, as she described an atmosphere of deprivation and mind control that sounded like a precursor of Jones-town. Even here, food is part of the drama; she recalled living on nothing but creamed corn and ice cream for months.

A recent trip to Japan, where she was writing the introduction to a book on classical Japanese cuisine, also took a dramatic turn when she and her sister decided that their rooms and the cars provided for them were bugged.

Today, she lives in a cottage that was built for her on the property of a friend in Glen Ellen, California. It is two big, airy rooms with curved wooden ceilings like the inside of a wine barrel. The first is for sleeping and writing. The second, with a view across the Sonoma Valley, is for cooking and eating and entertaining. A vast table is strewn with papers and new copies of the reissue of "With Bold Knife and Fork," the closest she ever came to writing a real cookbook, and some handsome, giant crookneck squash.

The kitchen is perfectly ordinary, a lineup of stove and sink and refrigerators along one wall.

She said happily, "I wanted a perfectly banal kitchen. I think some people were disappointed. They wanted me to have all kinds of imitation oak, so that it wouldn't look like a kitchen."

There is no Cuisinart, not even a toaster, in sight.

"You see, I live as if I were on a houseboat, and I don't have room for a lot of things."

One senses, too, that modern gadgetry is not part of her personal joy of cooking, especially when she describes the way she "baked that chicken last night and tore it off the bones."

The kitchen tools on display require more personal, physical involvement than clicking on a food processor. There's a group of mortars and pestles, both French and Japanese, and two lines of sharp French knives, the kind mad Ora probably used.

There are some 5000 books tucked into nooks and crannies around the house. Some of them are cookbooks, of course, and there are shelves of travel books. There are also books on gypsies and on old age and dying. One of her current projects is a book on the elderly.

"I've always been interested in old people, and I've been working on a book on old age since the 1930s. At first it was supposed to be a learned tome, but now I've decided to do a series of short stories on old people."

She's also working on a collection of articles about places, to be published next spring.

She seems to be writing less about food these days, which is perhaps the natural result of growing older.

Recalling the lengthy, rich meals of her first years in France, she said, "I think it's great, but I couldn't possibly eat it now. My metabolism has changed, and I want less to eat as I grow older."

As the Lingo Languishes
M. F. K. Fisher/1980

From *The State of the Language*, ed. Leonard Michaels and Christopher Ricks (Berkeley: University of California Press, 1980), pp. 267–276. Copyright © 1980 The Regents of the University of California.
   This essay is in response to the editors' question, "What is the state of the language?"

Hunger is, to describe it most simply, an urgent need for food. It is a craving, a desire. It is, I would guess, much older than man as we now think of him, and probably synonymous with the beginnings of sex. It is strange that we feel that anything as intrinsic as this must continually be wooed and excited, as if it were an unwilling and capricious part of us. If someone is not hungry, it indicates that his body does not, for a time and a reason, want to be fed. The logical thing, then, is to let him rest. He will either die, which he may have been meant to do, or he will once more feel the craving, the desire, the urgency to *eat*. He will have to do that before he can satisfy most of his other needs. Then he will revive again, which apparently he was meant to do.

It is hard to understand why this instinct to eat must be importuned, since it is so strong in all relatively healthy bodies. But in our present Western world, we face a literal bombardment of cajolery from all the media, to eat this or that. It is as if we had been born without appetite, and must be led gently into an introduction to oral satisfaction and its increasingly dubious results, the way nubile maidens in past centuries were prepared for marriage proposals and then their legitimate defloration.

The language that is developing, in this game of making us *want* to eat, is far from subtle. To begin with, we must be made to feel that we really find the whole atavistic process difficult, or embarrassing or boring. We must be coaxed and cajoled to crave one advertised product rather than another, one taste, one presentation of something that we might have chosen anyway if let alone.

41

The truth is that we are born hungry and in our own ways will die so. But modern food advertising assumes that we are by nature bewildered and listless. As a matter of fact, we come into the world howling for Mother's Milk. We leave it, given a reasonable length of time, satisfied with much the same bland if lusty precursor of "pap and pabulum," tempered perhaps with a brush of wine on our lips to ease the parting of body and spirit. And in between, today, now, we are assaulted with the most insulting distortion of our sensory linguistics that I can imagine. We are treated like innocents and idiots by the advertisers, here in America and in Western Europe. (These are the only two regions I know, even slightly, but I feel sure that this same attack on our innate common sense is going on in the Orient, in India, in Brazil . . .)

We are told, on radio and television and in widely distributed publications, not only how but what to eat, and when, and where. The pictures are colorful. The prose, often written by famous people, is deliberately persuasive, if often supercilious in a way that makes us out as clumsy louts, gastronomical oafs badly in need of guidance toward the satisfaction of appetites we are unaware of. And by now, with this constant attack on innate desires, an attack that can be either overt or subliminal, we apparently feel fogged-out, bombed, bewildered about whether we really crave some peanut butter on crackers as a post-amour snack, or want to sleep forever. And first, before varied forms of physical dalliance, should we share with our partner a French aperitif that keeps telling us to, or should we lead up to our accomplishments by sipping a tiny glass of a Sicilian love potion?

The language for this liquid aphro-cut is familiar to most of us, thanks to lush ads in all the media. It becomes even stronger as we go into solid foods. Sexually the ads are aimed at two main groups: the Doers and the Dones. Either the reader/viewer/listener is out to woo a lover, or has married and acquired at least two children and needs help to keep the machismo-level high. Either way, one person is supposed to feed another so as to get the partner into bed and then, if possible, to pay domestic maintenance—that is, foot the bills.

One full-page color ad, for instance, shows six shots of repellently mingled vegetables, and claims boldly that these combinations "will do almost anything to get a husband's attentions." They will "catch

his passing fancy . . . on the first vegetables he might even notice."
In short, the ad goes on with skilled persuasion, "they're vegetables
your husband can't ignore." This almost promises that he may not
ignore the cook either, a heartening if vaguely lewd thought if the
pictures in the ad are any intimation of his tastes.

It is plain that if a man must be kept satisfied at table, so must his
progeny, and advertisers know how to woo mothers as well as plain
sexual companions. Most of their nutritional bids imply somewhat
unruly family life, that only food can ease: "No more fights over who
gets what," one ad proposes, as it suggests buying not one but three
different types of frozen but "crisp hot fried chicken at a price that
take-out can't beat": thighs and drumsticks, breast portions, and
wings, all coated with the same oven-crunchy-golden skin, and fresh
from freezer to stove in minutes. In the last quarter of this family
ad there is a garishly bright new proposal, the "no-fire, sure-fire,
barbecue-sauced" chicken. Personal experience frowns on this
daring departure from the national "finger-lickin' " syndrome: with
children who fight over who gets what, it would be very messy . . .

It is easy to continue such ever-loving family-style meals, as
suggested by current advertising, all in deceptively alluring color in
almost any home-oriented magazine one finds. How about enjoying
a "good family western," whatever that may be, by serving a mixture
of "redy-rice" and leftover chicken topped with a blenderized sauce
of ripe avocado? This is called "love food from California," and it will
make us "taste how the West was won." The avocado, the ad goes
on, will "open new frontiers of wholesome family enjoyment." And
of course the pre-spiced-already-seasoned "instant" rice, combined
with cooked chicken, will look yummy packed into the hollowed fruit
shells and covered with nutlike green stuff. All this will help greatly to
keep the kids from hitting each other about who gets what.

The way to a man's heart is through his stomach, we have been
assured for a couple of centuries, and for much longer than that,
good wives as well as noted courtesans have given their time and
thought to keeping the male belly full (and the male liver equally if
innocently enlarged). By now this precarious mixture of sex and
gastronomy has come out of the pantry, so to speak, and ordinary
cookbook shelves show *Cuisine d'amour* and *Venus in the Kitchen*
alongside Mrs. Rombauer and Julia Child.

In order to become a classic, which I consider the last two to be, any creation, from a potato soufflé to a marble bust or a skyscraper, must be honest, and that is why most cooks, as well as their methods, are never known. It is also why dishonesty in the kitchen is driving us so fast and successfully to the world of convenience foods and franchised eateries.

If we look at a few of the so-called cookbooks now providing a kind of armchair gastronomy (to read while we wait for the wife and kids to get ready to pile in the car for supper at the nearest drive-in), we understand without either amazement or active nausea some such "homemade" treat as I was brought lately by a generous neighbor. The recipe she proudly passed along to me, as if it were her great-grandmother's secret way to many a heart, was from a best-selling new cookbook, and it included a large package of sweet chocolate bits, a box of "Butter Fudge" chocolate cake mix, a package of instant vanilla pudding, and a cup of imitation mayonnaise. It was to be served with synthetic whipped cream sprayed from an aerosol can. It was called *Old-Fashion Fudge Torte*.

This distortion of values, this insidious numbing of what we once knew without question as either True or False, can be blamed, in part anyway, on the language we hear and read every day and night, about the satisfying of such a basic need as hunger. Advertising, especially in magazines and books devoted to such animal satisfaction, twists us deftly into acceptance of the new lingo of gastronomical seduction.

A good example: an impossibly juicy-looking pork chop lies like a Matisse odalisque in an open microwave oven, cooked until "fall-from-the-bone-tender." This is a new word. It still says that the meat is so overcooked that it will fall off its bone (a dubious virtue!), but it is supposed to beguile the reader into thinking that he or she (1) speaks a special streamlined language and (2) deserves to buy an oven to match, and (3) appreciates all such finer things in life. It takes *know-how*, the ad assures us subliminally, to understand all that "fall-from-the-bone-tender" really means!

This strange need to turn plain descriptive English into hyphenated hyperbole can be found even in the best gastronomical reviews and articles, as well as magazine copy. How about "fresh-from-the-oven apple cobbler," as described by one of the more reputable food writers of today? What would be wrong, especially for someone who actually knows syntax and grammar, in saying "apple cobbler, fresh from the oven"? A contemporary answer is that the multiple adjective is more . . . uh . . . contemporary. This implies that it should reach the conditioned brain cells of today's reader in a more understandable, coherent way—or does it?

II

The vocabulary of our kitchen comes from every part of the planet, sooner or later, because as we live, so we speak. After the Norman Conquest in 1066, England learned countless French nouns and verbs that are now part of both British and American cooking language: *appetite, dinner, salmon, sausage, lemon, fig, almond,* and on and on. We all say *roast, fry, boil,* and we make *sauces* and put them in *bowls* or on *plates.* And the German kitchen, the Aztecan: they too gave us words like *cookie* and *chocolate.* We say *borscht* easily (Russian before it was Yiddish). From slave-time Africa there is the word *gumbo,* for okra, and in *benne* biscuits there is the black man's sesame. Some people say that *alcohol* came from the nonalcoholic Arabs.

But what about the new culinary language of the media, the kind we now hear and view and read? What can "freezer-fresh" mean? *Fresh* used to imply new, pure, lively. Now it means, at best, that when a food was packaged, it would qualify as ready to be eaten: "oven-fresh" cookies a year on the shelf, "farm-fresh" eggs laid last spring, "corn-on-the-cob fresh" dehydrated vegetable soup-mix . . .

Personal feelings and opinions and prejudices (sometimes called skunners) have a lot to do with our reactions to gastronomical words, and other kinds. I know a man who finally divorced his wife because, even by indirection, he could not cure her of "calling up." She called up people, and to her it meant that she used the telephone—that is, she was not calling across a garden or over a fence, but was calling up when she could not *see* her friends. Calling and calling up are entirely different, she and a lot of interested amateur semanticists told her husband. He refused to admit this. "Why not simply *telephone* them? To telephone you don't say telephone *up,*" he would say. Her phrase continued to set his inner teeth, the ones rooted directly in his spiritual jaw, on such an edge that he finally fled. She called up to tell me.

This domestic calamity made me aware, over many years but never with such anguish, how *up* can dangle in our language. And experience has shown me that if a word starts dangling, it is an easy mark for the careless users and the overt rapists of syntax and meaning who write copy for mass-media outlets connected, for instance, with hunger and its current quasi-satisfactions. Sometimes the grammatical approach is fairly conventional and old-fashioned, and the *up* is tacked onto a verb in a fairly comprehensible way. "Perk up your dinner," one magazine headline begs us, with vaguely disgusting suggestions about how to do it. "Brighten up a burger," a full-page lesson in salad making with an instant powder tells us. (This ad sneaks in another call on home unity with its "unusually delicious . . . bright . . . tasty" offering: "Sit back and listen to the cheers," it says. "Your family will give them to this tasty-zesty easy-to-make salad!")

Of course *up* gets into the adjectives as well as the verbs: *souped up chicken* and *souped up dip* are modish in advertising for canned pudding-like concoctions that fall in their original shapes from tin to saucepan or mixing bowl, to be blended with liquids to make fairly edible "soups," or to serve in prefab sauces as handy vehicles for clams or peanuts or whatever is added to the can-shaped glob to tantalize drinkers to want one more Bloody Mary. They dip up the mixture on specially stiffened packaged "chips" made of imitation tortillas or even imitation reconditioned potatoes, guaranteed not to crumble, shatter, or otherwise mess up the landscape . . .

Verbs are more fun than adjectives, in this game of upmanship. And one of the best/worst of them is creeping into our vocabularies in a thoroughly unsubtle way. It is *to gourmet up*. By now the word *gourmet* has been so distorted, and so overloaded, that to people who know its real meaning it is meaningless. They have never mis-used it and they refuse to now. To them a gourmet is a person, and perforce the word is a noun. Probably it turned irrevocably into an adjective with descriptive terms like *gourmet-style* and *gourmet-type*. I am not sure. But it has come to mean fancy rather than fastidious. It means expensive, or exotic, or pseudo-elegant and classy and pricey. It rarely describes a person, the gourmet who knows how to eat with discreet enjoyment. It describes a style, at best, and at worst a cheap imitation of once-stylish and always costly affectation.

There is gourmet food. There are gourmet restaurants, or gourmet-style eating places. There are packaged frozen cubes of comestibles called gourmet that cost three times as much as plain fast foods because, the cunningly succulent mouth-watering ads propose, their sauces are made by world-famous chefs, whose magical blends of spices and herbs have been touched off by a personalized fillip of rare old Madeira. In other words, at triple the price, they are worth it because they have been gourmeted up. Not long ago I heard a young woman in a supermarket say to a friend who looked almost as gaunt and harried as she, "Oh god . . . why am I here? You ask! Harry calls to say his sales manager is coming to dinner, and I've got to gourmet up the pot roast!"

I slow my trundle down the pushcart aisle.

"I could slice some olives into it, maybe? Pitted. Or maybe dump in a can of mushrooms. Sliced. It's got to be more expensive."

The friend says, "A cup of wine? Red. Or sour cream . . . a kind of Stroganoff . . . ?"

I worm my way past them, feeling vaguely worried. I long to tell them something—perhaps not to worry.

There are, of course, even more personal language shocks than the one that drove a man to leave his dear girl because she had to call people up. Each of us has his own, actively or dimly connected with hunger (which only an adamant Freudian could call his!). It becomes a real embarrassment, for example, when a friend or a responsible critic of cookbooks or restaurants uses words like *yummy,* or *scrumptious.* There is no dignity in such infantile evasions of plain words like *good*—or even *delicious* or *excellent.*

My own word aversion is longstanding, and several decades from the first time I heard it I still pull back, like the flanges of a freshly opened oyster. It is the verb *to drool,* when applied to written prose, and especially to anything I myself have written. Very nice people have told me, for a long time now, that some things they have read of mine, in books or magazines, have made them drool. I know they mean to compliment me. They are saying that my use of words makes them oversalivate, like hapless dogs waiting for a bell to say "Meat!" to them. It has made them more alive than they were, more active. They are grateful to me, perhaps, for being reminded that they are still functioning, still aware of some of their hungers.

I too should be grateful, and even humble, that I have reminded people of what fun it is, vicariously or not, to eat/live. Instead I am revolted. I see a slavering slobbering maw. It dribbles helplessly, in a Pavlovian response. It *drools*. And drooling, not over a meaty bone or a warm bowl of slops, is what some people have done over my printed words. This has long worried me. I feel grateful but repelled. They are nice people, and I like them and I like dogs, but dogs *must* drool when they are excited by the prospect of the satisfaction of alerted tastebuds, and two-legged people do not need to, and in general I know that my reaction to the fact that some people slobber like conditioned animals is a personal skunner, and that I should accept it as such instead of meeting it like a stiff-upper-lipped Anglo-Saxon (and conditioned!) nanny.

I continue, however, to be regretfully disgusted by the word *drool* in connection with all writing about food, as well as my own. And a few fans loyal enough to resist being hurt by this statement may possibly call me up!

III

It is too easy to be malicious, but certainly the self-styled food experts of our current media sometimes seem overtly silly enough to be fair game. For anyone with half an ear for the English-American language we write and speak, it is almost impossible not to chuckle over the unending flow of insults to our syntax and grammar, not to mention our several levels of intelligence.

How are we supposed to react to descriptive phrases like "crisply crunchy, to snap in your mouth"? We know this was written, and for pay, by one or another of the country's best gastronomical hacks. We should not titter. He is a good fellow. Why then does he permit himself to say that some corn on the cob is so tender that "it dribbles milk down your chin"? He seems, whether or not he means well, to lose a little of the innate dignity that we want from our gourmet-judges. He is like a comedian who with one extra grimace becomes coarse instead of funny, or like an otherwise sensitive reader who says that certain writing makes him drool.

Not all our food critics, of course, are as aware of language as the well-known culinary experts who sign magazine articles and syndicated columns. And for one of them, there are a hundred struggling copywriters who care less about mouth-watering prose than about filling ad space with folksy propaganda for "kwik" puddings and suchlike. They say shamelessly, to keep their jobs, that Mom has just told them how to make instant homemade gravy taste "like I could never make before! *Believe* me," they beg, "those other gravies just aren't the same! This has a real homemade flavor and a rich brown color. Just add it to your pan drippings." And so on.

Often these unsung kitchen psalmists turn, with probable desperation, to puns and other word games. They write, for instance, that frozen batter-fried fish are so delicious that "one crunch and you're hooked!" Oh, hohoho ha ha. And these same miserable slaves produce millions of words, if they are fortunate enough to find and keep their jobs, about things like synthetic dough that is "preformed" into "old-fashioned shapes that taste cooky-fresh and crunchy" in just fifteen minutes from freezer to oven to the kiddies' eager paws and maws.

When the hacks have proved that they can sling such culinary lingo, they are promoted to a special division that deals even more directly with oral satisfaction. They write full-page ads in juicy color, about cocktail nibbles with "a fried-chicken taste that's lip-lickin' good." This, not too indirectly, is aimed to appeal to hungry readers familiar with a franchised fried chicken that is of course known worldwide as finger-lickin good, and even packaged Kitty Krums that are whisker-lickin good. (It is interesting and reassuring, although we must drop a few g's to understand it, that modern gastronomy still encourages us to indulge in public tongueplay.)

Prose by the copywriters usually stays coy, but is somewhat more serious about pet foods than humanoid provender. Perhaps it is assumed that most people who buy kibbles do not bother to read the printed information on all four sides of their sacks, but simply pour the formula into bowls on the floor and hope for the best. Or perhaps animal-food companies recognize that some of their slaves are incurably dedicated to correct word usage. Often the script on a bag of dry pet food is better written than most paperback novels. Possibly some renegade English instructor has been allowed to explain "Why

Your Cat Will Enjoy This." He is permitted tiny professorial jokes, now and then: "As Nutritious As It Is Delicious," one caption says, and another section is called "Some Reading on Feeding," and then the prose goes all out, almost euphorically, with "Some Raving on Saving." The lost academician does have to toss in a few words like *munchy* to keep his job, but in general there is an enjoyably relaxed air about the unread prose on pet-food packages, as opposed to the stressful cuteness of most fashionable critics of our dining habits.

Of course the important thing is to stay abreast of the lingo, it seems. Stylish restaurants go through their phases, with beef Wellington and chocolate mousse high in favor one year and strictly for Oskaloossa, Missouri, the next. We need private dining-out guides as well as smart monthly magazines to tell us what we are eating tonight, as well as what we are paying for it.

A lot of our most modish edibles are dictated by their scarcity, as always in the long history of gastronomy. In 1979, for instance, it became *de rigueur* in California to serve caviar in some guise, usually with baked or boiled potatoes, because shipments from Iran grew almost as limited as they had long been from Russia. (Chilled caviar, regal fare, was paired with the quaintly plebeian potato many years ago, in Switzerland I think, but by 1979 its extravagant whimsy had reached Hollywood and the upper West Coast by way of New York, so that desperate hostesses were buying and even trying to "home-make" caviar from the Sacramento River sturgeons. Results: usually lamentable, but well meant.).

All this shifting of gustatory snobbism should probably have more influence on our language than it does. Writers for both elegant magazines and "in" guides use much the same word-appeal as do the copywriters for popular brands of convenience foods. They may not say "lip-smackin" or "de-lish," but they manage to imply what their words will make readers do. They use their own posh patter, which like the humbler variety seldom bears any kind of scrutiny, whether for original meaning or plain syntax.

How about "unbelievably succulent luscious scallops which boast a nectar-of-the-sea freshness"? Or "a *beurre blanc,* that ethereally light, grandmotherly sauce"? Or "an onion soup, baked *naturellement,* melting its knee-deep crust of cheese and croutons"? Dressings are "teasingly-tart," not teasing or tart or even teasingly tart. They have

"breathtakingly visual appeal," instead of looking yummy, and some
of them, perhaps fortunately, are "almost too beautiful to describe,"
"framed in a picture-perfect garnish of utter perfection and exquis-
iteness," "a pinnacle of gastronomical delight." (Any of these
experiences can be found, credit card on the ready, in the bistrots-of-
the-moment.)

It is somewhat hard to keep one's balance, caught between the
three stools of folksy lure, stylish gushing, and a dictionary of word
usage. How does one *parse,* as my grandfather would say, a complete sentence like, "The very pinkness it was, of minislices"? Or "A
richly eggy and spiritous Zabaglione, edged in its serving dish with
tiny dots of grenadine"? These are not sentences, at least to my
grandfather and to me, and I think *spirituous* is a better word in this
setting, and I wonder whether the dots of grenadine were wee drops
of the sweet syrup made from pomegranates or the glowing seeds of
the fruit itself, and how and why anyone would preserve them for a
chic restaurant. And were those pink mini-slices from a lamb, a calf?
Then there are always verbs to ponder on, in such seductive reports
on what and where to dine. One soup "packs chunks" of something
or other, to prove its masculine heartiness in a stylish lunchtime
brasserie. "Don't forget to special-order!" Is this a verb, a split infini-
tive, an attempt of the reporter to sound down-to-earth?

Plainly it is as easy to carp, criticize, even dismiss such unworthy
verbiage as it is to quibble and shudder about what the other media
dictate, that we may subsist. And we continue to carp, criticize,
dismiss—and to *eat,* not always as we are told to, and not always
well, either! But we were born *hungry* . . .

M. F. K. Fisher: *How to Cook a Wolf* and Other Gastronomical Feats

Ruth Reichl/1981

From *MS.*, vol. 9, April 1981, pp. 90+. Used by permission of Ruth Reichl.

. . . the most interesting philosopher of food now practicing in our country.

—Clifton Fadiman, 1954

She writes about fleeting tastes and feasts vividly, excitingly, sensuously, exquisitely.

—James Beard, 1976

I do not consider myself a food writer.

—M. F. K. Fisher, 1980

"You actually met her?" people say. Sometimes they add, "You mean she's still alive?" Always they add, "What did she give you to eat?" I answer yes, very much so, and split-pea soup. If they insist I tell them that there was ham in the soup and good sourdough bread with sweet butter and a local white wine that I could not identify and fruit compote and two kinds of shortbread cookies. Occasionally I add that there was too much sherry in the soup, and that I found this reassuring rather than disappointing. And that she whistled while she cooked.

Then people ask about her kitchen; she is, after all, the writer who has made reading about food palatable even to people for whom the eating of it is a chore. This is because her many books—14 to date—maintain that food is more than merely something to eat. "There is a communion of more than our bodies when bread is broken and wine is drunk," she once said, when asked why she wrote about food. And she has written, "I cannot count the good people I know who, to my mind, would be even better if they bent their spirits to the study of their own hungers. There are too many of us, otherwise in proper focus, who feel an impatience for the demands of our bodies, and who try throughout our whole lives to deafen ourselves to the voices of various hungers."

Nevertheless, when people ask about her kitchen, I tell them about her bathroom instead. It is the nicest one I've ever been in. There is a large tub right in the middle of the room. On the floor there are carpets, and on the walls pictures in a friendly jumble. If you were in the bathtub you would be facing a long, low, uncurtained window, and you would be able to see the trees outside. Great piles of towels wait to be used, and books wait to be read, and the contents of the most amazing assortment of jars wait to bubble and perfume and smooth and soothe. "Sometimes," says Fisher as she shows me around the small beautiful house amidst the vineyards of northern California, "my friends disappear into my bathroom for hours." She says it admiringly, as if she likes herself better for having friends who know how to use a good thing when they find it.

"Yes, yes, but her *kitchen,*" my friends insist. M. F. K. Fisher is the author of books with titles like *Serve It Forth, The Gastronomical Me,* and *Consider the Oyster.* They like to think that the book she wrote during World War II, *How To Cook a Wolf,* is a cookbook, although the wolf in question is the proverbial one at the door. They quote the conclusion to this book: "I believe that one of the most dignified ways we are capable of, to assert and then reassert our dignity in the face of poverty and war's fears and pains, is to nourish ourselves with all possible skill, delicacy, and ever-increasing enjoyment. And with our gastronomical growth will come, inevitably, knowledge and perception of a hundred other things, but mainly of ourselves. Then Fate, even tangled as it is with cold wars as well as hot, cannot harm us."

Today our greatest food writer cooks at one end of her large living room where there is a stove (electric), a refrigerator (ordinary), a few commonplace cupboards, and a sink that looks out over fields and trees. Plates dry in a plastic dish drainer, and a few vegetables ripen on the windowsill. There is a large, round, beautiful table, but still this kitchen, devoid of the latest gadgets, wouldn't interest *House and Garden.* It is a kitchen that you or I would probably be happy to cook in, but I prefer cooking with gas.

"I usually eat late when I'm alone," she says, "around eleven. And I love to read while I'm eating, so I cook dishes that will hold. I eat according to what I really find easiest to do—usually I find myself eating rice and vegetables, things that are already cut up, so I've got a book in one hand and good stuff in the other."

"Good stuff" is what you expect M. F. K. Fisher to eat, and you expect her to eat it on her own. In essays like "On Dining Alone," she writes about teaching herself to enjoy her own company, of ordering dishes and good wines as if she were "a guest to herself." It surprised me to learn that she was *reading* during all of this singular splendor. When I tell her that I had always imagined her to be unaccompanied, even by books, and that it seemed to me that the truly complete person ought to be content with the contemplation of one's dinner, she snorts, "Oh, ridiculous! People *are* alone. Everyone has to eat alone. And one has to do it, I think, or die, gracefully. You know— with a certain amount of panache—pizzazz."

At 72, M. F. K. Fisher is often referred to as one of America's greatest living writers. "I used to say that by the time I was fifty, I would have written a good book," she remarks. "And I got to be fifty, so I raised the ante to fifty-five. And I took a good look at myself and I said, never. I don't like to read the stuff I've written. Never have, never will." Asked to name her favorite of her own books she un- hesitatingly replies: "The best thing I've done is the translation of Brillat-Savarin. I like it, I respect it. I did it because his French was so good. It was so pure, so not effusive. He was just straight good prose.

"There are two kinds of books," M. F. K. Fisher says, "those that try to imitate Brillat-Savarin's, and those that try not to." He wrote *The Physiology of Taste* in 1825. It can *still* tell you just about every- thing you ever wanted to know about food, and a lot more that you didn't know you wanted to know.

Pressed further, Fisher will admit that she likes her own *A Cordiall Water,* which she calls "a nice little book—amusing, interesting, informative." The book, about folk medicine, is a collection of "odd and old receipts to cure the ills of people and animals." It has long been out of print, but a paperback edition is being considered. "I don't think anybody buys my books before they go into paperback— you know—years later. I don't know *why* publishers keep publishing me. So many publishers have lost their shirts on me. It's very mys- terious. The only way I've paid the bills is by free-lance writing."

A surprising lot of this writing—for someone who is often told, even today, "Oh, you're the woman who writes the cookbooks"—

had nothing to do with food. Fisher has written short stories and essays for *The New Yorker* for 35 years. "It was a great education for me," she says. "Mr. Shawn is so fussy—God, every comma counts." She also wrote for *House Beautiful, The Saturday Review,* and about a dozen other publications, articles for which she was never particularly well paid, and for which she never received an expense account. "They just didn't do it in those days," she says. "I never got a check for travel or expenses or anything until I was about sixty-five."

It is odd to hear M. F. K. Fisher talk about money. It is even odder to hear her talk about her lack of it. She has been to so many places, and written so much about traveling and eating and living abroad that she is generally assumed to be affluent. And yet, even now, when she speaks of her agent, Robert Lescher, she says, "I get broke, he gets sad. So I work and he sells it. That's the way it is." Of her former agent (of 35 years), Henry Volkening, she says: "Poor man. One year I made thirty-seven dollars. We used to call it the martini fund. All he ever said was 'Do not be discouraged if you can eat and feed the kids, don't worry. Everything will be all right.' "

Things always have been more or less all right for Fisher. She was born Mary Frances Kennedy in Albion, Michigan. Her family moved to Whittier, California, when she was three; her father was the editor of the local newspaper, and her mother was an extremely well-educated homemaker. She married at 20, and with her husband, Al Fisher, who later became dean of English at Smith College, spent three years, from 1929 to 1931, living and studying in France. Back in the States, they "sweated out the Depression" by living in her family's beach shack and cleaning other people's houses. "It annoyed the hell out of me," she says, "because he got fifty cents an hour and I only got thirty-five cents because I was a woman.

"My husband was writing the great American novel and he was an absolute nut. I was, too. I was carving wood to make money— wedding chests and things like that, and I was doing quite well. I liked working with the tools, but I wasn't working with any kind of inspiration. I guess I wrote my first piece because I was so bored. I illustrated it, too—and when the check came it really gave me pause. I got ten dollars for the piece and fifteen dollars for the illustration. I thought—am I a writer or am I going to be a sort of mediocre illustrator for the rest of my life?"

Mary Frances Kennedy Fisher may not like to read her own work, but as she says, "You do what you do best. I never remember making a decision about it, things just happened. I really believe that some things are decided for you, by forces outside yourself—your genes, whether Pakistan gets invaded, you know it. It depends on so many things."

She also believes in bowing to the inevitable. "For instance, when I left my first husband, I was terribly sad about it. But I didn't hesitate for a minute because I knew it was inevitable." What had happened was that she had fallen in love with a friend, and he with her, and after getting over her "mid-Victorian attitude about Hopeless Passion," they were married.

In libraries, many of Fisher's books are still filed under "Parrish, Mary Frances Kennedy." Right in front of her card is that of Dillwyn Parrish, author of 11 books. He was a better painter than he was a writer, and he had two exhibits in California just before he died of a disease that progressively destroyed his circulatory system. The couple had a few idyllic years in Switzerland before returning to California, where Parrish succumbed.

"I was very much in debt and I didn't know what to do," Fisher remembers. "Some concerned friends of mine got me a job in Hollywood. I wrote gags for Bob Hope, Bing Crosby, and Dorothy Lamour. The first time I wrote one, my producer said, 'I want you to do a three-minute gag line.' So I trotted across the lot, went into my office and dictated it to my secretary. She typed it up and got a messenger—everything was very protocol—and sent it to the producer. He looked at it and said, 'This is impossible. Pure plagiarism. Nobody could write this in a half hour.' So it was rejected. When I asked my business manager what I had done wrong, he said, 'Too fast, it should have taken two weeks. They would have accepted it immediately.' "

Less than a year later, the Screenwriters Guild managed to get Fisher out of her seven-year contract. It was one of the rare times that a union wasn't battling for money. As M. F. K. puts it, "I was a writer who was not writing what I could write."

What she could, and did, write was The Gastronomical Me, a book that is less about food than it is about good people and good places and the extraordinarily good times that are possible for those who

know how to live with all their brains and all their beings. It is also
a book that has some of the most loving passages that one human
being has ever written about another. "Chexbres was there, of
course. We celebrated with the first of 10,000 completely enjoyable
drinks. . . . Everything was all right after that, for as many more years
as he was on the earth, and I lived secure and blessed for those years
too, through many terrors."

"Calling Dillwyn 'Chexbres' was an affectation—I wouldn't do that
now," she says. "It was the name of the town in which we had lived.
It is the old spelling of the French for 'goat,' and he did have a kind of
goatlike look. But I didn't think how odd the word would look
printed in English."

When I ask M. F. K. Fisher what happened after Hollywood, she
answers, "I acquired a husband and two children, and I worked very,
very hard." About her third husband, publisher Donald Friede, she
says little and has written less. In book circles he is known as "one of
the first publishers who understood modern literature." Of her two
children, Anna and Kennedy, Fisher says simply, "They're good
girls," and that she considers them a great blessing. As for the work—
she wrote four books in quick succession and then, not believing in
alimony and with two children to support, she went back to free-
lance writing.

"I was never a working parent, in the sense of having a nine-to-five
job and having to ensure proper child care." The family was, in fact,
quite mobile. They lived for a time at the Kennedy ranch, and Fisher
helped her father put out his paper. Then, "because I wanted my girls
to learn new ways and new languages," they went abroad. The franc
was down then, and the three lived in France and then Italy for four
years. "I don't know if I could have done it with a husband," she
says.

Fisher's sense of independence and "differentness" as a woman,
never an overt issue in her work, recently surfaced in *Newsweek*'s
"My Turn" column, where she wrote: "Women continue to think,
speak, act and react, conduct their inner and outer lives, in a completely different pattern from any that has been imposed on them,
with small success, by the so-called opposite sex. (This usually
includes fathers, teachers, brothers, lovers, husbands.)" The article,
called "Why We Need a Woman's Party," chronicles the many ways

in which Fisher believes women differ from men. "I was surprised by the amount of comment the article aroused," she says. "It didn't occur to me that people would be bothered by it. I just thought that's the way things were; I've always assumed it to be so. Women do everything differently from men, given the chance. We're taught by men to be like men, and to compete with men, but this is ridiculous. Why not train women to recognize their own strengths? Why, even our metabolisms are different. Men wear out quicker than women. That's why there are so many widows."

Fisher has started working on a book about aging. (She is also in progress with a book about "places I've been to.") "I think it's something we should prepare for—like anything else. Most women *are* going to end up alone; it shouldn't come as a surprise. You slow down as you get older, and you have to learn to live with pain. These are physical facts of life. It doesn't help to pretend that it's not going to happen."

Her hands are crippled by arthritis, but the pain does not apparently bother her. She does not believe in taking pills. Her vanity is nonexistent. "I feel sorry for any photographer who has to take my picture. There's all of this. . . ." She pinches at her face, which still bears the traces of a beautiful youth. She speaks easily of "when I die," and meanwhile she works, "most of the time." She cherishes her solitude. While her refrigerator is covered with her grandchildren's drawings, she says, when speaking of one daughter, "I let her call me. I try not to intrude." Charlie, the cat, strolls about the house and scratches at the furniture. "I wouldn't feed him anything I wouldn't eat," she says, but Charlie knows that the table is off limits. There is no nonsense about Fisher; she has made her rules and sticks to them.

She also sticks pretty close to home. "I love living in the country, and I love this house." The house, consisting of two big rooms (a workroom/bedroom and a living room/kitchen), and the bathroom, is one that she traded for a "great big house" in St. Helena, about 40 miles away. "We could sleep nine, and after the children left, I felt I was running a sort of dining room and inn. I couldn't get any work done."

Since her children have left home, Fisher's book output has increased. She's written about Aix-en-Provence, an autobiography of

her childhood, a book about Marseilles, and the first volume of the
Time-Life *Foods of the World* series. About this, *The Cooking of
Provincial France,* Fisher says, "I did it mostly for the money. That
was the first time I ever had an expense account. I told them very
bluntly that I didn't need to go to France, that I could do it all at
home. But I had French friends who were sort of dying on the vine,
and I didn't have any money to get over there. That's why I did it."

Of that trip she remembers: "I damn near starved. My friend liked
to eat deli food, and his wife lay in bed all day drinking tea. I was
living in Julia Child's house, but she and Paul are very tidy. I kept
ferreting around in the cupboards thinking that certainly she would
have hidden a little old can of tuna or something, but there was
nothing. So finally I made a very good friend of a chauffeur, and he
would come up for me secretly and take me to the market in Grasse.
Oh, it was heaven. I'd bring back a little bag of green almonds
because that was the season, but there was no reaction at all to them.
Nobody gave a damn about green almonds. Then we'd go out to a
three-star restaurant which was no good at all that time of year. Jesus,
I was hungry!"

She says it happily, as if contemplating past hungers were a great
joy. "We were born *hungry,*" she once wrote. Other people may
have found ways to appease or assuage or diminish their appetites,
but Fisher has emphatically not. She has *stayed* hungry.

Showing me out, she points to a little bronze plaque on her
wooden gate. A friend brought it from Paris. "It was a mistake," she
says, "but I like it." The plaque reads, "Mary Frances KFisher." She
says the last word slowly, rolling the letters voluptuously off her
tongue. "Sounds like a sneeze, doesn't it?" She closes the door, and
as I leave I can hear her whistling.

How to Cook a Life

David Eames/1981

From *Quest*/81, June 1981, vol. 5, no. 5, pp. 38–42.

Why do all the other food experts in America pay such close attention to M. F. K. Fisher? She is not a famous chef. She doesn't teach, appear on television, or produce syndicated columns. She has never written a cookbook as such. "Recipes in my book will be there like birds in a tree," she declared early on, "if there is a comfortable branch." No, she is a writer who cooks—and writes magnificently about eating, as well as loving and living and dying. Clifton Fadiman has called her a philosopher. W. H. Auden said of her: "I do not know of anyone in the United States who writes better prose."

What sets M. F. K. Fisher apart is her gift for savoring the relationship between food and other human concerns. "It seems to me that our three basic needs, for food and security and love, are so entwined that we cannot straightly think of one without the other," she once wrote. "So it happens that when I write of hunger, I am really writing about love and the hunger for it . . . and then the warmth and richness and fine reality of hunger satisfied . . . and it is all one."

Disciplined, elegant, often passionate, Fisher's writing has taken the form of short stories and essays—many published in *The New Yorker*—travel articles, memoirs, a novel (*Not Now But Now,* long out of print, "and no great loss to the world," *she* says), and a distinguished translation of Brillat-Savarin's *The Physiology of Taste,* in which the translator's glosses are often as piquant as the text itself. Perhaps her best-known work is *The Art of Eating,* a collection of five earlier culinary books reissued several years ago in paperback. Thirteen titles in all, reflecting a sophisticated delight in everything from oysters to ocean voyages, from love affairs to literature, from bullfights to bachelorhood to bouillabaisse.

Her first book was published in 1937, long before Americans were used to woks and whisks, much less gazpacho and spinach quiche. A slim volume entitled *Serve It Forth,* it is fat with scholarship, opinion, anecdote, humor. And she has been instructing and entertaining us ever since. If this country has experienced some gastronomical growth over the past 40 years, it is partly because Mrs. Fisher has been at our elbow—scolding, cajoling, insisting that we try the new, try just one bite.

Example: for lunch at her house recently there was, to begin, a small plate of chilled braised celery dressed with oil and lemon and minced shallots and possibly a touch of anchovy, surrounded by halves of little plum tomatoes, each filled with a dollop of Chinese oyster sauce. Sound awful? In fact, it was delicious.

The first thing I remember tasting and then wanting to taste again," she writes in *The Gastronomical Me,* "was the grayish-pink fuzz my grandmother skimmed from a spitting kettle of strawberry jam." Mary Frances Kennedy was then about four. She is now 72. Born in Michigan, she grew up among the orange groves and vineyards of southern California. "I have always lived in wine country," she says, and she still does. Her father was a small-town newspaper editor (and son of another) who "pounded out at least a thousand words a day. My family was extremely articulate. Writing seemed a completely natural thing to do. In fact, I wrote a novel when I was nine. I used to read chapters aloud to my parents, but I stopped because they laughed so much, and it wasn't meant to be funny. I couldn't spell 'hopping,' so my characters were forever 'hoping' in and out of bed."

But from that time on, during stints at proper boarding schools, throughout her student days in France at the University of Dijon, then years of living in the Swiss countryside near Vevey, and later a term as a screenwriter in Hollywood and another as a teacher in a black school in the Deep South, and for all the years since, she has been writing and tasting, tasting and writing.

The rich ingredients of her life include three marriages, two children, and long periods of full-time living in Europe. Through it all, she has written unsparingly of worldly pleasures and personal pain. So it is not accurate to say that M. F. K. Fisher is a food writer, although she has always written about food. Her travel writing is seasoned with evocative mentions of eating, just as her food writing is flavored with places and people.

Mrs. Fisher can describe the tiny grilled ham-and-cheese sandwiches once served to her in the old Palm Court of the Palace Hotel
in San Francisco in a way that makes you long for a trip back in time.
With equal zest she tells of a salad of early summer vegetables once
eaten in Venice, or recalls a dessert of pears baked with honey and
kirsch and topped with sour cream, a special slice of pâté shared with
a special friend in Paris, *truite en bleu* in Lausanne, a particular bottle
of Chambertin '19.

In 1929 she went to France with her first husband, Al Fisher, whom
she had met at UCLA. "We were both from small towns, and felt an
almost desperate need to escape that kind of environment." The
escape was successful; she lived in France almost continuously for
three years. And when she left Fisher in 1936 to marry Dillwyn
Parrish, a gifted artist, she returned to Europe to live again, settling
in Switzerland until the outbreak of World War II. Mrs. Fisher has
made the crossing many times since. She has written a book about
Provence, *Map of Another Town,* and her most recent work, *A
Considerable Town,* is all about the city of Marseilles—"because I
love the place." Europe was her testing ground, and France her early
gastronomic mentor.

But Mrs. Fisher is no snob. She likes a simple bowl of soup. She
likes plain rice (although she would probably cook it in a good stock,
not water), she likes asparagus on toast, canned shad roe, saltines,
rice pudding. She can enjoy a grilled lamb chop, although she
chooses to eat less meat these days. She even admits that she once
had a secret craving for . . . mashed potatoes with catsup.

Whatever it is, from caviar to kasha, Mrs. Fisher gives loving
attention to her subject: "The best way to eat fresh peas is to be alive
on the right day, with the men picking and the women shelling, and
everyone capering in the sweet early summer weather, and the big
pot of water boiling, and the table set with little cool roasted chickens
and pitchers of white wine."

Driving across the Golden Gate Bridge and up into the Sonoma
Valley where Mrs. Fisher lives, one is quickly affected with a sense of
peace and well-being. The smooth hills in a misting spring rain are an
almost oily green—the color of the first pressing of olives for oil.
Eucalyptus trees line stretches of the road and ancient oaks dot the

pastures, where fat cattle graze. Surely the Italians who first settled here experienced a certain resonance—it was Umbria or the gentler slopes of Tuscany: wine country. And gradually rows of grapevines begin to appear. Pruned, hacked back, gnarly, they lie across the landscape like giant strands of old rope.

The house is small and white, set in a lush meadow full of lupins and poppies. The property is part of a larger one, a ranch belonging to a friend, which is in turn set in the midst of an Audubon preserve. If it sounds idyllic, it is. A place to live and work and rest, a land of milk and honey.

There is, however, no suggestion of retirement or reclusion in the manner of the lady who opens the front door. Her gray hair tied back in a neat bun, she is tall and slender, intelligent and poised. A slightly hesitant step is her only apparent concession to troublesome eyesight. Her voice is gentle, almost whispery, and cordial. She offers a glass of wine and a quick tour of this place she quite obviously loves.

It is an odd house, designed to Mrs. Fisher's specifications. There are just three rooms. A large central area serves as living room, kitchen, and dining room. Along the far wall are sink, refrigerator, dishwasher, cupboards, counter space. No monster commercial range, no hanging battery of hammered copper, no Cuisinart. No pungent, heavy smells. No real assurance that any meal will appear at all. But the dining table, a big, handsome round one, is set for two people.

This is a room that will be cool in summer, cozy in winter. Cool because of the glistening black tile floors and the graceful arc of the ceiling and the generous windows on three sides; cozy on account of the comfortable chairs, the Oriental rugs, the handsome Franklin stove—now with a vase of long-stemmed carnations set on it.

Through the front hall and up a couple of steps, one finds the bedroom, which is also Mrs. Fisher's study. At one end is a bed and at the other a desk covered with a jumble of books and piles of paper. A page from a work in progress is stuck in the typewriter. "Have a look," Mrs. Fisher says, waving toward the machine. "I'm trying to do a book about places—calling it *Places,* I think. But, gee, I don't know, sometimes I wonder if I have the energy to finish it. My advice is, if you have something important to do, do it *now,* while you still have the energy."

All the walls in the house, including those in the enormous bathroom, are covered with paintings, some by friends, many by her
second husband. "He died in '42 of a very painful and debilitating
disease. If he had lived, I'm sure we'd still be together. He was the
love of my life. Have another glass of wine and look around while
I see about lunch."

Where there are no paintings there are books—about 5,000 of
them. Cookbooks, of course; novels, history, psychology; books
related in some way to food and drink. Shelves of them in the
hallway, in the bedroom, in the living room. Stacked on desks,
arranged haphazardly on tables, piles of them everywhere. Many
are in French.

From her conversation and from her written work, it is safe to
suppose that Mrs. Fisher has read all the books on her crammed
shelves and a great number of others besides. She quotes appropri-
ately and confidently from Shakespeare, Lewis Carroll, Santayana,
Hemingway, Edmund Burke, La Rochefoucauld, Seneca, Talleyrand,
and Dr. Johnson, to mention only a few. Scattered between hints on
how to pep up a can of baked beans and information about eggs are
notes on the way Lucullus arranged his banquets, speculation about
what the Crusaders ate, homage paid to the Chinese Emperor Shen
Nung (2873–2689 B.C.), curious scientific facts about the chemistry
of the human body and the sex life of the oyster.

The rain has disappeared, and from a small veranda one has a fine
view of fruit trees, an old bell tower, and the main ranch house a
comfortable distance away. Chicken wire has been tacked up to keep
the cows from nibbling at the planters. The cat, Charley, wanders
past, intent on some movement in the farther field. Whistling comes
wafting from inside the house, followed by a surprised, annoyed
matter-of-fact "Ouch!" And lunch is served.

After the vegetable hors d'oeuvres comes a dish of potatoes baked
in a custardy base with cheese. For dessert, ice cream and cookies.
Both are homemade—the cookies thin and crisp and sugary, the ice
cream rich with hunks of plum preserve. More wine, a light local
white, is poured from a heavy, squarish glass jug that looks like an
elegant old-time milk bottle and always seems to be full.

Mrs. Fisher's talk, like her writing, is characterized by anecdote and
allusion, emotion and wit. She is casual about chronology, vague

about dates, but precise when it comes to nuance and detail. She is
candid, sometimes downright blunt, in arresting contrast to her gentle
voice and manner.

"You know, recently I've been discovered by the young. They
think I'm a 'liberated' woman. I've always been liberated, I hope. But
I never thought of myself as part of a movement, just a liberated
person."

She was sufficiently liberated to travel to Mississippi as a volunteer
teacher in a black school in 1963. "Both my children were out of the
nest and I was free. I wanted to see if the South was as rotten as I'd
heard it was, and it was. Oh, it was worse! Of course, I chose the
'long, hot summer.' "

But although she has incorporated much of the experience of a
complicated life into her prose, she has never mentioned that
sojourn. "I wish I could write about it, but I just can't—yet."

Nor has she given more than passing mention to her days in
Hollywood. "It was during the war. I was newly widowed, and I
wanted to see if I could manage on my own. I was just part of the
stable of writers at Paramount. There was really nothing for me to do.
I didn't fit in. I kept being introduced to people who were interested
in meeting 19-year-old blondes. They were *not* interested in a tired,
32-year-old widow with two children. But I did make some marvelous friends, including the Marx Brothers."

She has written extensively about her brother, but not about his
suicide at the age of 22. "He was about to be called into the army,
and he refused to wear a uniform. He was a wonderful artist. If he
had lived he might have been the Daumier of today."

Mrs. Fisher sighs and takes a bite of cookie. "I've gotten some
letters lately that are actually disapproving because I haven't told
more about myself. Well, I don't see why I should. Especially when
you think of all that soap-opera junk that people write about themselves these days. Still, it's nice to get mail."

Fisher: Past, Present, Future Together
Robert Davidoff/1982

From *The Lost Angeles Times,* 8 September 1982, pp. 10–11.

What is a California writer? If by a California writer we mean one who has lived from an early age in California, who returns to it as home and who has written about it well and over a period of many years, then M. F. K. Fisher is a notable California writer, though seldom recognized as such. Known as a food writer and read for her wonderful style, her keen observations, her high and lively temperament, her supremely evocative and descriptive gifts, as well as for her vast knowledge of good cooking, eating and drinking. Mary Frances Kennedy Fisher makes one look again at what we mean when we claim a writer for a region.

Although she was born in Michigan three-quarters of a century ago, Fisher considers herself an "almost native" Californian. She grew up in Whittier, about which she has written her wonderful and foolishly neglected *Among Friends* (Knopf, 1971), still the best account of life in Southern California in the early 20th Century. She thinks of herself as a Californian, and it is West that she has always returned to from sojourns abroad. Returning to California "intensifies things. I love to get away from this country, from the West, because whenever I come back, I'm more American than when I left." Needing, missing an older culture, " part of me needs to feel that the bench I am sitting on has been there, 2,000 years," she said. But the salient aspect of California life for Fisher, as for so many, remains its newness. "We're very new. The soil is new and the trees and the architecture; and the people are even newer."

Fisher resists the notion that a California writer has certain traits or special subjects. She does not recognize in them the regional sense of the Southern writer, although Steinbeck, for one, gave a good feeling for the country. Southern California writers have been too tied up with Hollywood for a real regional literature to develop. Talking with her, reading her books, where she grew up, where her family lived,

66

where she got her bearings. Fisher's California is a distinctive place but not a crazy one. One could live there, she did.

Throughout the *Art of Eating,* a compendium of five of Fisher's best books (available in a Vintage paperback) are striking vignettes of an earlier Southern California. She tells of eating a fresh baked peach pie and fresh cream with her father and sister en route home to Whittier in a model T after a weekend during harvest time at a family ranch near Lancaster. The emotions of a daughter and her father, the tastes and other sensations that linger through the years make unforgettable reading. In Fisher's writing, the good things in life are never separate from life itself. And the place is California, a real place, sanctified by the drama of human lives.

"In *Among Friends,* Fisher gives our sprawling, crowded Los Angeles world a comprehensive and charming history. We can borrow from her a past of family, upbringing, childhood, weather, neighbors, the circus coming to town, that makes it possible to imagine that we too might have had a Los Angeles history, to imagine our own pasts in this city where so many of us have come already grown up.

M. F. K. Fisher writes an uncommon and distinctive prose. She has an unmatched capacity to convey taste, smell, feel, the physical experience of food and weather and buildings and place and of people, not only the people one knows and loves or hates but the people one comes up against here and there—a waiter, a passing stranger, someone else's lover, her own passing fancy. She conveys the essence of a place encountered and remembered as few other writers can. Among her works in print are the *Art of Eating,* her translation of Brillat-Savarin's extraordinary *The Physiology of Taste* (HBJ), her book on Marseilles. *A Considerable Town* (Knopf), and last year's reissue of her compendium of home remedies and country nostrums. *A Cordiall Water* (North Point Press). This Californian has to hope that *Among Friends* will be reissued; Fisher's writings spur one on.

As They Were (Knopf, 1982) collects 19 of Fisher's pieces from over the years. It is a splendid place to begin reading her and a varied and rewarding collection. Several of the pieces take place in California: her first published piece, an account of Laguna Beach in everything but name, a haunting memory of the Mission Inn in

Riverside, a concise memoir of the "inner ghetto" of Whittier and
xenophobia in larger form during the First World War and a
charming piece on her life now in the Sonoma Valley of Northern
California. Other pieces range from accounts of kitchens in France
to an arresting story of isolation and confrontation with self during
a winter storm at the ocean's edge. They share an interest in places
and how life resolves itself into experiences. Every sense and every
season and every sensation has its moment. These writings, especially one about the gathering and preserving of food in Provence,
reveal Fisher's awareness of the flow of life and of nature. What other
writer about civilized life has so intense a feeling for what one might
call the interaction of the natural with the social processes? Food and
drink and making oneself at home in the world keep even the most
modern people in close touch with nature and the elemental in life.
Fisher's vivid interest in this makes her the most compelling writer
about an American high bourgeois style of life that has reached its
apotheosis in California, what we call (but she never would) life style.

This month, North Point Press will republish her one novel, *Not
Now But Now,* originally published in 1947. The novel tells the story
of Jennie, a character who has adventures in different places and
historical periods. Jennie is beautiful, narcissistic, adventurous, cold,
punishing and, perhaps, vulnerable; she has a kind of independence
but is as cut off from her traditional moorings in the moral world as
she is unconfined by ordinary historical time. Fisher's notion for the
book enabled her to concentrate on a certain sort of female character, a little like others who have appeared in her writings and who
have seemed to fascinate and repel her. At the same time, her lush
observational fancy roams through some memorable scenes from the
past: Gold Rush San Francisco; turn-of-the-century Chicago; Switzerland between the Wars.

Fisher undertook *Not Now But Now* at the urging of friends and
under pressure of circumstances: "I am not a novelist," she told them
at the time. "Why should I write a novel?" She wrote the novel, "five
novellas" really, but "was determined not to make it anything about
me." There are things in the book that Fisher's readers will recognize
as familiar, "because I don't know anything much, you know, except
myself."

The story set in Gold Rush San Francisco has especially the ring of

Fisher's best work with the added dimensions of history and fiction. With her delighted sense of what, in any age, made life worth living, Fisher fashions the textures of old San Francisco, when its charm was neither so established nor so safe as it is now. One enjoys in *Not Now But Now* the profusion of life's bounties and the concentration on one character's greedy embrace of it. Jennie isn't Fisher, surely, but a made-up character, whose adventures offer another view of a world Fisher has experienced so fully in her own voice.

Fisher is something of a moralist of experience, encouraging one to try things out, advocating, in the pioneer American way, that one live a life. In this time of sudden affection for the ways and things of life that sprawl and change have doomed, Fisher's books may have a particular nostalgic interest and a piquancy for Californians. She writes about what may have been the last old-fashioned times from which so many of our tastes and manners derive, about Dijon, Provence, Marseilles and California before the world had shrunk and generalized to its current state, when these were still pungently, demandingly individual places with their own people, customs, foods and charms, about sea voyages, trains, waiters, manners, the countless things that made up life before the spread of technology enforced uniformity. She was lucky to have lived in that Europe that so beguiled our older generations, but that is as different from Europe now as we are from America then. Fisher also writes with the same power about the California of those times, when it was isolated, traditional, quieter, rough, perhaps the best American place to live, old and new, full of adventure and charm.

It would be misleading to say that Fisher's work is primarily nostalgic. Talking about what a writer might do, she said, "my main interest in writing, although I never do it deliberately, is to be evocative so that it'll make other people say, 'Oh yes, I remember, I remember.' " But hers is a special kind of nostalgia, because she does not aim merely at the past. "I want to be evocative of either the past or the future." Her undimmed interest in life as she and we now live it evokes for us how our lives might be if we have the courage and imagination to live them.

Perhaps Fisher is most a California writer in her evocation of each reader's future as she writes about her own past and present.

M. F. K. Fisher

Maya Angelou/1983

From *People Magazine*, 24 January 1983, vol. 19, pp. 63+.
Maya Angelou/*People Weekly;* © 1983, Time Inc.

She is beautiful, of a generous size, and life has used her, sometimes beautifully, and in all ways generously. She has had a Great Love, immobilizing tragedy, good health until recently, fame, and enough time to learn and explain the art of cooking and the art of eating. She was also given a hearty good humor.

Mary Frances Kennedy Fisher has been called the greatest food writer of our time. W. H. Auden, the revered English-born poet, said of her, "I do not know of anyone in the United States today who writes better prose." Her books and articles are studied by serious cooks and cherished by serious lovers of the English language. A near recluse now, she has always been an extremely private person, avoiding the glitter track, traveling at her own pace and choosing her own destination.

Today she is 74 years old and still as sensual as mocha cheesecake. Her voice is light but strong, rather like good lace, and her large gray-green eyes look directly out at life, still challenging and still amused. "It is very simple: I am here because I choose to be," she declares in her latest book [*As They Were,* Knopf, $13.95]. It could easily be the motto of her life.

She was born in Albion, Mich, to Rex Kennedy, an adventurous journalist, and Edith Oliver Kennedy, who was tall, willowy and, according to Mary Frances, "a really beautiful Gibson Girl." When Mary Frances was 2½, Rex, half owner of the *Albion Evening Recorder,* sold out to his brother, Walter. Gathering his wife, his younger daughter, Anne, and Mary Frances, he traveled West to brave a life of beachcombing and other high adventure.

The Kennedy's roamed along the West Coast from Washington to Oregon, then south through California. "We could have been called hippies," says Mary Frances, "had the word been created in 1912."

There is a wistful pride in her voice as she speaks of her family. After a year and a half, her father bought a tottering newspaper in Whittier, Calif. (the Quaker hometown of ex-President Nixon) and settled down to the provincial life of a small-town newspaper publisher. Unlike their neighbors, however, the Kennedys were neither Quakers nor provincial. They were given, by popular consensus, one year to be run out of town, broke and broken. Forty-two years later, Rex Kennedy died not far from his newspaper office, still publisher of the *Whittier News.*

During Mary Frances' girlhood, her brother, David, and sister Norah, now her closest friend, increased the household, along with a maternal grandmother and a live-in cook. Grandmother Holbrook ruled the family's large Victorian kitchen and was, in Mary Frances' words, a "gastronomical dictator appointed by her own vision of Righteous Christian Living and a Nervous Stomach." The offerings of boiled dressing (served over wet shredded lettuce) and "sip and go easies" (custards and strained stewed tomatoes) seem hardly the foods to train the palate of a young gastronome-scholar.

At 18, Mary Frances had to get away, not from the large loving family but from the small town that enclosed her. Hating the idea of college, repelled by the thought of joining a sorority, she asked her father to help her find a newspaper job, somewhere far away. "Timbuktu, anything, and I wanted to travel," she says. "To see something besides Whittier." After he refused, she and a cousin did manage to arrange a semester at Illinois College in Jacksonville. "It was dreadful, just sad," she recalls, "but we were together."

Then back to Whittier and a summer semester at UCLA, where she met and fell madly in love with Al Fisher, the handsome son of a Presbyterian minister. "Well, I fell . . . something. . . . Anyhow, I was dying to get out of the trap and he brought me out." And she brought him out. He was a Princeton graduate who wanted to be-come a college professor, to speak better French and to understand another culture. When Al won a fellowship, the young American lovers escaped to France and the good life.

French became her second language, and she speaks it today without a flaw. The exquisitely prepared foods of France developed her taste for the "pure and the fresh and the kindly." After a few days in Paris, the Fishers moved to Dijon and set up housekeeping in a

pension ruled over by another gastronomical tyrant. Madame
Ollagnier, however, was the absolute opposite of Grandmother
Holbrook. She knew good food, Mary Frances recalls like milk-fed
lamb à la mode printanière." For three years Mary Frances studied
at the University of Dijon, polished her French, and ate the most
voluptuous foods available in the city Burgundians consider the
gastronomic capital of the world.

Her palate learned to appreciate 10-year-old pâtés and roasted
birds, which had hung until they were so tender they fell from their
hooks and then were served on toast softened by a paste of rotted
innards and brandy. She consumed, with appreciation, grilled steaks,
snails green and spitting in their shells, oysters embedded in seaweed
that were "so fresh," she recalls, "their delicate flanges drew back at
your breath upon them."

After her husband earned his doctorate in Dijon, the Fishers
returned to Laguna Beach, Calif. in 1932. That Mary Frances had
become a woman of passion and courage is evident in the choices
she soon had to make. While still married to Al, she fell in love with a
close friend, the painter Dillwyn Parrish, cousin to the already famous
Maxfield Parrish. He was also married. But she was disciplined: still
profoundly attached to her husband, she kept silent, holding her
feelings in check for four years and remaining loyal to Al. And she
was audacious. With Al's encouragement, she took a sea voyage with
her new love (not yet her lover) and his mother. After spending a few
months in France, the strange ménage à trois returned to the United
States, and Mary Frances returned for the last time to Al Fisher and
duty.

When her emotions would not be controlled any longer, she set
sail again for Europe and Parrish. The next three years at their home
in Switzerland were glorious. Mary Frances was in love and was
loved in return. She was writing well—her first book, Serve It Forth,
was published in 1937—and after divorcing Fisher, she married
Dillwyn.

They played near Vevey, entertaining themselves by gardening,
canning their own crops, cooking and serving sumptuous meals to
visiting friends. When Mary Frances wasn't preparing fresh home-
grown produce or complicated Burgundian dishes she had learned
in Dijon, she spent her time writing, or talking to Dillwyn. "The only

man I've ever really known," she says. "We talked more in our short time together than I have talked in my life." Dillwyn painted his glowing oils in a studio connected to their house, and they drank the thin local wines.

It was well for them to live so intensely, for Dillwyn soon lost a leg to a nameless but ever-encroaching disease that led to his death in 1941. "For several months after he died I was in flight, not from myself particularly nor of my own volition," says Fisher. "I would be working in my little office and suddenly go as fast as I could out the door and up the road until I had no breath left."

Although drained and changed, a more mature Mary Frances knew she had to survive the loss. She visited Mexico, where brother David, with his new bride Sarah, had taken a house with Norah. Guadalajara, its music and musicians, and searching the markets for food filled the days. Drinking, eating, and singing with her family filled the nights. Mary Frances was recovering.

A few months later, at the beginning of World War II, David committed suicide. Mary Frances, with a look so direct it could be called hard, says of the tragedy, "Well, he told me he would never wear a uniform."

Further grieved by the new loss, the young widow went back to work. Her second book, *Consider the Oyster,* was published in 1941. *How to Cook a Wolf* came the next year and *The Gastronomical Me* the year after that. Meanwhile she met and married publisher Donald Friede; had two daughters, Anne and Kennedy; wrote articles on food for the *New Yorker* and other slick magazines, and went to work in Hollywood writing screenplays for Paramount. She divorced Friede in 1951. "He was more trouble than the children," she says.

When they were only 8 and 10, Mary Frances took her girls to France to see the land their mother had loved in her youth. As if the ability to learn languages could be inherited, the children quickly acquired French. After they spent a year in a local school, their mother let them run free, unrestricted by lessons, exposed to the countryside and its culture. "As I watched my daughters turn sweeter and rosier in the pure air and heard them gossiping with the old shepherd, I knew I was right to let them have their freedom. My demon was worth listening to that time."

Her child-rearing ways may have been unorthodox, but the results

have proved successful. Anne, 39, the mother of three, lives in
Oregon and works in a social center caring for the unemployed.
Kennedy, 36, mother of one son, is a respected stage manager under
contract to a Berkeley, Calif. repertory theater. Mother and daughters
remain comfortably close. Once Mary Frances plied her way between
California and France with the regularity of a scheduled steamer,
encouraging cooks and eaters toward wise and sensual experimenta-
tion, writing constantly and writing well. She now has 16 books to
her credit and a much-admired translation of *The Physiology of Taste*
by Brillat-Savarin. But she has surrendered France and the large
cities of America to live in somnolent Sonoma County in Northern
California.

Now housebound most of the time by various illnesses, she
continues to fill her days with work. Memories are as thick in her
combination living room-kitchen as the fine odors of her cooking
which weigh on the air. The lush paintings of Dillwyn Parrish hang on
the walls, along with numerous works of art by old friends. Hundreds
of cookbooks are snug in their shelves, and fine old pots rest in
cupboards. Freish flowers abound.

Culinary awards and literary tributes are absent from view. The
house, designed for her by the British-born socialite architect David
Pleydell-Bouverie, is a remarkable portrait of its owner. Its exterior
is calm, lovely and totally lacking in gee-gaws, and only the careful
observer would suspect that inside the pacific structure black tile
floors glisten like fat Greek olives, and flocked wallpaper, as red as
young wine, covers an enticing sitting room-bath. Likewise, those
who have not read her books, or watched her captivate a table of
guests with delicious food and comfortable wit, might imagine that
this quiet, still beautiful woman has lived in a life of humdrum
routine.

As the years have passed, bringing arthritis, a weakened heart and
other maladies, Mary Francis has stopped driving her trim little car.
Once weekly a young friend takes her into the town of Sonoma,
where she still selects "the honest fruit, fresh vegetables and purest
meat." She continues to write, to laugh, to cook and to entertain,
although not as frequently or on such a grand scale. "I will not bow,"
she declares. "Absolutely not bow. I say. 'Brother Pain, come in and
sit down, you and I are going to take this thing in hand. And I will not

give in.' "—As a kind of proof, she has just finished a book entitled *Sister Age*. "I took liberties with Saint Francis, who wrote songs to his brother the sun, his sister the Moon. My book is about old age. I think it is something you must welcome, and I welcome it as a sister. And I am grateful. Other people have done much more and much better, but I'm glad I've lived this life and I expect to be around for many others." Expectantly, she smiles at the promise.

M. F. K. Fisher: Philosopher-Poet of the Stove

Betty Fussell/1983

From *Masters of American Cookery* (New York: Times Books, 1983), pp. 23–29. © 1983 Times Books, a division of Random House. Reprinted by permission of Times Books, division of Random House, and Betty Fussell.

I was alone, which seems to be indicated for many such sensual rites. The potatoes were light, whipped to a firm cloud with rich hot milk, faintly yellow from ample butter. I put them in a big warmed bowl, made a dent about the size of a respectable coffee cup, and filled it to the brim with catsup from a large, full vulgar bottle that stood beside my table mat where a wineglass would be at an ordinary, commonplace, everyday banquet. Mine was, as I have said, delicious.

—from "Once a Tramp, Always . . ."
With Bold Knife and Fork (1968)

Who could make mashed potatoes and ketchup sound like *that*, invoking Mark Twain on the one hand and the secret life of Frank Harris on the other? Whose words were both so bold and so curiously devious that the poet W. H. Auden had called the wielder of them one of the best prose writers in the United States today?

Who in fact *was* the mysterious M. F. K., whom the gastronome Lucius Beebe assumed was "a wispy young Oxford don" and with whom he promptly fell in love until the truth was exposed? I am wary as I search for a nearly invisible house on the Bouverie Ranch near a dinky crossroads called Glen Ellen, California, in the Valley of the Moon.

The person who comes to the wrought-iron gate at the sound of my bell is surprisingly tall, surprisingly young. Mary Frances Kennedy Fisher, born July 3, 1908, is full of surprises—like her prose. She wears a loose cotton smock over trousers and walks slowly. A snub nose, a red cupid's mouth, and a girlish whisper contradict the gray hair pulled back from an imperious brow and the cool of gray-green eyes. I am right to be wary. I remember her writing about a great-grandmother who was "part witch, part empress." Fisher's disguise as a simple girl of the West doesn't fool me a bit.

We enter a room of such simplicity that I instantly sense a trap. Along one wall is the "kitchen"—a stove, sink, refrigerator lined up a step away from the round oak table set with a centerpiece of Santa Rosa plums. A floor of black tiles, a ceiling of weathered redwood, a sofa covered with mirrored Indian cushions: It is all too comfortable, too real, too inviting. A Siamese of infinite breeding, whose name is Charles II, pretends to sleep beneath a Spanish arch that looks west to the hills where Jack London built Wolf House in 1906. From Bouverie Ranch he had hauled red lava rock by ox sled. Fisher, I note, enjoys telling how London's macho bohemianism had shocked the citizens of Sonoma Valley in the days when the California wine country was inhabited by a handful of Italians and Russians and the odd Scottish Presbyter. This is her room for food and people, she says, simply, to throw me off the track.

She shows me the room for work and sleep. A typewriter, a clutter of manuscripts, a purple spread on the bed, and some 5,000 books— Colette, Virginia Woolf, Thackeray and Dickens, Simenon and Maigret, Shakespeare, Blake and Donne, books on gypsies, persecution, and old age. And cookbooks, of course. "I consult Irma Rombauer and Julia and Escoffier or Larousse and then I go ahead and do it my way." It is all too plausible.

Then, she shows me the room between. At last, a clue. A bathroom of Roman splendor—a six-foot tub, Oriental rugs, an easy chair beside the books and magazines, Pompeian red walls covered by the brilliant canvases of her second husband, the painter Dillwyn Parrish. I remember how she has written about the strategies of food in confronting grief, after his slow and painful death. "I ate with a rapt, voluptuous concentration which has little to do with bodily hunger, but seemed to nourish some other part of me," she wrote in The Gastronomical Me. "Sometimes I would go to the best restaurant I knew about, and order dishes and good wines as if I were a guest of myself, to be treated with infinite courtesy." Anyone who could eat like that could bathe like this, with voluptuous concentration. She is a voluptuary. She said so herself.

When she pours me a glass of Johannisberg Riesling 1981 from Napa, in the room for food and people, she recalls the toast of her newspaper father, Rex. "Here's to myself. A good man is scarce." I remember her envying his "great beak of a nose," but I also remember how she's written of the women in her family, a strong matriarchal line: "women like Mother and Grandmother and Baunie and even Aunt Gwen and Isobel and my little sister Anne and—yes, and me."

On the ranch in Whittier, where she'd been raised and where her father published and wrote 1,000 words a day for sixty years of the *Whittier Daily News,* the battle lines were drawn between women. On one side were her Anglomanic mother, Edith, joined by Aunt Gwen of the delicious Fried-Egg Sandwiches and French-Fried Onion Rings. On the other was Grandmother Holbrook of the Nervous Stomach and Ritual Enemas and Puritan Hunger for White Sauce. Grandmother Holbrook, when she was not refurbishing her bowels in Battle Creek, Michigan, oversaw the series of kitchen hirelings who were all women, "trying to survive among savages." The story of Fisher's life, I realize, is the story of a woman's struggle, setback, and eventual triumph over Grandmother Holbrook's Boiled Dressing and White Sauce. That is the person who could make the eating of mashed potatoes and ketchup a pornographic rite.

I realize that all of Fisher's thirteen volumes, from 1937 to 1982, comprise a unique autobiography. They are kitchen allegories about A Cook's Progress from cradle to grave with Pilgrim stops along the way in Aix-en-Provence, Marseilles, Switzerland, beginning and ending in California, a wholly allegorical place. Her initials are part of her disguise, like the invented name of Samuel Clemens. Yes, she is as tricky as Mark Twain, who pretended to write simple stories about the Mississippi in order to lure us into experiencing something else. Fisher and Twain were both writing about the American journey from innocence to knowledge and about all the hungers, yearnings, and cravings of that perilous trip.

If Twain disguised himself as a tramp, Fisher disguises herself as a kitchen tramp. Once a tramp, always . . . And if Twain measured his powers by plumbing the depths of the Mississippi River bottom, Fisher measures hers by plumbing the depths of her family kitchens. She discovered at twelve, she wrote, the pleasures of kitchen power when she began to cook dinner on the cook's night off. "I felt powerful," she said, "and I loved that feeling."

She was the natural leader of her savage tribe of two younger sisters, Anne and Norah, and a brother David. Their 100-acre ranch, halfway between country and town, mountains and sea, seemed an ideal place for savages. They grew everything—oranges, blackberries, mirabelles, guavas and dates, asparagus and artichokes. They raised everything—pigeons, chickens, turkeys, a pig, a cow, even a horse named "Hi-Ho Silver." They cooked everything—they canned fruits in Aunt Maggie's Cookhouse in the desert beyond Mount Baldy. They collected mussels in ten-gallon cans on the beach at Laguna. When they slept out after their barbecues, they circled their bedrolls with a lariat of horsehair to keep out the rattlesnakes. It was the savage West, where *la vie mondaine* meant a trip to the Victor Hugo restaurant in Los Angeles to order grandly a chicken à la king.

But there were other snakes in this Eden. The Whittier that produced Richard Milhous Nixon was entirely Quaker. As Episcopalians and mid-western Campbellites, the Kennedy family was heathen. She titled her family memoir *Among Friends,* but she had wanted a stronger less ambiguous title. "I wanted to call it *Child of an Inner Ghetto,*" she tells me, "because it was a lesson, she says, that she never forgot. That lesson took her to Mississippi in the long hot summer of 1962 to teach black students, age seventeen to twenty-two, at Piney Woods Junior High School. It took her six months to win their trust and when the whites discovered the barriers were beginning to melt a little, she was asked not to come back. Her voice is still whispery, but I feel the cutting edge of her rage.

To escape the Friends and Grandmother Holbrook's Boiled Dressing, Fisher, at nineteen, married a son of a Presbyterian minister, Alfred Fisher, and fled to France. They lived in Dijon on $25 a month each. They were tramps and innocents abroad, and she writes of their wonderment on first biting into a hot croissant on the Quai Voltaire. Or on first ordering a *dinner deluxe au prix fixe* at a fancy Dijon restaurant because they were unable to read a French menu. They learned French at the University of Dijon and they learned food in the marketplace and kitchen. She learned how to buy hard cheese by the kilo and grated cheese in grams. She learned how to cook a simple meatless casserole of cauliflower, with bread and fruit afterward. And she learned, when she returned to America to get a divorce, that everything in America was different—the cauliflower, the bread, the marriage. "It was never so *innocent,* so simple," she wrote of those days, "and then where was the crisp bread, where the honest wine? And where were our young uncomplicated hungers, too?"

She had fallen in love with "Timmy," cousin of the painter Maxfield Parrish. And when they went to live in Switzerland, in the small town of Vevey, she learned anew the power of the kitchen. They built their own onto the living room "so that we, the owners of the place, could be its cooks and servants." Their conventional Swiss neighbors were shocked and disbelieving. After one dinner party, the Parrishes were accused of concealing the cook so that no one else could hire her.

She also learned from this idyllic place, where fresh green peas seemed to pop from the garden into the pot, the power of food to evoke our senses. Later she would write of the way contemporary American women seemed to have lost that power and that pleasure by shunning contact with food as such, by pretending to live like aristocrats above the kitchen matters of servants. Long before est or other voguish sensory therapies, Fisher was writing about the therapy of food, how one might recover the immediacy of lost senses "by touching an egg yolk, smelling a fresh lettuce leaf or berry, tasting either the product of their own hands, such as a fresh loaf of bread, or a fresh body."

In the early forties, the idyl ended. The death of her husband, the suicide of her brother, the outbreak of war required new strategies of survival and once again she found them in food. When the wolf is at the door, ask him in, seduce him, and cook him up for supper. *How to Cook a Wolf* (1942) is a book like no other, with excursions on How to Boil Water, How to Keep Alive, How Not to Boil an Egg, How to Make a Pigeon Cry. It is a parody of American how-to-books with a bucketful of anti-recipes. Here the artful strategist contrives recipes for Prune Roast and Mock Duck, for Aunt Gwen's Cold Shape (which turns out to be headcheese) and Addie's Quick Bucket Bread, for Rice Fats Waller, and Eggs in Hell (garlic and tomato sauce, ketchup will do). And, of course, her famous anti-recipe for Sludge.

"Borrow 50 cents," her anti-recipe begins, along with a food grinder and a kettle. Spend 10 cents on whole-grain cereal and the rest on vegetables—the withered, battered, or big ugly kind are cheaper. Grind everything together, cover with water, and cook slowly until the sludge is a "stiff cold mush, and a rather unpleasant murky brown-gray in color." You can make it *look* better, she assures us, by adding a blob of Kitchen Bouquet, but why bother? Gastronomically speaking, sludge is the means to an end "like ethyl gasoline."

A wolf-seducer, she was caught by a wolf in gastronome's clothing in the form of her third husband, Donald Friede. "He was expert in caviar and smoked salmon and had never eaten a muffin in his life," Fisher said. "I was his fifth wife and we lasted seven years." Fisher had one daughter, Anne, and now she had a new daughter, Kennedy. Their marriage broke over children. "He was appalled by babies," she says, so she took them to Aix and wrote, in *A Map of Another Town* (1970), about the strategies of food in combating loneliness. ("Place three tangerines on the sill above the radiator until they have distilled their juice.")

Her strategies with food were never simple. The rites of cooking and eating were her way of coping with the "atavistic realities" of man's essential cannibalism. Since eat we must, what and how we eat is everything. She turns the eating of snails, for instance, into an erotic and disturbing act of necrophilia:

> Then there were snails, the best in the world, green and spitting in their little delicate coffins, each in its own hollow on the metal plates. After you pulled out the snail, and blew upon it cautiously and ate it, you tipped up the shell for every drop inside, and then with bread you polished the hollow it had lain in, not to miss any of the herby butter.

"Their little delicate coffins"? Another ambush of the seductress. I recall that her one adult novel, with the intriguing Samuel Beckett title *Not Now But Now,* is about a modern Lilith, "a wandering wanton."

And I remember the entrapments that lay in the depths of even the most ordinary of her institutional kitchens. She wrote about the kitchen of Miss Huntingdon's School for Girls, which the young Mary Frances attended until she was sixteen. Mrs. Cheever ran Miss Huntingdon's kitchens. "She ran her kitchens with such skill," Fisher wrote, "that in spite of ordinary domestic troubles like flooded basements and soured cream, and even an occasional extraordinary thing like the double murder and harakiri committed by the head-boy one Good Friday, our meals were never late and never bad." I begin to

understand fully why I was uneasy when I found out that Fisher's
present kitchen lay in the Valley of the Moon.

I remember, too, that even in the security of her own childhood
kitchen, there were insights of what was to come. Fisher recalled the
elderly spinster cook named Ora whom her Grandmother Holbrook
disliked. She disliked the affectation of Ora's long "French" knife and
the way she was always polishing and sharpening it. Grandmother
Holbrook thought Ora way above herself when she failed to return
after her Sunday off. Grandmother Holbrook was not surprised to
learn that Ora *could* not return: She had cut first her mother into neat
pieces and then her own wrists and throat without inflicting a single
scratch or nick in the knife.

Even so, I did not make the full Fisher connection between
strategies of survival and "the dark necessity of eating" until the
reissue, in 1981, of a very small book of recipes called *A Cordiall
Water,* first published twenty years earlier. I know that writing was as
natural as sneezing to a woman born into a fifth generation of
journalists and broadside pamphleteers, including a great-grandfather
who fled Ireland to escape being shot for printing tirades against the
queen. "With my own discovery of the printed word I came into
focus," she once said, and proceeded to write a novel at age nine
and short stories all her life. But her real writing is halfway between
essay and meditation, meditations like those of Brillat-Savarin in *The
Physiology of Taste* she has so finely translated. Her meditations, she
tells me, are little ways of saying "what I think about omelettes or
nosebleeds or warts." And the meditations she likes best, "the pick
of the litter," are those collected in the "Garland of Odd and Old
Receipts to Assuage the Ills of Man & Beast" that she has titled *A
Cordiall Water.*

"While writing about horny cats and aching bones . . . and all that
clutter of life," she writes in her preface, "I was stripped of banality,
and I wrote simply in my native tongue . . . ." She wrote simply and
purely of recipes for healing our wounded condition as human
beasts. She wrote of recipes For a Consumption, or To make ye
Green Ointment that cured Lady Probyn's Coachman's Back, or
a Sure Cure for a Scorpion Bite—all of them incantations com-
pounded of age-old science, magic, poetry, faith—the true ingredients of our recipes for death and life. She wrote of an Elizabethan

receipt that called for thirty garden snails and thirty earthworms, and of a contemporary French workman's receipt that called for the Laying on of Hands. "Both spoke," she said, "of incantation, and mystery, and ageless faith: the essentials of healing." She wrote of cures using urine and dung, "the liquid and the solid, which all animal bodies must make and then excrete in order to exist."

Finally, I had reached the truth of her siren song. Her strategies were addressed to a single overwhelming question: "What must we do in order to exist?" She was a philosopher in an existential kitchen, a poet who saw Plato in a bean pot, love in a baked potato, death in a bowl of chicken soup. With cunning and daring, she wrested food from the exploitive hands of pseudo-science, commerce, and industry, from the wasteland of mass mediocrity, from the corruptions of greed and self-loathing, to restore it to its rightful place at the center of those "ageless celebrations of life" expressed in feasts and fairs. She was a philosopher who believed in "Nothingness probably, like an oyster or a seed." But she was a poet for whom an oyster or a seed is everything.

As a poet, she observed precisely her fellow creatures, a toad's throat pulsing like a baby's fontanel, the three stiff hairs by the single nostril of a bifurcated *tête de veau*. As a philosopher, she wrote about hunger instead of about wars and love because "There is a communion of more than our bodies when bread is broken and wine drunk." Food was, in truth, a sacrament, and she has seduced me like Circe into confronting that hard fact as I sit at her round oak table with the plums she will pickle that night.

By this time I would willingly eat mashed potatoes and ketchup but she is too canny for that. She serves forth a Moroccan *chermoula,* a dish of green and red peppers bonded by oil, garlic, and coriander. There are thin slices of smoked salmon prepared by an Eskimo friend in nearby Petaluma, exiled for a year from his tribe because of a death in his family. "Not a bad custom," she says. There is a loaf of sourdough wheat bread from a family of Basque bakers in the village of Sonoma. "Like the bread in Marseilles," she says. There are blueberries from Alaska macerated in brown sugar and a very crisp shortbread. "Just put a little too much sugar on before you bake it," she says. Her receipts are exact.

"I went to the woods because I wished to live deliberately," Thoreau wrote in *Walden,* "to front only the essential facts of life, and see if I could not learn what it has to teach." What Thoreau learned in the woods, Fisher learned in the kitchen. The essential facts that Thoreau fronted in the wildness of nature, Fisher fronts in that "art which may be one of our last firm grasps on reality, that of eating and drinking with intelligence and grace on evil days." Her cook's progress begins and ends in that real and symbolic kitchen in which she took the measure of her powers, tasted the fruits of her passion, and learned her place in the world. She has caught me by the throat. I am spooked by her powers and food will never again be entirely innocent of them. As she says, "Once a tramp, always . . ."

M. F. K. Fisher: A Profile

Elizabeth Hawes/1983

From *Gourmet*, November 1983, vol. 43, pp. 50 +. Reprinted by permission of Elizabeth Hawes.

When Mary Frances Kennedy Fisher heard a critic suggest that if Americans followed the Japanese custom she would be designated a "living national treasure," she responded with an airy chortle. "Ridiculous," she said. "I'm becoming marbleized. And my bones are so creaky, I shall soon turn to stone."

M. F. K. Fisher has a peculiar eminence. Proclaimed America's greatest food writer, she has been quietly turning out fine, precise, and evocative prose, full of sensuality and touched with wit and humanity, for nearly half a century. She has written seventeen books and been published in a wide spectrum of magazines: *The New Yorker, The Atlantic Monthly, Vogue, Gourmet, House & Garden,* and *Family Circle.* Over the years she has acquired a very special and ardent group of fans, and more often than not they refer to her as M. F. K., for her prose has a pungent intimacy that tempts many into an unusually close reader-readership with her. And yet, until the 1982 publication of her collection of essays, *As They Were,* which was deemed autobiographical, she was something of a literary secret.

Mrs. Fisher is very modest about her work. She laughs away compliments and is neither surprised nor impressed by the recent attention focused on her. "Things just happen, that's all," she might say, with a rather mystical far-off gaze. Or "I don't know, I don't care, I don't read reviews," with a set of her mouth, and "I just cook and talk and have fun" about the number of interviewers she has indulged for the past six months, having relaxed only briefly her stern dictum about privacy. Moreover, she would point out, it is both odd and ironic that *As They Were* is responsible for all the fuss because the book was meant to be simply about places.

Mrs. Fisher is settled deep in the lap of a Victorian chair before a wood-burning stove in the living room of her house in northern

California. Her cat Charlie paces. A luncheon guest is arriving. A new
poster, designed by a friend for the San Francisco Culinary Fair, is
tacked to the door. Entitled "UFO," it shows a dark purple and blue
landscape above which floats a lustrous pearl-white pattypan squash.

That Mrs. Fisher is the food writer extraordinaire of the twentieth
century is indisputable. But her title is too narrow a fit, for when she
is writing about a solitary meal in the Gare de Lyon or a ritual tasting
of fresh peas in Switzerland, her kitchens in Provence or the last
virgin truffle hunter, she is writing about far more than food. Accord-
ingly, her admirers insist she *is* more, and reach for other labels—
philosopher, social critic, poet—often settling for the adjective
unique. Familiarity with her work breeds complexities. She is both
feminine and a feminist; she loves men but celebrates independence.
While writing intimately, she doggedly eclipses the facts of her
personal life. She is consummately "truthful," yet a puzzling mysti-
cism pervades her work.

As if to jostle the categorical reader, Mrs. Fisher's solitary novel,
originally published in 1947, has been recently reprinted. Called
Not Now But Now, it follows a beautiful hedonist through a time
warp. *A Cordiall Water,* a small gem of a book about elixirs, nostrums, restoratives, and fortifiers—a work Mrs. Fisher considers "the
pick of the litter"—has reappeared. And in April of this year Alfred A.
Knopf published *Sister Age,* a volume of short stories about aging in
which food is the most minor of characters.

James Beard's first brush with M. F. K. Fisher was his reading of *How
to Cook a Wolf,* which was brought out during World War II in a time
of shortages and rationing. It might pass for a cookbook because ever
so casually recipes are adjoined to the text: "like birds in a tree—if
there is a comfortable branch." But as the title promises and the
chapter heads tease (How to Be Sage Without Hemlock, How to
Distribute Your Virtue, How to Boil Water, How to Be Cheerful
Though Starving, How to Carve the Wolf), it is also a witty and sym-
pathetic dissertation on both the wartime table and the wartime
mentality.

"I was hooked," Mr. Beard says in his "Appreciation" in a late
edition of *The Art of Eating.* "Oddly enough, though we eventually
moved in the same professional sphere, corresponded, talked by

telephone long distance, and shared a number of friends, it took
twenty-five years more for us to meet. By then I had long been a
captive to her prose, her charm, and her taste for the better things
of this planet."

"There have been so many changes in the food world and our
sensibilities in the last twenty years," Mr. Beard says. He is sitting in
the lofty greenhouse attached to the kitchen of his Greenwich Village
town house. "In 1961 I don't think the general public was ready for
Delights and Prejudices [his volume of memoirs]. I don't think it was
ready for M. F. K. either.

"Mary Frances has had a secure place in the food establishment,"
he ventures, "but now I think she rests on her laurels as a critic and
as someone who uses the English language the way it was meant to
be used. It's as if she had her portrait done; food frames it, yet is not
a vital part of the composition. I think of her as a goddess, Juno
maybe, who descends to earth now and then. She doesn't write
about food the way I write about it, or Julia [Child] does, or Marcella
[Hazen] does. It's a means to an end with her."

North Beach is a part of San Francisco that M. F. K. Fisher has
haunted for most of her life and might choose to live in if she were
twenty years younger. It is a neighborhood of abundant warmth and
a sweetly perverse nature, the bookstores and food vendors now
mixed with pornography shops and transistor palaces. Though the
area is frayed and fragmented, its Italian character still holds on, most
conspicuously in great old restaurants like Vanessi's, on Broadway.
At Saturday lunch the place is a haven for regulars of thirty years'
standing, an unpredictable array of types united in the obvious
pleasure they take at the table. Seated at the counter a big man,
neither florid nor beefy but whose face brings both adjectives to
mind, has polished off an order of antipasto, *linguine* with clam
sauce, steak *pizzaiola* with vegetables, and plenty of the bread,
radishes, olives, and tiny hot peppers that are lined up next to the
salt, pepper, and sugar shakers. His chin glistens with olive oil as he
offers a taste of his remaining pasta—and conversation—to a new-
comer on the next stool. He is in the advertising business, he says,
travels a lot, plays the horses, and has sumptuous gardens in Marin
County. Has he ever heard of M. F. K. Fisher? "Sure. I have three of

her books. I open them anywhere and read at night. She's an angel,"
he says, "a real gutsy angel."

Not too long ago in America food was food—not quite a hand-to-
mouth matter, but hardly sensual. To be sure, in the inner sanctums
of mahogany-paneled clubs and quaint old inns there existed a
special breed of eater who discussed with authority Bordeaux versus
Burgundies and perhaps the appealing qualities and even cultural
significance of an extraordinary plat. Elsewhere, though, the word
"gourmet" was tinged with pomposity, and the straight thinking of
Fanny Farmer and The Joy of Cooking held sway. The aphorism
"You are what you eat" was not in the national idiom.

It is evident that M. F. K. Fisher has led the way to the current
sophistication about food, or at least greased the wheels of the
culinary revolution that has swept America in the last twenty-five
years. In the beginning, Mrs. Fisher was a rarity in a gastronomic field
that produced hundreds and thousands of cookbooks but few
expressive writers in the European tradition of Jean Anthelme Brillat-
Savarin. Now the country stirs everywhere with people who have
turned to the preparation, presentation, and even contemplation
of food as an expression of personality, aesthetics, and culture.
Northern California, where Mrs. Fisher now lives, is a hotbed of
original and passionate culinary enterprise. More profoundly than
fashion, food, it is said, can turn the soul inside out.

There was no precedent for Mrs. Fisher's first volume, Serve It
Forth (1937), which even Lucius Beebe (a sophisticated but sometimes waspish reviewer who in his day was America's best-known
gastronome) described as elegant and original, although he was
disgruntled to find out that M. F. K. was a woman. Her subject is
"eating and what to eat and people who eat," and she is erudite and
writes easily as a person with passions, prejudices, and vulnerabilities,
drawing upon her memory with amazing clarity. Some stories are
historical reflections, others, musings on secret eatings or recollections of a snail hunt or dirty kitchens. Occasionally, recipes appear.

Mrs. Fisher's focus is wide and unpredictable and that is confirmed
in Serve It Forth, Consider the Oyster (1941), How to Cook a Wolf
(1942), The Gastronomical Me (1943), and An Alphabet for Gourmets (1949), all of which were later included in The Art of Eating
(1954). The concentration on food is constant, and details of fleeting

tastes and feasts are vivid and rich as if they had just happened. Sometimes they linger indelibly: a fried egg sandwich tucked into a child's pocket "tough, soggy, indigestible and luscious"; a tangerine drying delectably on a radiator with skin as "thin as one layer of enamel on a Chinese bowl, that crackles so tinily, so ultimately under your teeth."

In the foreword to *The Gastronomical Me* Mrs. Fisher explains her purpose: "It seems to me," she says, "that our three basic needs, for food and security and love, are so mixed and mingled and entwined that we cannot straightly think of one without the other. . . . There is a communion of more than our bodies when bread is broken and wine drunk. And that is my answer, when people ask me: Why do you write about hunger, and not wars or love?"

On July 3 of this year, M. F. K. Fisher turned seventy-five. (Had she been born a day later, her father had threatened to name her Independencia.) She grew up in small-town Whittier, California, the oldest of four children, happy and secure, well-fed and well-bred. She was influenced by her family's genteel exuberance and the social ostracism of being the only Episcopal family in a snug town of Quakers. She was affected by her father's devotion to his post as editor of the nonpartisan newspaper in a partisan town and her Grandmother Holbrook's nervous stomach. ("Even when I was a little kid," she says, "I noticed the difference food made to people's spirits. When grandmother left, we had such a different time.") A gallery of memorable characters—dowagers, politicians, cooks, and carpetmen—drifted in and out of the household. "Father's Lame Ducks" is how Mrs. Fisher traces her tolerance for and attraction to the odd and the down-and-out, in fact and in print. Other youthful experiences took hold too: Cooking made her feel important, and newspaper training made her orderly with words. Eagerly she swept through her father's bookshelves and the countless periodicals that filtered in to his attention, from *Photoplay* to *The New Masses* and Bernard McFadden's *Physical Culture*. At twenty, after several idling years at college, she married Albert Young Fisher, the son of a Presbyterian minister, and left behind a comfortable but complex conventionality for France.

Of all the influences in M. F. K. Fisher's life perhaps the most important is France. "I am more of me in France," she tries to explain, "more of the way I *think* I am. I'm more awake, more aware, and as far as senses and personality, stronger. Every minute is more of a minute there. Here, I'm really passing through." All told, perhaps two decades, and many lifetimes, have been spent there. In the late 1920s as a student at the University of Dijon with her husband Al, a scholar (who later chaired the English department at Smith), she responded to a new culture with all the spirit of adventure inspired by first love, a lean pocketbook, and a relentlessly curious nature.

The post-Depression years brought the Fishers back to America, to WPA jobs, and to emotional changes. By the time of her next stint in Europe—Switzerland, in the shadow of the French Alps—which came as World War II was brewing, Mrs. Fisher had divorced Al and married their friend Dillwyn Parrish, a painter and a novelist with whom she had an intense idyll of five years before he died in 1941. During these years she tells us in *The Gastronomical Me,* "I seemed beautiful, witty, truly loved, the most fortunate of women . . . with her hungers fed."

After Parrish's death Mrs. Fisher recuperated in Helmet, California, cultivating a vineyard and doing a stint as a Hollywood screenwriter. She also "took a gamble" on a third marriage to the publisher Donald Friede, with whom she had two children, and then divorced. In 1954 Mrs. Fisher returned to France, and with her daughters Anne and Kennedy in tow she took up residence in Aix-en-Provence, a place, she writes in *Map of Another Town,* that "is intimate to my being." There were good times, and bad. "I am somewhat like a cobweb there. I do not bother anyone . . . I can walk the same streets and make my own history," she muses, "my growing ability to be alone would protect and help me from being arrogant." When she left France to resettle in Saint Helena, an old wine town in northern California, in a big Victorian structure that bustled like a boarding house, she told herself, "I need not worry about coming back, for I [am] there anyway."

Once more, in 1961, Mrs. Fisher managed to live at length in France, this time on assignment to write Time-Life's *The Cooking of Provincial France* in collaboration with Julia Child, who became a lasting friend, and Michael Field. In other years, as "her demons called," she returned to Aix-en-Provence, Arles, and Marseilles, as if

to check up on them, and on herself. At times her company was her
sister Norah—her best friend—or Donald Friede, his new wife,
Eleanor, and the children (they called themselves "The Five Flying
Friedes"—an unconventional but very merry band); or Julia and
Paul Child, Dame Sybil Bedford, or simply her five senses. In 1978,
when New York City's Les Dames d'Escoffier honored her with a
title, she seized upon her proximity to France for a "final" visit.

M. F. K. Fisher has an impressive fortitude. Like other strong women
of the twentieth century she is self-contained. "Over the years, I have
taught myself, and have been taught, to be a stranger. A stranger
usually has the normal five senses, perhaps especially so, ready to
protect and nourish him." She is well nourished by small moments.
In *As They Were* she writes of a world contained in the sounds of the
Rue Brueys in Aix-en-Provence: "there was the feeling that I listened
to a whole carnival, blurred, just off a cosmic Midway . . . a huge
sponge dripping with sound. . . ."

Seen through her senses, M. F. K. Fisher's world has the romantic
impact of a wonderful earthy stew—gypsies, transvestites, California,
France, Mexico, freighters, wharfs, vineyards, friends who are food
people, revolutionaries, countesses, calligraphers, painters, ranchers.
Yet there is a chill in her stories as well as her life. Her puzzling mystical dimension is tied to sensual awareness: Lushness contains a
touch of evil, love cools, "sulky" peaches will go rotten.

To a certain extent the coincidental has shaped Mrs. Fisher's life.
She began writing gastronomic pieces for her husband Al when
someone in the library where she worked left behind a tempting
volume on the culinary arts. Her research into that field led to the
discovery of Brillat-Savarin's *La Physiologie du Goût,* which she translated in 1949 and which stands as one of her noblest accomplishments. (In the 1940s she might have devoted her life to translating
Colette, with whom she is often compared, had not the publisher
insisted upon emphasizing the sensational in the subject's life.) The
purchase, in Zurich in 1937, of an odd nineteenth-century painting of
an ugly old woman is responsible for *Sister Age.*

The way in which Mrs. Fisher approaches her work is revealing.
She is determined to be frank and unsentimental and insists upon
calling her stories or memoirs "reports." "They are meant as the

truth. I love to tell stories, but I can't fabricate," she says. "Everything happens for a reason, with a real beginning and an end. It may have started two hundred years ago and we don't know the end yet, but it has happened. Even the stories in *Sister Age*, which are told in the third person, were dreams of mine."

In the face of curiosity about her life and the resulting accusations of coyness leveled at her, Mrs. Fisher is adamantly private. "Cézanne felt that the light in his pictures was more important than the color. And Henry Moore certainly proved that space is more important than the outline of space. If I were writing the story of my life, I would put in names and dates, times and places, as I did in *Among Friends*. But, Good Hell, whether I am with my second husband or my third lover—who might be Artemis J. Swooney, who was born in Philadelphia, and whom I met in a café in Munich—has nothing whatsoever to do with the reason I am walking down a street in Zurich."

Mrs. Fisher is in fact evasive if not vague about what she has written because it is in the past. She doesn't read reviews, she rarely rewrites, and she does not reread finished work. When a psychoanalyst friend suggested that she look at her past work, she felt sick. Why? Judith Jones, Mrs. Fisher's editor at Knopf, who copes with her idiosyncrasies, says, "she simply sets very high standards. She is a perfectionist, with great modesty and an old-fashioned sense of propriety." Mrs. Fisher says, "Well, I get so self-critical. I get sick. I think, 'I have to pull this thing back,' but I can't; it is over. Writing is the only thing I know how to do, the only thing that makes me very happy. I write all the time—my house is bulging with things that will never be printed. If we survive another fifty years, these pieces might have some value—they might not. I don't care. *I really don't care.*"

"The Last House" is what M. F. K. Fisher calls her stucco cottage nestled in the front corner of a large ranch in the Valley of the Moon, fifty-two miles north of San Francisco. She is not being dramatic, merely honest about the fact that with troublesome eyesight and creaky bones, she can no longer travel. (She has already envisioned "the queer old-lady authoress, found quietly dead between the stove and the icebox, with a glass of vermouth in one hand and an overripe pear in the other.") To lure her out of her oversized house in nearby Saint Helena, this house was built to her specifications a

decade ago by David Pleydell-Bouverie, an English architect-friend
who owns the five hundred acres of vineyards and wild country
outside her high arched windows. Essentially two rooms and a bath,
it is described by Mrs. Fisher as a *palazzina*. California light rushes in;
the Sonoma Mayacamas to the east. Cobwebs hang here and there.
The ceilings of the bedroom-workroom and the living room-kitchen
rise up to unfinished redwood domes. The bathroom is practical but
voluptuous and is outfitted with the largest tub in the region, a
rocking chair, Oriental rugs, and on one wall, painted the same
Pompeian red as the ceiling, an art gallery that includes several large
oils by Dillwyn Parrish, a Rouault, and a tiny valentine. In every
room are books, artwork, and mementos. There are no photographs
or gadgets. And although Mrs. Fisher's kitchen is streamlined and
compressed into one long counter, it quietly dominates.

"When I can't work, I read; when I can't read, I cook," is how Mrs.
Fisher explains her days. Apart from a weekly marketing excursion
with a helpful young friend, she remains at home, supplied with a
bounty of fresh produce by local farmers and with social intercourse
by a steady stream of friends and admirers. Although she lives alone,
she is not afraid of isolation and is unwilling to depend on others.
Invariably Mrs. Fisher prepares meals for her visitors—soup, salad,
and cookies, perhaps, or a ragout and a fruit *dafouti*. She is a
practical and inventive cook who shuns pretension. Though there are
three thousand cookbooks carefully ordered about the room, she
would prefer to draw inspiration from the season or her own stash of
recipes, many of which appeared in her early books, in particular
With Bold Knife and Fork. (She is well known for her vegetable
soups.) The contents of her refrigerator are telling: small packets and
bowls of leftovers, a pitcher of a fruit juice brew, a bag of tiny potatoes scavenged by a friend from the fields of Long Island, a tin of
caviar, and open bottles of wine.

Mrs. Fisher has readied a supper for two friends who own a
kitchen shop in Sonoma: sliced tomatoes sandwiched with *pesto*,
scalloped oysters sprinkled with nutmeg at James Beard's suggestion,
a salad of baby lettuces, and fresh fig ice cream. Dressed in a purple
velour outfit and her long silver hair arranged in a neat twist, she sips
a glass of vermouth. With prominent cheekbones, high arched
eyebrows, and bright, rather imperious eyes, she is still beautiful. In

her youth a food critic once described her as "a blond gorgeous enough to eat." Clifton Fadiman, who wrote the introduction to *The Art of Eating,* tells of falling in love with both her picture and her prose.

Nonetheless, Mrs. Fisher says she has aged faster than she anticipated and feels that most Americans are unprepared for old age. "We are helped by wise parents and teachers to live through our first couple of decades, to behave more or less like creative, productive social creatures, and to withdraw from the fray, if possible on various kinds of laurels. And then what?" For forty years Mrs. Fisher accumulated notes and clippings to write a book on the art of aging, and recently she shipped the material off to Radcliffe's Schlesinger Library, where her other papers and manuscripts are stored. What came out of this research are the stories contained in *Sister Age.*

M. F. K. Fisher has a very special place in the California food establishment and in the wine community, for which she has written two books. She is a wine connoisseur. France aside for practical reasons, northern California is the right place for Mrs. Fisher to be. The fields smell of eucalyptus, rosemary, and fennel. It is surprising that Mrs. Fisher hasn't written more about California, because the state's lore and history are the ingredients of her casual conversation and her wide circle of local friends could be characters in her stories.

Alice Waters, owner/chef of the celebrated Chez Panisse in Berkeley, whom Mrs. Fisher calls a phenomenon, shows deep affection for M. F. K. On visits to Mrs. Fisher's ranch she brings rare mushrooms, evocative flowers, handfuls of the young bitter lettuce known as *mesclun,* and old Marcel Pagnol movies and a projector. "Few people have stirred my culinary feelings deep down and provoked me the way M. F. K. Fisher has," she says.

In 1978, to commemorate Mrs. Fisher's seventieth birthday, Alice Waters, with James Beard, planned a surprise party for her in San Francisco. Mrs. Fisher's close friends were present as well as a number of admiring restaurant patrons, one of whom recited spontaneously from her works. The menu was contrived by Alice Waters to celebrate M. F. K. Fisher's books. The first course, called *Consider the Oyster,* consisted of eight varieties of the shellfish on the half shell. Next, *A Considerable Town,* featuring Marseilles, presented

California *escargots* with Pernod, tomatoes with garlic, whole Pacific rockfish charcoal-grilled with herbs and anchovies, spit-roasted pheasants with new potatoes, a bitter lettuce salad with goat cheese croutons, and three plum sherbets in orange rind boats. *A Cordiall Water* suggested the last course, a Muscat de Beaumes-de-Venise, coffee, and cordials.

M. F. K. Fisher, for once, accepted the deeply felt tribute. Mr. Beard commented, "It was one of those exciting times that you never expect to happen, but when they do you feel as if a magical moment has been created."

✓

A Conversation with M. F. K. Fisher
Joan Nathan/1986

From *The Washintgon Post,* August 24 1986, pp. 16+.

The themes of her writing, M. F. K. Fisher once said, were always the same—food, warmth, love. By elevating the act of eating to among the loftiest of human endeavors, Fisher has established a special place for herself as an elegant and witty observer of food and society. Writing prose that W. H. Auden said was the best of any American author, the newspaper editor's daughter from Albion, Mich. has produced 18 books, including *The Gastronomical Me* and *The Art of Eating.*

Now 78 and nearly immobile, Mary Frances Kennedy Fisher lives in a two-room white stucco home in the midst of wide fields and vineyards 52 miles north of San Francisco. Seated in a large, comfortable Lazy Boy within easy reach of her telephone and dictation machine, surrounded by thousands of books on floor-to-ceiling bookshelves, Fisher receives a stream of visitors who come to hear her wisdom about food and life.

How have your feelings about eating and food changed through the years?

I think I have always liked the basic things. Good seasonal foods. Now it's called California cuisine or something ridiculous like that. And of course American cuisine is familiar to me because we ate it all our life. Lots of awfully good food, milk and fresh vegetables. Always had good cows and I was very fortunate because the first really bad American food I ever ate was when I went to college.

What do you think of the so-called New American cuisine?

It's always been here. It's made from every influence in the world. It's international. That's why it's American, I suppose, a real melting pot cuisine. The best simple stuff from every cuisine in the world was handed down. I got a wonderful recipe for *biscotti* the other day. People have had so many cuisines thrust at them that the word cuisine is kind of banal now. First we had the revolutionary things of *nouvelle cuisine* and *la cuisine minceur* and then the American cuisine and then the California cuisine and the Cajun cuisine. They've all been here all the time. They'll always be here.

What do you think will be next?
I have no idea. Depends a lot on politics. We're trying to prove we're real Americans now. We're making a whoop-de-do about it. You know, the Statue of Liberty, the Fourth of July. The tall ships. Fine, great. It's to divert us as a circus. When in doubt, throw a circus. The Cajuns have been cooking that way for 200 years or more. We have had American cuisine here at least since California had white people in it. The secret is right there. Fresh good stuff. Simple. American cuisine has still to be thought out.

Are there any foods that can be savored in no other country but this one?
There are some foods that are unique here, like avocados. Nobody eats avocados. They grow beautifully in Australia and in Mexico, but I think we have made a thing of avocados. Local things like Maine lobster, bay scallops, dungeness crabs—they're marvelous stuff. Oysters along the Bay of Mexico are quite different from our crisp oysters. We don't have oysters naturally. The Japanese started with the cold waters of Oregon and Washington. Little oysters. They're good. People love them. Bear. Who eats bear except in Russia and America? We don't eat bear anymore. I don't know where they eat buffalo except in Nevada. Just like beef, you know. We've borrowed a lot. Cranberries are definitely American. You can have them. I don't like cranberries. I drink cranberry juice. I'm drinking some right now. Well, we do have things that are very American. We've evolved some cuisines that are completely American like Tex-Mex, all these amalgams of the Orient with the western world. Fascinating! Out here on the coast especially. I love sashimi.

You wrote, "The story of a nation's life, from its simple innocence at the beginning to its final corrupt, decadent end, can often most clearly be charted by its gastronomy." How so?
It is very obvious. You can see in the decline and fall of the Roman Empire, for instance, that the more decadent their habits and politics,

the more unreligious they became, the more they ate and drank. And their emphasis was on the perverse side of gastronomy rather than on the healthy, good side. That's why I feel basically quite encouraged by the last-ditch hysteria—unwittingly—that we're going back to natural good foods. Maybe it's too late, you know. We're not decadent anymore but it could have been. Then the *nouvelle cuisine* swept in, and they did all sorts of weird things. Even tycoons have to have truffles. Truffles are marvelous, but [they're part of] all that fancy stuff that the rich people could have in the old days. Nobody bothers about that anymore, even very rich people. We're getting simpler.

How do you explain the American interest in food?

I think it's because we are so desperate to think about something besides an atomic bomb or something like that. It's very easy to get people to think about something that's a fad, if it's stylish. If it's in to eat kosher pickles, the whole nation will want kosher pickles. It's all hype to divert us a bit.

Do you think there are foods we are kidding ourselves about?

Oh gosh, yes. Organic foods. You must have corn that is off the stalk in half an hour, but you can't always have that if you like corn. You just take the old tired corn and enjoy it if you can't have any other.

What do you think of flavorings?

Natural flavors are best. I love the flavor of good chocolate. I think bad chocolate has a lousy taste to it. Lousy smell. I think taste and smell and touch, all those senses should be pleased by anything you eat or drink. I don't like most extracts. For instance, I was brought some really good macaroons, but there is no almond in the extract of almond at all. It is rather bitter and so badly overused. It stinks a bit. Lemon extract: I can't imagine using it because I use lemons. Be discreet about it. A lot of people just dump it in.

What about milk?

Awful, terrible, partly [because of the] government. Overpasteurized, overhomogenized. No reason at all. Enriched milk is so ridiculous, like enriched flour. You keep adding stuff to make it taste like flour. Do that with wines, too. With a filter you get everything out so there is no chance that it's ever turning rotten in the bottle. The same mediocrity that is safety.

Gamble with raw milk and unpasteurized wine that doesn't ship very well. In France, if you bought a case of wine in the old days, before they pasteurized it, you'd count on sediment always. That's what made great, great wines. There are very few great, great wines now. Mediocrity has taken command. Mediocre is good now. If it is above mediocrity, it is marvelous, superb. Too bad. You don't gamble. If you buy a case of wine, by God, every bottle has to taste like every other 11 or you feel cheated.

What do you think of McDonald's?

Only once have I eaten there. It was interesting. I ate french fried potatoes, of course, and the kids [her two daughters] ate a Big Mac. They tasted marvelous at first. Hot, wonderful smells. Halfway home they said, "We can't finish these now, we'll finish them at home." Four miles from home, the whole car stank of this strange, cold, dead, bad oil. The girls opened the windows. Without mentioning it they dumped all this stuff in the garbage pail.

If you're starved or a truck driver, they taste very good. That was our experience with McDonald's.

What do you think of the microwave?

I wouldn't have one for a million bucks. I don't know why I think that, I'm just superstitious, or old-fashioned. I consider it a gadget, you see, but with my children it's a necessity.

What should we stop eating tomorrow?
Coca-Cola and french fried potatoes.

Are there any foods you don't like?
Oh yeah, there are lots of foods. I don't care for parsnips. I don't like rutabagas.

What should we drink?
Water, next to that, wine.

How do you think we can educate children to grow up with food?
I don't believe in cleaning off your plate, then you can go to the pictures. Not at all. I never think that food should be used as a bribe or as an inducement or as a handicap to hold people back. If children

don't want food, they'll eventually develop a taste for it. Don't force it on them. If the parents enjoy it, they'll eventually say, 'Can I have a taste' some time. A lot of kids don't know how to eat at the table. They like french fries and hamburgers because they can eat them with their fingers. They've just never sat at a table with more than a spoon or a fork and a knife. They don't know how to behave.

You talk in many of your stories about your two daughters and eating with them in France. Did you have trouble teaching them to eat?
I didn't have any trouble with my own children. My 16-year-old grandson wrote me a log of a two-week trip when he went back to Maine. From his reports he ate nothing but french fries. You can't live on french fries. That's all he ever talked about, that they were wonderful. It was shocking to me.

Would you say that people's tastes change during different cycles of their lives?
Oh, sure. I think it's kind of silly to say that babies want everything bland because a lot of them don't. Lots of children love to be puzzled or excited or thrilled or scared, even, by food flavors. This feeding them Pablum is ridiculous. It shapes their whole lives. Their first years they're eating all this horrible stuff, yuck, and then when they get older they want guck, easy to swallow. I think it's awful to feed babies this guck. I never will forget my older child Anne's face when I gave her a spoonful of Gerber's strained beans. Incredulity! She looked as if to say, 'Are you doing this to me?' I never did it again.

As you have gotten older, have things you have liked to eat changed?
Oh yes, enormously. Yes, well, not only what I like to eat but what I can eat. We're dictated to by the size of our tummies, and all that, and also I can't eat very hot things, which I love because they make me cough. But I remember going to a little college in Illinois [Illinois College in Jacksonville], and after everything, of course, we were all half starved. We'd go out and we'd eat chili at what they'd call a "chili hut," and we'd drive out there in these beat-up old cars because everybody was poor in the community I lived in. We'd get out there somewhere and everyone would buy a bowl of chili for 15 cents and for a quarter you'd get a bigger bowl and a piece of bread. We

lived on that stuff. In the dormitory, we had such awful stuff. We had
canned parsnips—that's about all. It was starvation almost. We loved
that hot, hot gutty chili with lots of spices. It was probably bad beans.
We sat down, and it filled us up. We lived on it practically. Couldn't
do that now. Wouldn't want to do that now. No, you change with
where you are and your age.

What's your favorite way to dine?
I don't think that's fair. I am older now. I like to eat all by myself
and have a dainty meal. I like things nicely served. For example, my
breakfast, which I have not eaten, is a pear. For lunch it doesn't
matter. Simplicity. Last night for supper I had an artichoke with a
mixture of yogurt and bought mayonnaise, you know, add a little bit
of Tabasco and a little bit of lemon juice and I had those long tiny
beans, cold and marinated, and 3 or 4 tiny little carrots and new
potatoes with their skins on with butter and salt and pepper and so
forth. I read or listen to music or the radio, news or talk shows.

Do people know how to eat alone in America today?
I don't think they do. Most people eat to survive . . . to exist. It has
nothing to do with esthetics or pleasure. It's a feeding of the maw, to
keep the body alive; you could do it just as well intravenously or
quicker. Oh it's terrible, a bore. I have a friend who is 94. She still
doesn't know what she puts in her mouth. She just likes something to
go down to feed her. Most older people love sweets. She might just
as well be having water.

What was your favorite meal?
One time I was standing on a lonely hill in Burgundy. I shared a
piece of chocolate with an old Burgundian. It was so cold it broke off
like gravel in my mouth. It was wonderful.
I've had lots of wonderful food. Delicious. One time Al Fisher [her
first husband] and I were in Paris and we got dressed up and went
out. We had spinach and never had we seen spinach done so
beautifully. The head waiter himself came in and melted it in a great
chafing dish. It cost an incredible sum. It was memorable to me
because it was beautiful.
Another was the first time I ate potatoes without meat. It was
special because the potato was being honored, It was kind of a soufflé

of mashed potatoes with cheese. God, it was so good. It was in a courtyard in Avallon.

What are your favorite cookbooks?
Well, they have to be good. I don't have very many favorites, but if I had to consult anything, I would consult Mrs. Rombauer's the *Joy of Cooking,* Julia's *Volume Number I* and the *Larousse Gastronomique.* Then I would do it my own way, different timings and adapting old methods and new methods. Those are some of my favorite volumes, I guess.

I know Julia Child cooks beautiful, simple food but she's so complicated in telling you how to do it as if we were idiots. I know a lot of good cooks. If you do exactly what Julia says in every inch of the way, you can't fail. I know people who say they have tried that recipe, but it was no good at all. "Well what did you do?" "Well, I just skipped Stage 3 and I added a little something," you know.

Of course, it's not [just] Julia's [recipes]. It's all laboratory stuff. That's why I really loved chemistry when I took it because I was really amused to think that I had been doing it in the kitchen all this time. The problem of how does the white of an egg turn solid; why can it be as hard as rubber and inedible or if you know how, through heat, to break down that white of an egg, it can be gentle and tender and digestible as a baby's bottom or better . . . It's all chemical. The kitchen is a chemical laboratory.

Is there a food writer out there who you think might carry your torch?
I don't have any footsteps. God, no. No, I can't imagine thinking that ever. There are so many people who think you are wonderful. It's a little bit the cult deal. And so they worship what they're told to worship. Some people write me that I have influenced them greatly. I think I could say that about a lot of people, too. Whoever wrote the alphabet influenced me enormously. E. B. White—I love the way he treats the American language, a witty look at what's already there. I think that's good. I've read voraciously all my life, and I've sorted out what I thought was good and bad. Kids do. If they're left alone, especially. I had no limitations to what I read.

In the foreword to The Gastronomical Me *you wrote, "There is a communion of more than our bodies when bread is broken and wine drunk." What did you mean?*

It's like religion. If you have a glass of water and a crust of bread with somebody and you really share it, it is much more than just bread and water. I really believe that. Breaking bread is a simile for sharing bread. Of course, in the Orient they test more than they do here. In Arab countries they serve tea. If you won't drink tea, it means you are an enemy. You cannot swallow if you are angry or hateful. You choke a bit. I choke easily now. I have only one vocal chord and a cracked voice box so that's why I have such a small voice. It's very true. The Orientals serve mint tea and watch you very closely. When you're bargaining for a rug—I never bargain—they serve mint tea. They watch you like a hawk if you are drinking or sipping or choking it down a bit politely. It means you're an enemy.

It's all very betraying, how we eat.

Eating Well Is the Best Revenge:
A Conversation with M. F. K. Fisher
Julia Reed/1986

From *U. S. News and World Report,* 8 September 1986, vol. 101, pp. 62+. Copyright, Sept. 8 1986, U. S. News and World Report.

The text of this piece consists of M. F. K. Fisher's responses to Julia Reed's questions, which were not included.

People ask me very seriously, "What is California cuisine?" or "What is the American cuisine?" I tell them very seriously, "It's what we've always had but we're just more aware of it now." Suddenly we have to have labels and talk about American cuisine, our regional cooking, and there are dozens of books out about it.

I think it's plain that we are too big ever to have a national cuisine, because we've got wonderful regional foods. But they're regional forever. Just because people in the South eat corn pone doesn't mean that every American eats corn pone. We can't do it. It depends on the region. I think it's just that people are trying desperately to find some roots somewhere. We're all kind of rootless. Most Americans are; it takes more than one generation to put down real roots.

Somebody assured me very solemnly yesterday that the American cuisine is passé and that California cuisine is out, out in New York. I said, "So. It's been in forever, and now it'll be out forever."

But one very good thing about all these fads, I think, is that something good lasts. We're going back a bit to simpler things, and people are satisfied, whether it's stylish or not, just to have a grilled steak instead of steak with béarnaise sauce and truffles. Whether that's stylish or not, it's here to stay. People love it, and I think it's wonderful to be simple. In fact, I get simpler as I get older.

I think some people take food much too seriously and too pompously. [Cookbook author] Craig Claiborne said to me he gets bilious when he goes to San Francisco because people talk about nothing

but food. Well, for him it's an occupational hazard because they think
they have to talk about food with him. But still, I know what he
means because people take it terribly seriously, and they talk about
"there's this old place where you can get wonderful polenta," and so
on. They get kind of carried away.

But, in general, I think we just face the cold fact that we have to eat
to live, and we might as well do it with fun and panache and style, or
we might not. Some people go overboard, and they just drive it into
the ground. You feel indigestion is right around the corner, just listening to them.

We celebrate almost every one of our main events like birth and
death and marriage and all that with food, don't we? I was really
touched when my mother died and the girl from the leading Quaker
family, who had never come in our house, came to the back door.
She had a pie because she knew mother died and she thought we
didn't have pies. They didn't eat pies at home, either, probably, so it
was just a ritualistic and very loving gesture of respect. I was deeply
touched—and amused. And it was a good time to be amused, too.
My mother would have laughed. It was nice.

My memorable meals have all been marked by great simplicity.
The first one I recall appalled and shocked and pleased me because
one course was nothing but potatoes. My husband and I were in
France—we had just married. Some nice old ladies took us as far as
Dijon in their car, and we stopped at Avalon on the way for lunch.
And at the Hotel de la Porte they served a kind of soufflé of potatoes
as a separate course. All my life I thought potatoes were an accom-
paniment for meat or fish, and here suddenly they were treated with
real respect and admiration. I thought, "My God, this is the way to
go." That really was important.

Fast food is cheap and quick and easy, and anything too easy is
not too good, really. I don't mean to sound puritanical here, but you
have to *feel* a little bit about food. You have to want to use it and
want to make it for yourself. You could eat fast food and not give one
damn. You don't have to work, you don't have to think. You just
open your purse and open your mouth.

I just happened to write about food. It could be love or it could be
politics or it could be finances, money, religion or any of the other
great things; but none of those can exist unless we've had something

to eat. First we have to breathe and then we have to eat, and then we get on with business.

There are two things I could do naturally, and one was to cook and one was to write. As a child, I loved to cook on the cook's day off. I had a little stool that I had to use to get up to the stove, and I was turning out pretty good food. I was a patsy and I loved the attention.

If people you love really like your food, I think that's a marvelous way of strengthening your own feeling of power. And yet you've given them real pleasure, which also pleases you, and you enjoy the good it does.

America's Finest Food Writer—M. F. K. Fisher: An Intimate Portrait

Bert Greene/1986

From *Food & Wine*, December 1986, vol. 9, pp. 28 +. Reprinted
by permission of Mr. Phillip Schulz.

We are, I must make clear, very good friends and are dead honest
with one another about all the eternal verities of our lives: sex, food
and money, too. The day I recently visited her in Sonoma County at
her simple white stucco ranch was an unexpectedly lucky one for me.
A royalty check for a whopping $18,000 from my last book had just
been deposited into my perpetually dwindling bank account in New
York. I could not wait to tell her of the windfall.

She was suitably impressed. She whistled a long fluty aria and the
famous Fisher eyebrows went skyward with delight. Earlier, we had
planned to go out for dinner at a local restaurant with the under-
standing that she be allowed to pay for the meal since I was a guest
on her turf and she was not feeling up to any serious cooking these
days. After I announced my good fortune, however, she rescinded
her offer. "On second thought, Bert, dear, I'll let you pay for dinner,"
she laughed. "For that is surely a heck of a lot of dough."

Shaking her head, she recalled that she had never received a
royalty check for more than $500 in her whole life. "Usually they are
well under that figure. Several hundred dollars. Never more. The
smallest amount I ever received was $10. It didn't depress me, but it
really upset my agent a lot!" At the look of utter dismay on my face,
she waved her arm to dispel any concern. "It's really all right. My
wants are very simple. This house was built for one occupant, and I
am it. There is food in the fridge and wine in the pantry. You don't
think I appear in need do you? Because I am not. When funds get
low, somehow something always happens, and they are replenished.
Most often I get left a stipend in some old friend's will. Though at the
rate of survival—theirs and mine—I think I am finally exhausting that
source of supply."

I have known M. F. K. Fisher for almost 20 years—good times and bad. We met when she came to dinner at my house in Amagansett, New York, one winter in the late 1960s. She had been staying "holed-up," as she put it, at a small and drafty cottage near the end of Long Island, attempting to finish her book *Among Friends.* I was then part-owner of the temporarily shuttered Store in Amagansett. I was giving cooking classes, catering parties and commuting to an advertising job in New York City from Monday to Friday in order to survive.

On a particularly frigid weekend, an acquaintance asked if he could bring his tenant—a lady who wrote cookbooks—over for a decent meal because pickings were pretty slim in Sag Harbor in February. I suspect he had no idea who M. F. K. Fisher was, and I doubt he had ever cracked open one of her books. But I had—all of them, in fact. Her exquisite prose intoxicated my senses from the time I was a late adolescent fumbling at the stove. I longed to meet this lady, but decidedly at *her* table, not my own. Frankly, I quaked at the idea of what to feed a legend. However, I cooked and I must have cooked well, for that meal is still a high point in both our memories.

Mary Frances (for that is how I came to know her) was and is a model for all dinner-guest decorum. She eats with obvious pleasure, savors conversation as much as any dish she is served, and listens when others speak. A human being of rare sensibility and amazing grace, she was also the most sensual creature I'd ever met—a physical knockout at 60—and long before the first course ended I fell madly under her spell.

That initial bread-breaking literally changed my life. At one point in the evening, under the cover of a cross-conversation, she asked me point-blank if I was happy. I shrugged, as I have always done when difficult answers need to be framed. I was certainly *not* unhappy. A playwright-turned-cook, I had stopped writing because I claimed the theater no longer gratified me. The truth is I was paralyzed by the idea of rejection. The same fear kept me in a static relationship that never progressed beyond the boundary of amicable accord. "I'm not completely satisfied," I remember telling her, "but then, who is? I am 44. It's too late to make changes now." Mary Frances looked me straight in the eye. "Oh, pooh," she declared, "You're a baby! Take it from someone much older and wiser, you can still do anything you want in this world. The thing is to make up your mind what you want!"

That was the sum total of our first serious conversation, but it burned a hole in my consciousness.

Sooner than later I made up my mind what I wanted and never regretted what followed. But then, my model, Mary Frances Kennedy Fisher, is not a lady much given to regret either.

Born in Albion, Michigan, on July 3, 1908, during the worst heat wave anyone in those parts can remember, she claims to have appeared only minutes before midnight, apparently a result of a supreme effort on the part of her mother, whose intemperate young husband had informed her their firstborn would be named Independencia if it arrived on the Fourth.

When she was three, her parents migrated cross-country to Whittier, California, an almost solely Quaker community, where her editor/writer father bought a foundering newspaper, the *News,* for a suspiciously low price.

In *Among Friends,* M. F. K. Fisher recalls growing up as a "heathenish Episcopalian" in a town of less than 5,000 people, which was, in her own words, "a ghetto." She was never, in the more than 40 years she lived there, asked inside a Friend's house.

The eldest of four children, Mary Frances grew up on a street "planted with bushes never seen today, and tall handsome trees brought as seedlings by the courageous homesick pioneers across the Great Desert." She was known as Dote or Dotey, probably because her father always called her Daughter, and her youngest sister, Norah (Nonie), couldn't pronounce the word. Her closest sibling, Anne, two years younger, was called Sister (Sissy). The youngest Kennedy child, David, was exempt from a nickname. "He was David from the time he was born until the day he died."

M. F. K. Fisher began to write almost from the time she learned to read and spell. At nine, having read every volume in the Kennedy family bookcase, she began a novel of her own, which, for better or worse, was abandoned by the time she was 10. But what really formed her was working for her father's newspaper.

"The darndest thing about growing up in a family like ours," she recollects, "was that there was never a proper vacation. I used to look forward to holidays with longing, for I was not a particularly model student. My father, however, always had other plans. 'Mary Frances,' he would announce, 'you will write up social events from July 1 through July 16 when the society columnist takes her vacation. David will do sports and Anne will compile the obituaries. When the social news writer returns, you may all switch assignments, but vacation posts *must* be filled first!' They were too. Sometimes I would write 14 or 15 stories a day on an old stubborn Remington standard. It was hard work, but I learned a lot."

One of the things she learned was that not every woman is cut out for a newspaper career. After a dispiriting term at Whittier College and even less satisfying experiences at Illinois, Occidental and UCLA, Mary Frances Kennedy gave up the scholastic ghost.

"In 1929," she later wrote, "the stock market crashed, and I got married for the first time and traveled into a foreign land across an ocean. All those things affected me, and the voyage perhaps the most." Barely out of her teens, she and a brand-new husband, Al Fisher, set off on a honeymoon in France. Eventually he would earn a doctorate from the University at Dijon and she would become a lifelong and passionate Francophile.

But she tells it best herself: "Paris was everything I had dreamed, the late September when we first went there. It should always be seen, the first time, with the eyes of childhood or of love. I was . . . much younger than girls are now, I think. And I was wrapped in a passionate mist."

She and Al Fisher stayed in a hotel on the Quai Voltaire. "That was before the trees were cut down. And in the morning I would stand on our balcony and watch him walk slowly along the book stalls, and wave to him if he looked up at me. Then I would get into bed again. . . . The hot chocolate and the rich *croissants* were the most delicious things, there in bed with the Seine flowing past me and pigeons wheeling around the Palace mansards, that I had ever eaten. They were really the first thing I tasted since we were married . . . tasted to remember."

The sights and smells that gastronomic territory first awakened and the alterations made in both of their young lives have been well chronicled by M. F. K. Fisher since her work was first published. While much of what she writes is autobiographical, it has always been purposefully blurred in sequence and vague in chronology—with many pertinent details withheld from any prying reader's eye. The effect, as through a glass darkly, is often brilliantly tormenting. But M. F. K. Fisher is her own person—on paper and off.

Longtime friends, we have never discussed any truly intimate aspect of her life unless she volunteers the information first. I have always half suspected that if I asked a question that she did not wish to answer, she would simply change the subject or smile enigmatically.

If one reminds M. F. K. Fisher (as I do) that her esteem in literary circles is immeasurable and that she is generally acknowledged to be one of the greatest food writers who ever lived, the lady's response is quick, old-fashioned and wholly irreverent.

"Oh, pooh!" she declares.

It is an expression she uses often, particularly when she suspects some icon or other needs cutting down to size. Sacred cows, like trendy food, best-selling cookbooks and college-trained restaurant chefs, are all worthy of a jot of her spleen. But the world's opinion of her talent seems the very least concern of her life at the moment.

When M. F. K. Fisher, at 78, sets out to write what she calls, "my tired old prose," it is as fresh and seamless as ever—less about food than fascination with the hunger of the human race. Her eye may fail from time to time, but her ear is acute as a dog's. She misses no footfall at her door or whisper in the room beyond. If her wrist pleads infirmity, her spirit ignores it entirely.

Using a tape recorder, in lieu of the typewriter she can no longer manipulate, she continues to work—summoning up the places she has lived and the people who have crossed her path here or there; the friends, lovers, family members and total strangers whose appetites she notes and matter-of-factly celebrates, just as she has done for over half a century.

Some years ago, the poet W.H. Auden paid her the ultimate literary compliment: "I do not know of anyone in the United States today who writes better prose."

When I asked her on what occasion Auden had singled her out for that encomium, M. F. K. Fisher shrugged her shoulders and eloquently lifted her pencil-thin eyebrows in surprise. "I don't remember. Did he *really* say that? How nice." Then she laughed, somewhat apologetically. When she laughs, it is a clear crystal sound, like wine goblets breaking. "I never seem to recall the good things they write about me," she confessed, "only the bad."

That is no case of false modesty. From 1937 when her first book (*Serve It Forth*) appeared, until 1983 when her latest (*Sister Age*) was published, she has written 16 memorable volumes, plus countless essays and short stories. All garnered enough critical hosannas to salve the egos of an army of lesser writers. But not hers.

"The truth is," she sighs without an ounce of rue, "I don't really like the stuff I've written. And I never have. I used to think that by the time I was 50, I would write a good book. Then I got to *be* 50, so I raised the ante to 55. Then 60. And up and up. Now, I try never to read a line I wrote the day before yesterday."

For the record, M. F. K. Fisher is neither a garden-variety recipe giver nor an epicurean food critic. What she writes are extremely personal, highly aromatic memoirs: recollections that attest to her enjoyment of the art of living as well as eating. This philosophy is summed up in the opening paragraphs of *Serve It Forth* (somewhat amended here): "There are two kinds of books about eating: those that try to imitate Brillat-Savarin's and those that try not to. The first substitute whimsy for his wit, and dull reminiscences for his delightful anecdotes. The second are gross where he would be delicate, and choose blunt statistics rather than his piercing observations. . . . Now I am going to write a book. It will be about eating and about what to eat and about people who eat. And I shall do gymnastics by trying to fall between these three fires, or by straddling them all."

Confronted with the preceding passage, which was written half a century ago, M. F. K. Fisher winces. Pressed to name a favorite work, she does not select either *Serve It Forth* or *The Gastronomical Me,* the book that cemented her reputation as culinary pundit and kitchen prophet to legions of fans. Instead, unhesitatingly, she chooses her translation of the same Brillat-Savarin's *The Physiology of Taste,* a project on which she worked, off and on, for more than a decade. "It's the best thing I've done because his French was so good and pure. I like it, and I guess others do, too, because it stays in print. Knopf is planning a new paperback edition soon so, happily, it will hang around for a while."

Sad to say, not many of Mrs. Fisher's other books hang around. "I can't think why they keep publishing me," she says. "So many

practically lost their shirts on my books!" It is slightly unsettling to
hear M. F. K. Fisher talk about money (or the lack of it), but it is an
old story to her.

I do know the most important relationship of her life began when,
still married to Fisher, she met and fell hopelessly (haplessly) in love
with the American writer and artist, Dillwyn Parrish. Together they
moved to Switzerland, bought an old stone house near Vevey,
planted a garden, then a vineyard, and lived sufficiently unto
themselves—much like the Italian-Swiss farmers who were their
neighbors on the hillside.

I learned most about their life together, not from reading *The Gastronomical Me,* but from a random conversation we once shared
about filial responsibility.

"When I was young," she confessed, "I always tried to find a way
to be friends with my parents, but I never did. They were good
people, you understand, but parents first, I could never manage to
have them treat me as an equal until I divorced my first husband. I
was living in Europe with Dill, and I felt I had to come home to
California to tell them in person that I was divorcing Al and marrying
Dillwyn. Somehow they accepted the fact. For the first time, they
accepted me as a person—not a child, not a possession, but an
equal. It was a good feeling, like an augury."

Mary Frances and Dillwyn Parrish's life together was full of good
things. She has written of their table and stove and storehouse; of
shallots, onion and garlic that she braided into long silky ropes and
hung over the rafters in the attic; of eating what they grew and
preserved or dried. There were three cellars filled with jars that she
had canned. "When I went down into that coolness and saw all the
things sitting there so richly quiet on the shelves, I had a special
feeling of contentment," she wrote. "It was a reassurance of safety
against hunger, very primitive and satisfying."

Three years into their marriage, Dillwyn Parrish died of a disease
that progressively destroyed his circulatory system. Before he died,
they sold the house in Vevey, gathered up their scant possessions and
returned to America, where M. F. K. Fisher began what has come to
be thought of as "a seminal literary output." For starters: *Consider
the Oyster* in 1941, *How to Cook a Wolf* in 1942 and *The Gastronomical Me* in 1943.

During the early Forties she also spent a brief moment in Hollywood. "I was hired to write dialogue for a Bob Hope-Bing Crosby opus, "The Road to Somewhere or Other," but they didn't trust my sense of humor, so I was fired." During the same time she also published her only novel, *Not Now But Now.*

That book (recently reprinted by North Point Press) was written at the urging of a New York publisher, toward the end of World War II. In time that publisher, Donald Friede, became her third husband and the father of her two children, Kennedy and Anna. Mary Frances talks about her daughters freely. On the subject of the late Mr. Friede, whom she expeditiously divorced, she is somewhat taciturn. "Being married to him was a full-time job of motherhood. I really had three children, you see, and he was the most difficult of all."

Mary Frances Kennedy Fisher is a lady who thrives on solitude. The house where she has lived alone for the past 18 years is almost unnoticed from the highway. A small sign proclaims the ranch name, but it is possible to drive past the solid stone post several times without noticing it. The way there is winding, carpeted winter and summer by dry grass and fallen eucalyptus bark. The house, designed to her specification, is white and small, or so it seems from the outside. Within, it sprawls endlessly, and wide windows, set in arches, turn every view into a stunning vista.

The list of arrivals here on any given afternoon is eclectic to say the least: Julia Child, a wine critic, a book publisher, a distinguished transsexual writer, and a neighbor from down the road bearing a jar of therapeutic lamb broth. Before any visitor reaches her door, he must announce his presence by clanging an old rusty bell and passing through an open courtyard protected from the elements by two carved wooden gates. Above each is a panel of stained glass: one bears a Gothic-inscribed M: the other, an equally upright F. They appear to be as well traveled as the occupant inside.

Still looking remarkably beautiful, if somewhat fragile, in her eighth decade, M. F. K. Fisher suffers from an obscure form of Parkinson's disease. "Actually they call me a Parkinsonian," she explains, "because there are so many infinite varieties." A lady of inquiring mind, she recently asked a neurologist about the nature of her particular strain. "It is such an imprecise disease," he replied, "the only way we can *really* tell is by autopsy." Mary Frances laughs with delight as she recalls her answer. "I can't wait!"

Once an intrepid traveler, her movements are somewhat circum-
scribed, if not entirely curtailed these days, after bouts with Parkinson's, two hip replacements and a cataract operation. Her only
permanent live-in companions are her two cats, but now an earnest
young woman looks in on her daily.

All of Mary Frances's possessions have stories attached. The house
is a virtual museum of her rich life, filled with personally inscribed
paintings, piles of friends' books and marvelous glittery objects that
cover every scintilla of space. I have visited her often—staying elsewhere, but taking meals at her generous table—and know my way
around without crashing into any bibelots.

Over her kitchen sink there are an infinite variety of curiously
shaped bottles and jars. Each contains some herb or dusty blossom
in a fragrant oil or compound—like elixirs of the past. The sight of
them brings to mind my favorite of all her books: *A Cordiall Water: A
Garland of Old and Odd Receipts to Assuage the Ills of Man and
Beast*. It was written in 1961 and reprinted again recently. In that slim
volume she records all the mysterious homeopathic cures she's collected from primitive souls who still believe in miracles, like both of
us.

I asked if any wartwort grew in Sonoma. For in the book she
relates how, on a French peasant woman's advice, she squeezed the
juice from a clump of wild Provence wartwort on her nephew's wart
and it disappeared in three weeks time. My interest was strictly
parochial. I had developed a bump on the knuckle of my index
finger. "Let me see that," Mary Frances beckoned me to her chair.
"That is not a wart. Wartwort—even if we had it—would not work
on that. I wish you had a nosebleed. It would be much easier to cure.
I could stuff your nose."

When I told her I was thankful my *schnozzole* was to be spared her
shaking hand, M. F. K. Fisher gave me a look. It was not unlike the
glances of mock dismay that Margaret Dumont always bestowed on
Groucho Marx in the movies. And we both laughed. She is absolutely
radiant when she laughs.

"I love you and I want you to be happy," I have confessed on
more than one occasion.

"I am happy," she has replied, "just deteriorating. But that's the
way it *has* to be. That is the way it was planned after all."

One of the times I came to her ranch, she was reading a book on reincarnation. "Everyone important throughout the ages had thoughts about this subject," she announced. "Julius Caesar admired the Gauls because of their thoughts on the hereafter. Do you know anything about the Gauls?"

"God, yes," I groaned, "I plowed through four years of the Gallic Wars in high school."

"Me, too!" Commiserating at the memory of all those intransitive verbs and pluperfect tenses, she tapped the book in her lap. "I doubt you will remember that Caesar and the Romans had no concept at all of life after death, but the Gauls did. They were savages and painted their bodies red, yet Caesar discovered one thing about them to envy." She pronounced the words slowly, like a child: "It was their concept of reincarnation."

"Do you believe in it too, Mary Frances?"

She smiled, "Oh, pooh. If I did, I wouldn't tell you!"

Loving Brillat-Savarin:
A Tale of a Tasteful Affair

Jeannette Ferrary/1987

From *New York Times Book Review,* 31 May, 1987, pp. 51+.
Copyright © 1987 by The New York Times Company. Reprinted
by permission.

First I did the arithmetic. M. F. K. Fisher was in her mid-30's when
she started the translation. She must have been reading, writing,
drinking and dreaming the man. It's no wonder he captured her
heart, that she fell in love with him "that way": the way you do when
you're married and have two daughters and no time to carry on an
affair properly.

To be honest, this is all my idea, or almost all. She does admit,
in the preface, that her "love for the old lawyer burns as brightly
as ever." Anyway I'll ask her all about it. As I drive toward her hide-
away in northern California, I have with me her 1949 translation of
The Physiology of Taste, originally written by the French lawyer-
philosopher Jean Anthelme Brillat-Savarin in 1825. But this particularly happy-looking book, with grapes all over the cover, is a new
edition issued by North Point Press.

I'm not sure what she'll say. How do you ask a woman if she was
in love with a man who died nearly a century before she was born?
Some women would find that ridiculous. But not this one. She's
good at falling in love, in all kinds of ways with all kinds of things:
people, ideas, moments. And that's what her writing is about: enthusiasms. People who think she's a food writer are merely concentrating on one of her enthusiasms. Of course food writers have a
vested interest in trying to make her one of them so they can plumb
her works for paragraphs about tangerines because they're the best
things anybody ever said about tangerines. Sensual, elegant, present.
But that's because, underneath it all, she's not talking about tangerines. Her tangerines lie in the subconscious, with all their primal
associations intact. She's a thinker, a wanderer, an absorber of life, a

117

philosopher even, but not a food writer. Food writers never quote
food writers anyway; there's the real proof. In fact the only other
person quoted as frequently about food and the art of eating is
Brillat-Savarin. And even then, it's often her translation.

Of course he wasn't a food writer either. He was a lawyer, a judge
and a raconteur. He had, she assures us, "handsome legs" and was
"a tender and sensitive lover." He was also fascinated with every
aspect of taste, from its effect on the senses to the niceties of dining.
For 30 years he kept notes, almost sub rosa, finally publishing his
work with his own funds just before his death. Did he consider his
interests inconsistent with his professional status? His translator-friend
will know his feelings on the matter. Her research was more than
thorough. In her translator's glosses, she introduces the reader to
bystanders at dinner parties, to the endless odd cousins that prolifer-
ated in 19th-century Paris, and, most significantly, to Louise, the
classic beauty who accommodated Brillat-Savarin's romantic fan-
tasies both by having consumption and by dying young. "Lost
forever when he was only twenty," is how Mrs. Fisher puts it.

She also supplies background information, indulges in more or less
relevant speculation ("If he were alive today, he might well be an
anesthesiologist"), or just writes whatever she pleases. So it is from
these lovely glosses that we learn what Charles Lindbergh ate during
his historic trans-Atlantic flight (one and a half sandwiches) and that
the French were appalled, if not insulted, that he didn't choose to
toast his success with the champagne they had waiting, but preferred
instead some milk and a roll and a good night's sleep. Another note
relates how her father's reputation as the family carver originated
prenuptially with the need to impress his father-in-law-to-be, who
considered carving the mark of a true gentleman.

Most of these stories do have their inspiration in the original text,
but translators generally do not become so intertwined with their
material. Yet it is the glosses that make her "Physiology" as much
a contemporary American commentary as it is French and classic.
Through them she can converse with her lawyer-lover, duel with him:
first he speaks and then, touché, and its's her turn. She can even, if
she chooses, ignore him. Her translation is a book within a book, the
difference between literal definition and literary dimension.

That brings up the well-known Edward FitzGerald question: is he translating or paraphrasing? FitzGerald's 1859 translation of *The Rubaiyat of Omar Khayyam* made an exquisite poem in English; so exquisite that it is now considered FitzGerald's own masterpiece, his inspired rendering of the Persian original rather than a true translation. This "Physiology" sounds so much like Mrs. Fisher that I can't help wondering if she has infused the work with her own style and wit or if they are there to begin with. Is this book her "Rubaiyat" or his? Even the most faithful translation can transcend its original. With my lapsed French I can tell that hers is much more than the kind of word-by-word translation we performed on Caesar's Gallic Wars. His words exuded death and fear and we worried about whether they were nouns, gerunds or verbs. She was after bigger game.

When I pull into the long driveway, I see her standing at the gate. Mary Frances Kennedy Fisher has red lipstick on and her face is a good pink with powdery blue lids. She's especially pretty today. Her bright eyes and the wind chimes attack the air's complacency. She leads me out to the porch and sets me up, tape recorder and all, makes me feel these intrusions are minor, though they are indeed intrusions. She introduces Mary Jane, who is helping out with the day's chores and who is, at the moment, surrounded by the smell of roasting nuts and burnt sugar. I have a thousand questions, but first we talk about *biscotti.*

"Mary Jane and I made this batch of *biscotti* this morning," she announces, pointing to a total of six brittle-looking Italian cookies. Hardly a batch, I say to myself. "But the minute we touched them, they fell apart." Now I notice the way Mary Jane is standing beside a platter piled with filbert-studded cookie-trash: as if she is mourning.

"What do you think we can do with them?" Mrs. Fisher asks. She's asking me? I know better than to answer questions like this. "Do you think they would make a good pie crust or something?"

I nod in a way that will not get me held responsible if things don't work out for these ill-fated *Italiani* the second time round. I try to change the subject to anything about Jean Anthelme Brillat-Savarin. But the next thing I know, we are talking about Maurice Chevalier.

"Because I'd done Brillat-Savarin, I was offered a job to translate the life of Maurice Chevalier called *Mon Paris.* I thought it would be fun to do two Frenchmen."

She tried to capture him as he really was, the man himself, not the

Maurice prancing across the screen. She was pleased with the translation. As for him: "He was horrified. He hated it. He wanted to come across just as he thought people expected, prance and all. He wanted it rewritten so it was the American image of him: the *gai boulevardier,* the *flâneur.* I didn't do it," she admits, shrugging her shoulders. "I couldn't do it. I wouldn't do it."

Besides, she was even more excited by another opportunity that followed the appearance of *Physiology*—the prospect of translating the complete works of Colette.

"I've always had enormous respect for her as a writer," she explains. "I thought of spending the rest of my life translating Colette. It's all I would ever have done. But, as it turned out, the publishers were only interested in the slightly lascivious, the little innuendoes about lesbians and gays, what they considered the dirty parts." So she said "absolutely not" and did her own work instead.

Although the publication of *Physiology* did not divert her into a life of translating, it did affect her career immensely. For one thing, her literary agent sold a few sections before publication to *Gourmet* magazine. This practice, which usually stirs up interest in a book, is today considered a coup, a boost to sales. But in her case, it was a disaster. *Physiology* was being published by the Limited Editions Club, whose members were paying $25 for a boxed, fine-paper edition. An unboxed edition was to be simultaneously released by Heritage Press for $5, also a lot of money at the time.

"George Macy, the publisher, was livid," she says. "He said he was going to lose all his members who wouldn't think of paying $25 for something they could read in a magazine."

The translation had one other important consequence. When Earle MacAusland, then publisher of Gourmet, saw it he said, "This woman's getting too classy for us" and virtually ended the magazine's relationship with her.

"Until then I'd written quite a bit for them. But they only took one or two more pieces after that . . . one with fine pictures of Marseilles, I remember. And that was it."

Strange how one always envisions everyone else's life as a nice tidy continuum leading from obscurity to renown with very few of the glitches that beset one's own career. Brilliant though this realization may be, I don't mention it. I think of something a bit more relevant:

"I understand with this reprinting of *Physiology* that, for the first time in years, all your works are currently in print." "Oh is that right?" she asks, as if this is the sort of thing that means more to publishers and publicity directors than to writers themselves. At 78, she's working on several articles, one long manuscript, and a "secret project."

I could ask her directly about being in love with him, but I opt instead for the oblique approach.

"The *Physiology,* I begin, "is such a unique work that it doesn't seem to fit into any category. It's almost a genre in itself. You seem the perfect match for it in that sense, a writer without a real genre to fall into. Do you think that's why you worked so well together, you and Jean Anthelme?"

"I don't know about that," she answers, looking pleased. "But it certainly was fun and I learned an awful lot—like how to keep everything clear and simple—from his prose. He wrote such beautiful prose. If you followed it you couldn't go wrong. It's rather like following a recipe by Julia Child: might be boring as hell, but if you actually do it. . . ." Her eye wanders over to the plate of crumbs.

"Yes," I say, turning off the tape. "But then you'll make such a great pie of it all in the end."

M. F. K. Fisher Is More
than a Cookbook Author
Susan Stamberg/1987

Weekend Edition Sundays, National Public Radio, 5 July, 1987.
Transcribed by David Lazar. © Copyright National Public Radio®
1987. This news report by Susan Stamberg was originally broad-
cast on National Public Radio's "Weekend Edition" on 5 July
1987 and will be published in Ms. Stamberg's forthcoming book
from Turtle Bay Press. The report is printed with permission from
National Public Radio. Any unauthorized duplication is pro-
hibited.

Interviewer: Was it very hard for you to get something published in
the beginning?

M. F. K. Fisher: No, it was too easy, much too easy. I never had
any trouble at all, and I think that was too bad because I didn't even
want to be a writer, really. It never occurred to me to be a writer, and
there I was one before I knew it.

M. F. K. Fisher, celebrating her seventy-ninth birthday this weekend,
and a half century as a published writer. She is often called a food
writer, but in a way that trivializes her work. Writing which W. H.
Auden once said was "unsurpassed by any other American author."
Mary Frances Kennedy Fisher's first published work, *Serve It Forth*,
was so different from what women were writing about food in the
nineteen thirties that many assumed M. F. K. Fisher must be a man.
Since then there have been countless magazine articles, and many
other books, five of which were collected in a volume called *The Art
of Eating*, all revealing her keen eye and her appreciation of what she
says are the three essentials of life: love, shelter, and food. Celebrations are also a big part of M. F. K. Fisher's life, especially her own
birthday parties, which sometimes go on for several weeks, even
though she is quite certain about when she was born.

MFKF: I was born ten minutes before midnight of the fourth, of the
third, and I was born that way because my mother was a very

conservative woman who called people George, and John, and Henry, and things like that, and father said, "Edith, if you don't hurry up, it's nine minutes to midnight, if you don't hurry I'm going to call this child Independencia," and she was so horrified, you know, probably thinking what will the nicknames be, or something, that she gave a great heave and there I was, you know.

M. F. K. Fisher lives in Northern California now. She spent much of her life in Europe, but her earliest memories come from Whittier, California, where her father was the owner and publisher of the local daily newspaper.

MFKF: I wrote my first novel when I was nine, you know that sort of thing, but we all wrote in my family because I'm a fifth generation newspaper person, and my father probably wrote two thousand words a day for his whole life, probably sixty-five years of his life.

Interviewer: Do you have any idea of what happened to that novel you wrote when you were nine?

MFKF: No, I don't. I don't think I finished it because I suddenly realized that my father and mother were very amused by it, and I didn't write to be amusing. They never did laugh at it, but I realized at every-noon after father came home from work, for lunch, and we had lunch, they'd say what's happening in that book or something and I told them gleefully, you know, about my chapter of the day, and then I realized I was amusing them, and I didn't want to amuse them at all.

Interviewer: Do you remember what the book was about?

MFKF: Oh yes, it was about all sorts of things I knew nothing about, like love and being older. It was during the war, of course, the First World War, so it was about a girl and a boy. The boy was a sailor, but he kept looking through his porthole window, and sending her Morse code signals. She was a nurse, I think, and I knew nothing about nursing or anything like that, but every day she "hoped" into bed, and then "hoped" out of bed. I didn't know how to spell, you know. So she was "hoping" hard. The whole novel she hoped. That's all she did was hope, I'm afraid. But I didn't know what else to have her do, you know, because I didn't know anything about anything then.

Interviewer: Very often people will describe you as a "food writer." But you are not that, are you?

MFKF: Oh no, I don't think I am, really. I think we're a little preoccupied with that aspect of living. People have fun eating. It's not a sin to enjoy food, but I think it has become almost an obsession. I think we're overdoing it a bit, really, but it's just indicative to me of the fact that we don't want to face other, uglier things, so we pace the kitchen stove or the parts thereof. It's an evasion, really.

Interviewer: Miss Fisher, as much as we may think of you as a food writer, I think of you as a travel writer. That is I've taken you along on some wonderful trips, and that has made a great difference to my travelling.

MFKF: Oh gosh, that's nice to hear. Thank you.

Interviewer: What about you? Are you still travelling?

MFKF: Well, I'm not travelling right now, but thank God I have travelled. I know what it's about, sort of. And I travel in my mind a lot.

Interviewer: Do you miss the physical travelling?

MFKF: Oh yes I do, but I hate travelling now because as I'm older it's a bore to get to airports and sit around, you know, and I don't go dashing from place to place. My husband Dillwyn Parish said that the best way to go from place to place is to get off a train, head right for the nearest and best bar in town, pub, this is in Europe, of course, where you sat outdoors a lot. And just sit there till the sun goes down. By then you know whether you want to stay or not. And if you don't want to you can get on the next train, but you usually stay. That's very true, you know. True for me, anyway.

Interviewer: I think I discovered a wonderful place in a railway station in Paris, thanks to you. I was reading you at the time. Do you know what it is?

MFKF: I think I know. The Gare de Lyon.

Interviewer: Can you describe that for us?

MFKF: The station was built just about the turn of the century, I think, and it was built for the Paris-Lyon Mediterranean Railway. It's very garish, and sort of grand, and long stairways, marble staircases, you know, and its very imposing in a funny, outlandish, extravagant way, like a rather faded, beautiful old courtesan, sitting there waiting.

As far as I can know or learn, no other railroad station in the world manages so mysteriously to cloak with compassion the anguish of departure and the dubious ecstacies of return and arrival. Any waiting room in the world is filled with all this, and I have sat in many of them, and accepted it, and I know from deliberate acquaintance that the whole human experience is more bearable at the Gare de Lyon in Paris than anywhere else.

Interviewer: And you go up a flight of stairs at one end of that station, and tell us where you end up.

MFKF: At the right hand side as you stand at the top of the staircase, which has always got palm trees on it, it's very elegant with brass rails and stuff, at the right side there's the train bleu part, which was named for the famous train that comes over from London, so most of the people were once there. English people.

It is one of the most amazing public dining rooms I've ever seen, or even imagined. The ceiling is very high and elaborate. The windows are tall, looking on one side upon a goodly part of Paris, and then to the right into and under the endless stretch of grey glass roof over all the tracks that come to a dead stop down below . . . Switzerland, Italy, Spain, the Near East, all France to the south. . . .

Service is swift or slow, according to one's logistical needs, and there is a comfortable feeling of bourgeois polish and sparkle everywhere: clean linen and brass, waxed floors, good plain food as well as a few fastuous dishes.

Interviewer: If I remember properly, you were particularly struck by the rolls, the hard rolls.

MFKF: Well it was the best bread in Paris, by far, and it was the only bread that was any good after World War II when the bread was pretty awful all through France. And then they had wonderful ham from Parma, which just smells like violets, you know, Parma violets, and they had beautiful little half-bottles of champagnes that are made by small wineries in champagne country. So that was my breakfast always: bread and ham and champagne, before I started out.

Interviewer: Miss Fisher, you say you travel so much now in your imagination. You've helped us to do that, too, I think.

MFKF: I hope so.

M. F. K. Fisher celebrating her seventy-ninth birthday, a celebration she says will last until Bastille Day, July fourteenth.

Excerpts from Miss Fisher's book *As They Were.*

It's Not Just Eating

Meg McConahey/1988

From *Santa Rosa Press Democrat*, 22 February 1988. © 1988
Santa Rosa Press Democrat. Reprinted by permission.

SONOMA—The grand doyenne of the culinary arts consumed a
bowl of breakfast flakes and a silver cup of milk Sunday afternoon
before delivering an unpretentious off-the-cuff talk about the experience of eating.

It was a rare public appearance for MFK Fisher, the first lady of
American culinary letters whose resplendent prose has, over the past
half century, helped elevate food writing to a literary genre.

Fisher, sharing the Andrews Hall stage with restauranteur John
Ash, rambled delightfully through a lifetime of impressions, many
only peripherally related to food. When the several hundred chairs
were vacated two hours later—one hour overtime—the audience
was left with a sense that taste is sometimes merely an afterthought
when it comes to the complex climate of consumption.

Fisher loves to eat, but that pleasure is not the driving force behind
her obsession to write. It is only a small part of her lifelong affair with
the bounties of the kitchen.

Eating, under the wide angle view of Fisher's eye is an event
marked by the people who set the table, who prepare the meal, who
serve it and who share in the board. It is the place where it is consumed and it is the context of the time in which it is savored.

If anyone ever sounded a timeless note on the sociology of dining,
it is MFK Fisher.

Dwarfed by an enormous antique chair and sipping a glass of
Hacienda Chenin Blanc, the writer, purposely without a written
"speech," fielded questions from Ash and responded to audience
comments on trends in cooking and eating.

"The price of wine is very unfair compared to the price of food,"
she said. She and Ash sympathized with restaurant patrons afraid to
criticize a meal or service; both endorsed the honest approach but

Fisher said she's too cowardly to practice it herself. And they both applauded the current trend of creating menus with fresh, locally-produced food products.

Fisher's audience seemed to seek her presence more than her opinion on the latest cookbook or culinary craze. The woman whom Bay Area writer Cyra McFadden once called "a living national treasure," suffers from rheumatoid arthritis and Parkinson's Disease.

Sister Age, as she calls it, has been kind to her, but she admits the body no longer works as well as the mind.

"Sometimes I can walk slowly but very well. And sometimes I just give up in the middle of a room," she said from her Glen Ellen living room just before leaving for Sunday's talk. "I think, 'My God.' What'll I do. How will I get to the other side?' "

Fisher, who faced her Sonoma audience with a cane, also relies on a walker and wheelchair at home because of the unpredictable nature of her disease. Sometimes it makes her unable to walk.

The worst part, however, is physical restraint on her writing. Fisher says she had to give up her typewriter 14 months ago.

"My writing is just shot to hell by my disease. I can sign my name but nobody would know it is me except the people who get the book I've signed. It's an awful feeling, you know."

Fisher, who has had a lifelong compulsion to write ("I'm writing now in my head"), told Sunday's audience that she has reluctantly taken to dictating into a tape recorder. She says she hates it.

Age has also diminished Fisher's pleasure in food. Not that she likes it any less. But she can't consume as much as in her younger days and her physical limitations have made cooking, for the most part, out of the question.

"I cook mentally," she says, seated at an unpretentious old table in a kitchen void of any of the trendy gadgets and machines found at Macys. "I love to cook. I find myself dreaming quite a bit in recipes. Like, what would I do if suddenly someone turned up with two ducks?"

Fisher says the humming motor of her mind can be a frustrating liability. "In a way I kind of wish I'd get a little dimmer mentally. I think it would be simpler because my brain is going chigity chig-chig-chig and I'm not doing much about it but talking.

"I'm not working but it's working. I've got all these stories I want to write for myself."

Fisher fans fearful that her works are completed can rest assured. She still is producing magazine and periodical pieces. Her 19th book, "Dubious Honors," a collection of all the introductions she penned for other authors, including an often humorous introduction to the introductions, is slated for release next month by North Point Press.

Fisher, who says she has a vast collection of unpublished work, also says she's never enjoyed book publishing. Magazines and newspapers are her media.

Fisher's life is simple now. Although she's accessible to those who manage to find her friendly door at the Bouverie Reserve, the writer rarely enters into Sonoma social activities, mostly because of her declining health.

Four years ago she tried to turn down the title of "Sonoma Treasure" because she felt undeserving of the honor. She says that her limited income from royalties and social security are not enough for philanthropy, so she consents to an occasional benefit appearance.

Sunday's event, sponsored by the Sonoma Valley Vintners Association, benefits the renovation fund of the Sonoma Community Center. Fisher also occasionally appears at Herbst Theater for Friends of the Library and plans to do so again this fall, "if I'm around."

As she approaches her 80th birthday, Fisher says she's no longer into long range planning.

Christmas with M. F. K. Fisher

Christine Vandevelde/1988

From *Savvy Woman*, December 1988, vol. 9, pp. 77–79.

It is possible, indeed almost too easy, to be eloquently sentimental about large groups of assorted relatives who gather for Christmas, for Thanksgiving or some such festival, and eat and drink and gossip and laugh together," wrote M. F. K. Fisher, in her classic *The Art of Eating,* in 1954. "The cold truth is that family dinners are more often than not an ordeal of nervous indigestion, preceded by hidden resentment and ennui and accompanied by psychosomatic jitters."

Indeed. Who better to understand the primitive, nostalgic and ambivalent feelings evoked by the hearty tradition of Christmas than Fisher, who for 50 years has been penning lush, vivid prose and poems to food. Now 80, she has authored sixteen books, all of which are still in print, beginning with the publication of *Serve It Forth* in 1937.

But Fisher is more than a food writer. She's a philosopher of food, a candid chronicler of life, interested in who *and* what graces a table, engaged by what precedes and follows as well as what occurs during a meal. As Clifton Fadiman wrote in his introduction to her *The Art of Eating,* "Food is her paramount but not her obsessive concern. It is the release-catch that sets her mind working. It is the mirror in which she may reflect the show of existence."

Still beautiful, her long silver hair twisted and held back with tortoise-shell combs, Fisher lives in Sonoma Valley in California wine country, where she is visited by a constant stream of "hungry and thirsty strays." On this day, her guests are offered cold white wine and served tomatoes drizzled with olive oil and speckled with basil, tender salmon, pickled cucumbers, brown bread and biscotti. Following Fisher's direction, the food is prepared and served by an assistant, as she regales her guests with stories about Christmas entertaining.

Adjusting her black-and-white silk caftan and picking up her 1-2-3, a drink she invented by combining one part Campari, two parts gin and three parts dry vermouth, Fisher says, "I love Christmas. I really do. I think it is very special. I took a vow long ago that I would never write another nostalgic thing about Christmas. But if I were 189, I would still get a special kick out of it."

The "cottage," as Fisher calls her home, is somewhat eccentric, with only two large rooms, a bath and a porch. The domed redwood roof soars over a kitchen/living room and a bedroom/office. The large, Pompeiian-red bathroom serves as a gallery in which Fisher rotates displays of Picasso oils or paintings by her late husband, Dillwyn Parrish. Books line the walls of every room. Tabletops are littered with mementos and vases of fresh flowers, a cat sleeps in a doorway, and a basket of beribboned preserves sits cockeyed on a chair cushion. Navaho rugs in dusky hues of ochre and moss green are thrown over daybeds. And at the back of the house, a large porch with a fan-back rattan chair faces a field in which cattle graze. It's clear that here lives a woman who understands home and hearth and celebration.

Fisher, who is currently "working on four or five secret projects," speaks as she writes, punctuating the air with her long, elegant hands and waving her arms to signify exclamation. Ask her a question and she answers with a five-minute story. Like her writing, her views on the subject of Christmas are clear-eyed and unsentimental. "I can't talk about creating those feelings everybody wishes they had at Christmas. If the feeling isn't there, you know, it isn't there," she says.

"I remember one Christmas when we didn't have any children, except one little misbegotten grandson. And Christmas should definitely be a time for children, the child in people," says Fisher. "And we felt terribly old and bored, and that was the only Christmas we ever drank too much. All the sadness crept up on us, and there was this one little boy and we were all being terribly, terribly gay for him. Nobody even got drunk. We just drank steadily, quietly, too much. And every now and then, we would try to revive and be happier. So we would have another little drink, just a wee one. And this little boy didn't give one small damn, because he didn't know. Maybe he had a wonderful time, maybe he forgot all about it, I don't know. . . . We kind of used him as an excuse to even have Christmas."

Fisher has written thousands of words on the subject of Christmas.

In *Among Friends,* her memoir of growing up in the Quaker community of Whittier, California, she recounts her childhood holiday
parties in the parish house and Elks Club as the first great debauches
in her life, where the "hot cocoa, with cookies brought by the Guild's
prize cooks, tasted exactly like Christmas itself."

When Fisher compiled the excerpts for *Here Let Us Feast,* a
collection of writings "concerned with man's fundamental need to
celebrate the high points of his life by eating and drinking," it pained
her to select only pieces of Charles Dickens's *A Christmas Carol,*
because "the whole foolish moving story is one of food, physical and
spiritual, and I would have liked to put it here as I best like to read it,
uncut . . .'" And in *As They Were,* she recounts a Christmas spent
alone at Arles, visiting the Roman sarcophagi and the Christmas
Market on Les Lices, walking by herself under the Christmas lights
that gave the streets a white glare without shadows. "I've spent many
Christmases alone. That one, nobody gave a damn about me," she
remembers. "So I just chucked around. I wasn't unhappy."

After all, as she wrote in *An Alphabet For Gourmets,* "It must not
simply be taken for granted that a given set of ill-assorted people, for
no other reason than because it is Christmas, will be joyful to be
reunited and to break bread together. They must be jolted, even
shocked, into excitement and surprise and subsequent delight. All
the old, routine patterns of food and flowers and cups must be
redistributed, to break up that mortal ignominy of the family dinner,
when what has too often been said and felt and thought is once more
said, felt and thought."

When Fisher used to celebrate Christmas by serving large meals to
large crowds, she would change the order of the meal, the location
and the dishes from year to year. Family dinners—"intramural
sport," she calls them—must be prearranged with care and caution.
Even then they may not quite turn out. But in the shake-up, memories can be made.

"I don't like turkey. Mother didn't like turkey. But we always had
turkey. Then when we had our own homes, we broke away from
that. One time in St. Helena [after World War II], there were about
twenty of us for Christmas and we decided we would have pot roast
with prunes. It's very German—it cooks all day, you know, rich and
dark and gravyish, and you have lots of noodles with it," says Fisher,

who describes herself as "foolhardy enough" to have actually staged family dinners more than once.

"So I got the pot roast and I worked on it for about a week," she continues. "It was an enormous thing, the biggest pot roast in the world. Well, about halfway through dinner we just gave up. I laughed. It was like mummy stuff. I could have taken an axe to it and hit it, but you couldn't cut it. Well, it had been preserved under infrared light. It was just after the war and you couldn't tell if the meat you got was infrared or not. When it's raw it cuts beautifully, you know. So it stayed exactly that way, the biggest, most beautiful pot roast in the world. And at the end of dinner, little John, who was then about 10, said, 'Dodie,'—that's me— 'this is the best gravy I ever ate.' And I thought, 'you darling kid.'"

Christmas is no longer a family affair for Fisher. Some time ago she decided her two daughters, who now have their own families, should have their own celebrations. "For a long time, we all met at the ranch where my mother and father were. After they died, then, as the oldest, they had come to me. They would and they did," she says. "Then I realized it was a terrible, terrible job for all of us. They wanted their own Christmases with their own families. So I remember thinking—for two or three months, I believe—and I finally wrote a family letter, which we never did, a parental ultimatum. 'Go to hell,' in a way it said. 'You have your Christmases where you want them and when you want them. I am going to, too.' We all love each other dearly—did, do and will. But a sigh of relief went up that you could have heard on Mars: 'Thank God we don't have to do that anymore.' It was terrible to keep up the old bluffs. We all decided we weren't going to pretend any longer. And it is now very nice."

This Christmas, Fisher would like to be in France. But wherever she celebrates, there is sure to be good, simple food and wine. "And there will be people," she says. "We always have people. I have always believed you should have at least one unknown person at any feast." And they will not just eat, they will dine.

Something of a Ghost:
Conversations with M. F. K. Fisher

David Lazar/1989

Transcribed by Julia Gail Innis and David Lazar. Copyright ©
1992 David Lazar.

David Lazar: I read your piece last fall in the *Antaeus* special issue on journal writing and diaries.

M. F. K. Fisher: Yes, I never read that.

DL: Have you thought of publishing your journals?

MFKF: No, they're very personal. I don't know, I've never read them. I'm just a compulsive writer, and I had to write, so I wrote journals because it never occurred to me to publish anything, you see.

DL: Have you gone back and used them as sources?

MFKF: No. The *Antaeus* people wanted something from my journals, so I just had my assistant pick out three pages of something. I didn't even look at them; I don't care to. I get embarrassed, but I know it's probably well written.

DL: Journal writing, especially by women, is getting a great deal of attention now because of the relative scarcity of women's voices before the nineteenth and twentieth century. Annette Kolodny, an historian and literary critic, has gone back and resurrected and published some of them, with commentary. It is fascinating material. But, of course, most of them are not self-consciously written. They aren't usually writerly. Don't you think there's a big difference? Are your journals a writer's journals?

MFKF: Well, I don't know about that. You have a writer like me, you just know she's a writer. There is a difference in my writing because I'm a writer and somebody else isn't. But I'm not self-conscious at all. It never occurred to me I was writing for anybody. Some people think that's impossible, that anybody who keeps a journal must keep it for somebody, something. That's not true.

DL: When did you first get a sense of yourself having writing as a career?

MFKF: Early on, I don't know.

DL: Because your father, Rex, was an editor?

MFKF: No.

DL: Then what gave you that sense?

MFKF: I knew that I had to write. It never occurred to me to write about myself, it's not like narcissism. I wasn't looking at myself. I just knew I had to make something, express what I was thinking about, you or me or anything. It occurred to me that no one cared, and I just had to put it down. Never re-read anything I've written. I don't gloat over things, gee this is good or that's not bad or this is terrible.

DL: How do you think you'd feel looking back now at some of your work?

MFKF: I don't want to. But I'd be completely detached if I had to. Not completely, but almost. I don't know if it would be deliberate. Probably now it would be slightly deliberate because I know that if I don't sort it out, somebody else will. And so probably that's why I kept those journals. That half of the room over there is all journals; I don't think I'll ever look at them. I've kept them and I don't know why except maybe someday they will be of some use to somebody. I don't know why, how. Depends on whose hands they fall into. Now if I were really an honest soul, I think I would have burned them. I found them recently. I didn't mean to keep them, I didn't even know they were there. Someone kept them, I guess. I certainly didn't have anything to do with it. I was appalled, I said there are some old cartons in there, take a look, and there were old journals in them I kept when I was first married. Starts about then, some even earlier, in childhood. Mother believed in journals.

DL: Did she keep one?

MFKF: Years, for thousands of years.

DL: Do you still have them?

MFKF: Yes, some. But they're very dull indeed. They have five years in them of "Twenty-two eggs today." They've got a code. "H" means headache. "FD" means feel dreadful. "R" is Rex. "BM," that was bad mood. Or "broke," stuff like that.

DL: Did she talk about you, about the kids at all?

MFKF: She'd say "lost baby," for a miscarriage, or "all five children have measles. Awful, terrible day." Just the bad stuff, awful, terribly boring. She kept a journal religiously, and she thought I should too, but I'd write the whole page in and there would be nothing left for next year or the year after. She'd say "Doty [Fisher's family nickname], now what are you going to do about 1922, this is still 1921." I'd say "oh god." But then she never did interfere, so I kept that sort of thing for her, for the family, but I didn't have any codes. I just said "went to Laguna," things like that, "drove over to Puenta." "Grandmother well." Then I'd go and write about Grandmother to myself, and sometimes I'd write it down in the journal, and sometimes I wouldn't.

DL: Do your journal writing and your published pieces cover the same ground? Do you think they were very different? How different, in other words, is your public writing from your journal writing?

MFKF: Oh, I don't know. I never thought about it. I suppose the journals are all very introspective. But for a long time, I didn't say "I" or "me." There are tons of old journals in that box. Could you tell me what's there?

DL: Quite a bit of Dijon material, pages and pages.

MFKF: Journal?

DL: Yes, 25 October. Want to hear it?

MFKF: Yes.

DL: 1929. "He says he will write an hour a day and I say so too. It is very good for him. But when I start, I decide to do it on a typewriter and spend most of my time hunting for letters or crossing out those too quickly found. The first sentence is an interesting result of seeing no written English for six weeks and then reading the America Mercury in two hours. It's a good thing I've never worked in a sweat shop. I'd camp on Mencken's doorstep. Perhaps simply being Jewish or Negro would do. This is the first time I've heard a typewriter since last May when I used to pretend I was the main support of a little college newspaper. I wonder which is worse. Conceit protruding with relish and frank gusto into a favorable atmosphere or that kind of conceit which masks itself in a cleverly revealing way, in a veil of charming modesty."

MFKF: This stuff, you see, Nonie [sister Norah] would not have any patience with at all. It's too introspective.

DL: That's too bad.

MFKF: I didn't even know I was keeping it. I didn't know I was saving it. I kept another journal at the same time, less personal.

DL: Even if Nonie doesn't like the introspection, you should go through this, because parts of it look like they'd be well-excerpted: "The courtdoor bangs, bang bursts the little balloon, and I think it is Al. Then I hear vast steps going into the kitchen. There's a quick rush of hard shoes on the cobble and the almost shrill calls of small boys running into the dark streets from their school. It's 6 o'clock."

MFKF: That's the way it was.

DL: And you go on to describe window dressings and that kind of thing. It's wonderful.

MFKF: Well, for a 20-year-old bride, it wasn't bad I guess. I just wrote naturally, you know.

DL: It's all very well-written. Listen: "Today I finished the second chapter of Our Shilling Shocker and went over the first. I'll rewrite it later. The story may turn out all right if I can keep it simple enough to bring all the threads together at the end. Cheap novels are about the best I'll ever do, I think. Maybe I can earn some money with them while Al's [Al Fisher, first husband] writing the Real English. Today is another anniversary, nine weeks. It doesn't seem possible that I have been married for so few days. It seems that I've been living with him forever. All my life that has any reality is connected with him. All that isn't exactly what I mean because my years at home are very happy things to remember." Want to hear some more? This is November 17, 1929: "We came up the stairs, Al with his leg pressed against mine and stepping with it, both of us laughing and muttering. I pulled off my gloves, hung up my coat, ran a comb through my cold hair and come noisily into the purple. And Al was sitting on the radiator with a manuscript in his hand, quiet as a wraith. I said I was sorry to disturb his muse though there is no excuse for such obvious flippancy as we both know. I sat down with a curious sense of fullness, of tensibility to say something that needs to be said before it wears a hole in the cloth. There was a typewriter, there was the page of pert, receptive paper. And there was I, as empty as a tipped up bottle. Without my knowing or feeling or hearing everything that pressed against my mind had melted like snow on a warm cheek but with no wet tracings, only a realization of its absence."

MFKF: How strange. I was writing another diary at the same time.

DL: So, how did you divide? The other diary had more of a sense of audience?

MFKF: No, it was more conservative—dinners and lunches and activities.

DL: December 4—the last line in this entry is "damn this type-writer." February 24: "This morning Al sent off a paper to his friend, he's been working on it for several weeks, chewing sentences. I knew damn well that what brain I have differs from the norm. Principally because it knows it is different from the norm which is that sentence in itself, a good example of what the brain is. But when Al asked with his usual interest that I read his paper and tell him what I thought, I was flattered but at the same time realized that's what I was meant to be by my mate. The article is good, I think, clearly written in a style that seems to me to combine real profundity thought with aim of ingenious naivete. I don't know though. And now it is after dinner. Al came leaping up the stairs at 6 o'clock and made me close my eyes. He was grinning with pleasure and our own kind of silliness. And when I opened my eyes, he had put a little pile of salt and two smooth round tomatos, still pink with newness on the table. They were good. We smiled to each other as we bit into them." It jumps to 1931.

MFKF: Two years later.

DL: January 10, 1931—"At 5:00. I go to meet Al for a lecture on the German stage of the 19th century, but in between then and now, I am filled with a sense of thwarted energy that I haven't had for months. I want to write something but my mind is too slow-moving. I have an awesome collection of holey stockings and worn out collars to mend. But my fingers yawn at the thought and turn numb. I wanted to thumb at some Mexican songs, a letter to Rex swooned at the second sentence, and now I tap painfully at nothing at all. It is very silly, Al can't understand this kind of thing." Listen to this, Mary Frances: "It would be interesting perhaps if I were to read this ten years from now to find that I had written less about my own illogical meanderings and more about the people I find so personally boring, so maddeningly useless and so interesting. I'm appalled at what seems to my American eyes the sensibilities, the cruel ignorance of these French of the lower middle class, their food, their personal habits, their ideas of obedience and common courtesy with children make me sad. I think of how much better I could do it. The Germans are better too. The French snarl at the Germans for their prepared-ness but they refuse to see that the children of the nation are the ones who, in twenty years, will have to fight to think, to live. Here they say, it's numbers that count. Soldiers will be killed therefore it's more useful to have more and more men no matter how sickly they are to fill up the breeches than to spend all your time fattening the first batch. Therefore on with procreation. If a mother bears more than six children, give the father a gold medal. I'm becoming a fanatic on the subject of children."

MFKF: I was, too.

DL: Can I read you another little piece? "It would be a joke if I died young."

MFKF: Ha! Some joke.

DL: Did your father keep a journal too?

MFKF: No.

DL: Too much newspaper writing?

MFKF: Never occurred to me. Well, I don't think he did ever.

DL: It's interesting that in some ways your own writing travels the path between, but also deepens, the kind of writing your mother did and the kind your father did. On the one hand, the daily copious newspaper stuff, public life, and on the other hand your mother's journal writing, which avoided introspection, but covered private life, although the public side of private life. Your writing has combined both in ways; it's been autobiographical and it's also been journalistic at times.

MFKF: Mother thought that a housewife—they had a household and a female had to keep tabs on what happened, she'd consult her own dictionary, her diary. She'd say "Grandmother Hobert came back." She'd do over the whole thing. It would be in the book.

DL: So, like your father in a way, and she needed to get that perfectly straight, on the record. What did your father think of your work?

MFKF: Nothing.

DL: Did he read it?

MFKF: I don't think so. But he thought it was too bad that I had to, thought that I should marry a man who'd take care of me.

DL: Life of leisure?

MFKF: No, never, but financially comfortable. Mother was never

leisurely, but I don't know what Father thought much. I think both
of them felt that if you had a gift or a talent you should develop it
in order to be a better person for the world. Not that they were
"Christ-y" at all, either one of them. Mother was a Christian, she
thought, but she wasn't at all in the good sense. She believed in the
divinity of Christ. I guess that was good, but she never practiced her
Christianity, I think.

DL: What you're saying also ties into what you've said about your
father's sense of predestination, your sense of once you know what
gifts you have, it's up to you to develop them, be it writing or anything else. Isn't one of the books you mentioned wanting to work on,
something like "Living Ghosts?"

MFKF: Yesterday I think we talked about it. I thought one good
title might be "Living Ghosts." No, I don't know what it was, that was
a very passing thing. It'd be amusing writing about observing what
was going on as if I were a ghost very much alive. How could you be
both, I don't know.

DL: It gets back so clearly to the piece I've mentioned to you in
Gastronomical Me, "The Flaw," which is about being with Dillwyn
Parrish [second husband] on the train and going back into Switzerland, and those are very much the terms you use to talk about it:
terms of ghostliness. And that's why the essay has a frightening
clarity in it. You describe yourself as a ghost, as being so removed
from the world's trauma, because of what was happening to Timmy
[Dillwyn Parrish], that you had a detached, perfectly clear-sighted
view of everything. Don't you think this ties into what you were
saying about your own detachment, about that ghostliness, and
about your sense of memory.

MFKF: Well, it's necessary to be detached or else you die; you just
grow up and die. Which one should not do at will.

DL: You would die because things would strike to the heart?
Would strike too painfully?

MFKF: What dear?

DL: You would die because things would be too painful?

MFKF: I don't know what I meant. All I'm thinking about is that
we should eat. I'll eat a potato chip.

DL: I see you have a couple of your books around: *The Art of
Eating* and *As They Were.*

MFKF: Nonie and I are going to go through them. Now, in *As*

They Were, I started out by mentioning that I have a secret map in my mind of Dijon. That's going to be the start of this book. That will be the book that I write now. Right up the street to La Rue De La Liberte. The rest of the book is already written, we're going to take other stuff I've written. Nonie says it's so fresh and good. *As They Were,* there's something there. But I don't know what it is.

DL: So you must be looking heavily in *Gastronomical Me,* there's so much Dijon in that.

MFKF: And it's not indexed at all.

DL: North Point soon will have republished individually all of *The Art of Eating*?

MFKF: By the end of October. Nice little books.

DL: Does *Serve It Forth* have the Man Ray picture on the cover?

MFKF: Yes, that'll be the last book they do. I thought they were going to do it chronologically like they would records. However, they didn't quite match up the picture with the text. But that doesn't matter either.

DL: What was your relationship with Man Ray? What was he like?

MFKF: Before Julia, his wife, came along, Man was in love with a woman whom Donald [Friede—third husband] took away. Man took shocking pictures of them together that Donald liked to show around. Man took the picture of her with a violin going out the back. Donald asked Man to take pictures of me after that. Every time Man came to the ranch he took pictures, of the ranch, and lots of pictures of us. Donald didn't realize that Man took very cruel pictures, cruel because they show the Nero side of Donald. Man took them just to tease me because he saw Donald just the way I did. That was cruel, too, but it helped me. We understood each other completely, but never much with words. I resented that Donald always patronized Man. And Man played up to him. But Man was a very gentle man, as well. With dark eyes. We used to go Sunday afternoons to jam sessions: Thelonious Monk, Janko Barnes, all part of the scene. I was the youngest one of them all. They were all very famous and I was nonfamous. I paid no attention to them.

DL: But what was the central tension in the relationship between Man and Donald? What was that all about?

MFKF: It was a funny relationship. I didn't like it at all. Perhaps because they were different kind of Jews. Very competitive.

DL: How do you mean, different kind of Jews?

MFKF: From different classes. Man was lower class, originally. Donald came from money. He and I played chess. I was cheating to pretend I was worse than I was. Man knew it. He made a chess board for me. He kept trying to get me to win. And then when we were in Paris at the same time, Donald would have Man and Julie cook for us; he treated them like servants. But Donald had impeccable taste and knew Man was very important.

DL: And perhaps that's why he treated him like a servant?

MFKF: Perhaps more than perhaps.

DL: We've talked about Dijon. Where else would you have liked to live?

MFKF: To have lived? Well, now I can't have imagined living anywhere but in here, or around Southern France you know. One time I thought very seriously about living and dying in Greece. I've never even been there. I had it all planned—I'd raise the family, then I'd go to Athens, get a job on an English newspaper. I'd learn modern Greek so that I could write in Greek. And after I'd learned that I'd work two or three years in a newspaper in Athens, a big town, then I'd go to the hillside. Live about halfway up the hillside in a little cottage, just one room and the dear old ladies from the village would come up with bread and soup or something. That's as far as it went. I would live and die there, never come back, never see anybody unless I wanted to. Well, then once long ago, I wanted to live in China. That was before the revolution. I wouldn't want to live there now, too aggressive I think. I'm of communist nature. But I would never really like to live in China, just half-assed communism. I think, sad to say it, but the Chinese accept things more than most people do. To a certain point, they do. I was thinking about Beirut the other day because it's just in shambles. I almost went to Beirut to live with my kids when I was, let's see . . . from France I almost went to Beirut.

DL: Why, what circumstances?

MFKF: To be a professor of French and English at the university there.

DL: Really. Well, they had a very good university there.

MFKF: French, mostly French. French was the second language, I think, there for a long time. French and English both. The kids

were already very French, and I thought it would be just perfect for
them to go to the university there. Come back to America or go to
England, France, they could go any place from there. I didn't think
they'd become Lebanese or anything. I like the Lebanese people
very much, the ones I know, anyway.

DL: Well, why did you decide not to take the job?

MFKF: I don't know. Something to do about the French system.
I would have had to teach at least two years in lycee before I went to
the university. And I didn't want to. Otherwise, I would have been
visiting, always on an uncertain stipend. I couldn't afford to do it that
way.

DL: Was the time in Mississippi the only time you've taught?

MFKF: Yes. I wasn't really teaching there either. But it was like
being in a foreign country. I tutored a lot. Now and then, I'd tutor
French, mostly French and English, but I never did teach classes.

DL: Why is that? I think you would be an exciting, and severe,
teacher.

MFKF: Oh I loved the time in Mississippi, very stimulating to talk
to people, to lead them all. But I don't qualify at all in America because I never graduated from anything but high school, you see, ever.
I never had any honorary degrees offered me, given me or anything.
So I just wouldn't qualify in America. I could have taught in England
as a visiting lecturer. I would have liked to go to University of Dublin,
could've too at one point. I suppose I could have. If I were myself
now, I could be tottering over there. I might just do that.

DL: Actually things have changed enough in the last couple of
decades so that now is the time when you could teach. Because of all
the creative writing programs around.

MFKF: I know, but I don't have the voice for it anymore. My own
health is too uncertain right now. That was a funny twist of fate to get
caught in that hospital deal. If I hadn't had that, I would've been a
strong old lady. Now I'm not. I think though I might get away from
here.

DL: Get away from Glen Ellen? To where?

MFKF: I don't know. See, it was easier when I was less dependent
on other people. But I don't think this is too good for me. Too comfortable, unproductive. Can't exactly scrub floors but I can, I should
be doing more. However, that's another cup of tea. I think we should

talk more about you now. Oh, there were two things for you. There's a poetry catalog and there's a catalog of books you might like to look at. I don't want either one. If I look at them, I'll buy them.

DL: I love looking at catalogs of books. Anatole France called it the most delightful easy reading.

MFKF: I like to, but now with my eyes. . . . This is a new book on Dijon I've been sent. It makes it look much sunnier than it is there. They have a terrible climate. Thick, heavy, dark, rainy most of the time, greasy, greasy air.

DL: Other than the greasy air, it doesn't sound too bad for me. I've never minded rainy climate.

MFKF: Oh, it isn't. That's my memory of it, but it didn't matter one bit because I was very happy there. Wouldn't want to live there now, though. When I went back twice, we decided no, no, if we had to choose.

DL: I've meant to ask you, one place it seems that you never seem to talk much about is England. You've spent a bit of time over there, haven't you?

MFKF: Oh yes, I've been there a lot. Timmy and I were very happy there. We were mostly down in Cornwall.

DL: Oh, I love Cornwall.

MFKF: Yes, I do too.

DL: Where in Cornwall?

MFKF: Well, we lived in Penzance. We stayed for months there. We walked out to Land's End often, but he had some Cornish friends, and I had some Cornish friends and some Welsh friends near the border there. Of course, he was of Welsh decent. Dillwyn is the name for Richard, I think. His ancestor came over with William Penn; he was a surveyor for Penn. So he was of old Pennsylvania people. But they're very, still very, English, his family. They are all gone now, every single Parrish. Maxfield I guess has two kids maybe. I don't know. But the branch that Timmy belonged to is all gone. Seems odd that his whole family died out. You think they'd go on forever.

DL: It also seems strange when you consider that they've gone on for six, eight hundred years. Traceably. For them just to die out does seem somehow like it shouldn't happen. I love that walk though that goes all the way around the Cornish coast. From St. Ives all the way around to Penzance. When I was there a few years ago, I was staying in St. Ives, and I would get up and take a part of that walk. Not very well marked but you just follow the coast and you can do it.

MFKF: We walked the whole time. He had to go on the tops of the cliff there. Mussells, Mousehole. Mussells is down there near Plymouth, I think. Yes.

DL: Oh, it's wonderful. The thing I loved about Cornwall in general was the idea of having those splendid gardens right by the cliffs. I just thought that was the most wonderful thing. Those houses with these big, beautiful gardens by the cliffs.

MFKF: I don't remember that at all. What I loved when we were there was a long time ago, back in the 30s. I never went back to England with Timmy after the War. We were there mostly in the mid-30s. Maybe '30 to '35. And we went down to Switzerland, while I'd come back to this country several times with Al. I was married to Al until we went to Switzerland. That was in '36.

DL: The time in Switzerland with Dillwin that you've written about seems like it was best time of your life.

MFKF: Oh, it was because we were together. We didn't have any families or anything. Well we did—my family came over and Timmy's, and there were all kinds of people there all the time, but we were really together. Whereas always before when we were in England, we were with his mother. Which I hated. She hated me too.

DL: Why?

MFKF: Well, I just didn't like being with his mother. I didn't like being there with Timmy and her, but that was better than nothing. I was very nice and she was very nice. We loathed each other. I didn't really loathe her but she loathed me, she was scared of me. I wasn't scared of her at all because I was young and confident and she was old and tired and weary and scared.

DL: Was she scared of you because of the strength of your claim on Timmy?

MFKF: Yes, yes. Completely. She was very silly, a limited woman. She could have been a very fine artist though. I think I told you she was Mary Cassatt's friend, and they were in Paris together for years. And she came home and married Tom Parrish. Mary Cassatt never married. And Tom died when Timmy was, let's see, I think Timmy was six when his father died. A typical American English gentleman.

In debt up to here, you know. Charming guy. And Mrs. Parrish was rather self-righteous. Disapproved highly of him always. She was a martyr always, so she gave her life to raising her children in the style to which they were accustomed. She would be groaning and moaning every inch of the way. But she was a very good portrait painter. Excellent.

DL: Did you get to know Maxfield?

MFKF: Never met him, no. Didn't matter though. Timmy admired him enormously. He liked him as a person too. Of course, he was quite a bit older than Timmy. The first artist I was aware of was Maxfield Parrish, oddly enough. He'd just prostituted himself by doing the Masted Light series. I would sneak those covers, those advertisements out of the magazines and kept them all. We all read stories in the magazines all the time. Father and Mother read them. She said, somebody's cut this page out. Good god, this page is gone. She'd look around a bit. She knew that I was cutting out the ads. There was one other artist named Jessica Smith, Tandy Smith, something. Ivory Soap. It floats. She was wonderful, funny little fat children, never showed any of their private parts, water covered them. Which I thought was very silly. We all did, of course. Mother laughed at them too and Father did too. Kewpie dolls. Completely sexless. We said, what's wrong with them? They said, well, I don't know, what do you think? So we told them. No breasts, no penises, no nothing, no vulvas, nothing. And she said, would you like to be that way? And we said "yuuuck." So then we always covered up our dolls, to keep them modest, I suppose. They were so modest already. We were very overt about things like that. Which I suppose was rather odd. We never talked about them though. I realize now we just accepted them as silly.

DL: I think this is a tough time for families now. It seems to me raising kids now is like walking on eggshells about everything, about the dangers, the methodology of childrearing. In a way, everything's become so self-conscious and so theory oriented.

MFKF: Well, I don't know. Of course Norah's boys and her grand-children seem quite natural to me, and my kids do. Chrissie, I don't know, he's been down here a lot. He's my oldest grandson of the last batch of my own children's children. I have nothing in common with them really. They seem perfectly normal to me though. Maybe

they're throwbacks or something. But I'd hate to be a child now, just
hate it. All the menaces. I don't know. We didn't have any trouble
with dope at all or alcohol. No I can't say that, because my sister and
I were raised in Prohibition. We were both Prohibition children in a
way. But when she went to college, she could have beer. When I
went to college, all the kids wore flasks. You know, bathtub gin, body
warm gin. Ghastly stuff. We were used to good chilled wines. If we
wanted, which I don't think normal young people want to drink
much anyway. They don't need the stimulant. Unless it's forbidden to
them then they have to have it. Secret or something. Well, it never
was forbidden, but we always drank at home and so warm gin was
just horrible to us. When Sis and I were told we had to drink or we
would never have any dates at all, we said "yuuuck." We were very
popular, both of us. I know now we were. Good young men, but we
just didn't drink their booze. And they didn't care.

DL: This was in high school?

MFKF: No, in high school we went to boarding school. We went
to boarding school because Father didn't. I would have preferred to
go to high school but Mother thought no. We went earlier than we
were meant to because I became so insufferable. She said, I can't
stand to have Doty around anymore. She's suddenly so horrible,
rude, surly. I was. Family angel turned into a real devil. Sulky,
insolent. Oh, I was so unhappy. It was just terrible to be alive.
Suddenly I turned from a very happy child to terrible, morose, rude.
Well, my father and mother were so much better than I in every way.
I don't know, I just hated everything in the world, including myself
most, and them and everything. So Mother said, for god's sake I
can't stand to have Doty around. She's a different girl. So my poor
sister went along with me. She was not ready to go along at all. She
was too young, I think. But I was so happy to leave. I always wanted
to leave my family, get away from their influence. I suppose I longed
to leave because I had too much responsibility.

DL: Siblings?

MFKF: Yes, I raised them because my sister Anne was very ill. My
father didn't like to admit that any of us could be ill. So there was this
sickly child, but they wouldn't admit it. The only way she got any
attention was to pretend she was ill all the time. She could induce
anything she wanted to. She was very clever, much more intelligent

than I was. She was younger than I. The only way I ever got any attention away from her was by accepting responsibility. So Mother was delighted to have me do it. Too much, too soon. So that's what I was rebelling against. I think I wanted to be alone. They always sent Sis along, I always took care of my sister there. They didn't realize it, but she thrived when I wasn't there. Sneaky little bitch she was too. When I was not there she developed very well.

DL: What do you think about the fact that David and Anne somehow got the brunt of something that you and Norah managed to survive?

MFKF: Well, David and Norah were born in one batch and Anne and I in another. But Norah and I survived. One survived from each batch. David and I were very much alike. The youngest and the oldest, you see, were alike. He just couldn't and wouldn't take it. And I could and would. I had to dominate, had to be boss. For awhile, I didn't really like it at all. It was frustrating because Mother was a very lazy woman and very voluptuous, soft, easier for her to just let me run the family than for her to combat me. So she did. I didn't think she liked me to dominate her either. But I did for awhile. I realize she was much better than I, that she was a better person. I wasn't a person yet, I was just a force. She let me be a force without turning me into a person. So I got out as quickly as I could. I left home when I was 16. I never came back really.

DL: And in retrospect, do you think Al was a part of that too? Getting a way out?

MFKF: Oh yes, definitely, because he wanted to leave his family and I wanted to leave mine. He wanted to go to France and I wanted to go anywhere at all. Anywhere, France, anyplace. It didn't matter to me. Away, away. So we just beat it, two days after we were married, we just left. We went student third. Very cheap, cost only a hundred bucks to go from New York to Southampton, way down. Lower decks, god we were in the bottom of the ship. We didn't even have any deck seats in the student third. If we were nice, we were allowed to go to the third class. Third was really down in the bowels of the ship.

DL: When was the last time you traveled by ship? Do you remember?

MFKF: Nonie and I traveled first class on the Italian because we wanted to end in Cannes where we knew some people who would drive us right to where we wanted to be. We ended up in Palermo. It's a wonder we didn't end up in Quito, Ecuador. Because the officers struck, then the men struck. It was terrible, typical Italian. We knew better, we'd traveled on them several times. Travel on an Italian ship was mad. But we thought it didn't matter: first class on the Italian ship, like the QEII, only Italian. Terrible ship, worse than second and third class on a French ship. We traveled second class on the France. Timmy and I came over first though, we traveled on those little ones, DeGrasse, three of them, sort of elegant, intellectual ships.

DL: Do you miss ship travel?

MFKF: I loved it very much. Yes, I do. But now, the ships I really loved were the freighters. San Francisco and Los Angeles down the canal across, humpety hump stop at all the little ports along the way, all through the Mediterranean. No, the Caribbean. And, on the canal, we'd stop at Southampton, zigzag up and down. We got off in Brussels once and went down to Bruges. The kids and I did that once.

DL: Bruges is almost too wonderful. One of those places you feel you can't leave, and then refuses to leave you.

MFKF: I guess I know it is. I don't have a very good memory of it, though. Anne [her daughter] was so scared there, I didn't realize it at the time. I just thought she was a pill.

DL: What was she scared of?

MFKF: Life. I think. She was only eleven. Very mature. She knew that life was going to be very hard for her so it wasn't good for her. And then she was very hostile to everything and she'd do crazy things, show off. She showed a side of her nature that scared me silly. So I coped with that. Then it disappeared completely in France. She was very natural there. Then we came back to this country and she's wasted about 25 years of her life, which one shouldn't do. I think it was wasted anyway. But nothing I could do about it.

DL: How is she now?

MFKF: She's nice now. I think. She's leveled off, she's on lithium for the rest of her life. She's a real manic depressive.

DL: Tell me about other places that have intrigued you.

MFKF: Last night I dreamed a wonderful country near Mexico. Icy cold though wonderful. Whatever it was, I was in the subconscious but near consciousness most of the time.

DL: Do you remember the landscape?

MFKF: Oh yes, very well.

DL: What was it like?

MFKF: Very good, kind of French formal, informal. But I went to a store to get food to give to the other people. I knew I didn't need food, and the first thing there were a whole lot of peeled avocados for free and rotting. And I thought well, I'll just scoop these up in my bag. And there was a wonderful, fat Mexican woman. She didn't talk to me at all. I spoke to her in Spanish, pretty good Mexican Spanish. Now, Señora, I'm going to take these, I know you don't need them. So she said oh go on, do anything you want. Everything was in little dishes, stalks of wheat, all laid very flat, and I thought what a wonderful feast we'll have.

DL: Do you remember whom you were going to feed?

MFKF: Some friends, family, people. But the iciness, the icy cold river, great swirls of ice. And I went around the ice and was on the other side of the bank. All very significant. As I say this, it sounds very silly. I don't believe in determining things, you just accept them. Very pleasant though.

DL: You said—in the '40s, was it?—you kept a dream journal for years.

MFKF: Oh, no. Larry Powell was in, he was doing psychiatric experiments, on himself of course. His doctor said, make yourself remember your dreams because most people don't. Lots of people think they never dream but they do. My dream life has always been an important one. I dream all night long, usually six or seven periods of dreaming. But Larry said he could make himself see wisps of smoke, gradually remember more and more, which is true. In order to get Larry to do it, I did it too. But I didn't want to read his stuff, he didn't want to read mine. We just wrote. But I thought it was pretty silly for me so I never bothered with it. Very important to some people though. Makes them realize that they have a subconscious too, which I knew all along.

DL: I think the problem with the way some people try to interpret their own dreams is they almost forget all about dreamwork and try to be too literal in interpreting the symbolism.

MFKF: Larry never did try to interpret anything. I didn't either, I refused. I was not interested in his dreams, he was not interested in mine.

DL: You mentioned anesthesia, earlier. When I had the operation a couple of weeks ago, to repair my tendon, I had a general anesthetic, and I just hated coming out of it. It was just so perfectly still and dark, it was painful emerging from it.

MFKF: That's weird.

DL: I had one image to accompany the general anesthetic void, as I was waking up: a very, very dark small room, and a chair by a table, like the Van Gogh Arles painting, just this crooked chair by this crooked table. And I was very happy with it. I hated leaving it.

MFKF: Why did you leave it though? Could you take it with you?

DL: Well, no; I did of course take it with me in a sense. But I just hated emerging from the darkness of that room, it was so perfectly calm, so safe, and I have kept the image rather clearly. But not so clear the feeling of it.

MFKF: Did you ever read the letters of Van Gogh to his brother Theodore? Over there, all three volumes, you can take them if you want to, good amount to read.

DL: Sure, why do you mention it?

MFKF: Well, you said Van Gogh and I was thinking about Arles, and he was there before he died.

DL: Was Van Gogh a good writer?

MFKF: Not very, but I think he was. He was writing letters to Theodore. No point is proved that he wrote them to his brother, but Theo kept every one of them.

DL: It's surprising how visual artists, at least many of the ones I've read, seem to be pretty good writers, better writers than musicians. Cezanne wrote some beautiful pieces, some of his letters and journals, and Paul Klee's diaries are just wonderful. Playful but frequently dark and very well-written.

MFKF: Well, Van Gogh had no idea at all of writing, you know, but for some reason, kept every letter, every scrap he wrote. Sad to follow his madness, he did go mad, you know. Theodore did not. But it's a fascinating thing, I'm glad you have not read them yet because they're over there. All three volumes. You see, Van Gogh didn't think he was writing at all, he was just talking to his brother. And his brother didn't think they were very good either, but he kept them all, thank god. Timmy was very much influenced by them, I know. He got me to read them long before we knew we were in love. Fascination, every single word, I don't know why I particularly turned to them lots of times later in my life. Perhaps because we lived in that country.

DL: What was Timmy's effect on your writing?

MFKF: Good. Well, I don't know, he just wrote, naturally, so I did too. I don't think he had any effect at all except he encouraged me to go ahead and write. So I did, but I would have anyway.

DL: Having him as a reader, though, must have been difficult?

MFKF: No, he didn't read me. I never did write anything to be read. Just wrote. That's what surprises me so. People read me so I make a joke which is probably true: of course I know me but I don't know what I've said about me.

DL: Yes, you are different. You have a bit of Dr. Johnson in you.

MFKF: Yes, he's a marvelous old guy. Boswell didn't mean to be funny, but he was.

DL: Poor Boswell. So often is trying to make himself seem important in the scene, to pose himself as a great work.

MFKF: He always comes out pro-Boswell. But Johnson knew he was wonderful. I know people like that, very Johnsonian. Real pain in the ass too.

DL: There's a story of Johnson, got a group of people together and he'd just finished the "Vanity of Human Wishes." The crowd just sort of sat there in shock at the vituperativeness of it, and Johnson was in tears. It's a wonderful scene to think about, poor Johnson, having read his own poem in tears.

MFKF: Well, I can imagine it.

DL: Part of the fun of reading the *Life of Johnson,* is wondering, is putting yourself in Boswell's place and touring around with Dr. Johnson. I think that's what makes Boswell so much fun, too; he is so boneheaded at times, so thick that one can so easily put oneself in his place with Dr. Johnson. Am I performing as your Boswell, Mary Frances?

MFKF: No, dear. And I'm not Johnson, nor was meant to be. Someone sent me that Oxford Facsimile of Johnson's Dictionary. Love it but I don't ever look at it anymore.

DL: It's great fun.

MFKF: I liked the travel journals.

DL: We started out talking about journals, and this is true of letters, as well: one wonders if in a few years, since so much is being done on computers these days, and since the telephone has caused the letter to be so neglected, if the forms will even survive at all. How many journals will get wiped out by a bolt of lightning, and how many observations will just never be recorded because they're on the phone?

MFKF: My daughter Kennedy is a case in point. She hates to write. I can't remember seeing her name, can't remember getting a letter from Kennedy. She calls on the phone all the time, though. I remember once after she grew up, she was very independent from me, I just sent her a telephone bill, she couldn't believe it. "Well, Doty," she said, "you're cutting me off from you." I said, no I'm not, it's up to you.

DL: You wanted her to write.

MFKF: Well, she never could, she just couldn't. Let's talk about us. Are we talking now about us? Tell me something more about yourself. You talk. Your voice is softer than mine, you know.

DL: Whenever I go into restaurants, I have to repeat things three or four times because I don't project. I think it's a form of reaction. I come from a family of New York screamers, and I think my modulation is a lifelong reaction to that.

MFKF: Snobbish.

DL: You think so?

MFKF: Well, perhaps we all withdraw from reality.

DL: Some time in my teens I started feeling, maybe every teenager goes through this, I started feeling assaulted by my New York accent, and my family's, especially after I moved away and came back. Although I get a big kick out of it now.

MFKF: Assaulted by what? You were finer stuff, people were shouting, yelling at you?

DL: The intensity of family life and the noise level seemed inextricably intrusive. I grew up in very close circumstances. For the first twelve years of my life, we lived on the top half of this rowhouse, my brother's and my bedroom right next door to my parents with their little sliding screen door of their bedroom. Very little privacy.

And at some point, it all just seemed much too close. But I think lots of things I withdrew from most when I was younger are the things I'm most grateful for now.

MFKF: How do you mean?

DL: That extraordinary uncomfortably close intimacy of my family—for better and worse, somehow it was all very open.

MFKF: Well sure, because nothing else could be done, so they accepted it. You talk about the extraordinary closeness, but you mean person-closeness. It doesn't mean it goes mentally, since you're very detached in some ways.

DL: I think that I am but in some ways, my own sense of detachment comes from a sense of being a little bit of a split personality. And both are wont to come out unpredictably. I have a very robust ethnic New York side that bursts out, and I think can be very, very funny. And I have this kind of Don-ish side, retiring and, oh, perhaps, excessively analytical, but somehow they manage to live side by side. And my writing is best when they intersect, I think, but they're both there, both always there, sometimes trading center stage. Which may be why I'm usually either very comfortable or uncomfortable, socially. Very little middle ground. I don't feel particularly comfortable in the role of guest. Hard to relax. And it intensifies the sense that I'm an imposter, an interloper, the sense of masquerading, as though I had slipped in the back door.

MFKF: That's it, I've always been a masquerader too. That's what I mean about being a stranger, a ghost. You have a wonderful detachment which I've always managed to keep. You will too. Well, that's good. I'd like to stick around to see what happens to you.

DL: I'd like that too.

MFKF: I wish I could, I would really like to live to see the new century come in. If I did, though, I wouldn't be worth much, I wouldn't be seeing much. Eleven years. Too much. Because the actual living part is rather onerous now. Terribly tiring to live, you know. Which I'm not used to. If I think about crossing a room, crossing my legs. It's like having good legs, you only have them until you don't have them anymore. Being good looking, you never thought about being good looking, you assumed that all women are good looking, always. And you aren't and you think, my god, what happened to me? Well, I don't mind that so much but I know people do. I'm afraid I haven't done anything for you it seems except offer you my full heart, my hospitality.

DL: Well, that's been the world: the pleasure of spending time with you. What do you think about these last few weeks? How've they gone for you in terms of having me poking around?

MFKF: Oh, I liked it very much. I like you. I was thinking today, thank god you're . . . how wonderful it was that you're you and not just some guy. Because you're a person to me, very much so. I think we never really did introduce each other because there really was no need, which is nice.

DL: Why didn't you think you would live this long?

MFKF: I never thought one way or another, but I imagined 75 or something. I'm in my 82nd year now. I could have died, I could die. Sometimes I've been near dying and I've thought well, no, I don't think this is quite the time. I would've been dead if I'd stayed in the hospital, I know. Funny accident to happen to me. So the fact that I survived means that I was meant to, I'm sure. Write a big book, but I know I won't. I don't think I have. I haven't written anything to satisfy me yet.

DL: Tell me about the idea of writing about old age. You first thought of writing *Sister Age* quite a while before you actually wrote it.

MFKF: Oh yes, I've always been fascinated by it. And I think it's absolutely necessary, many bad things, boring you know. But it need not be as boring and horrible as people think. "Sister Age" is just an afterthought. We didn't call it that originally.

DL: Why did the idea fascinate you years ago when you first thought about writing it?

MFKF: It was very hard to find anything good to read about it. I knew a lot of good things I didn't personally know then, that I knew vicariously.

DL: That we're too busy denying advancing age? Trying to keep it away?

MFKF: Yes, I think that's so silly, not preparing for it at all. I find it very enjoyable, much better than being young in many ways. Also, I like to talk about things that people don't like to talk about, slightly shocking or challenging.

DL: Like the 1900 or pre-twentieth century treatment of the retarded, lock those subjects away. The decorum of things one does and does not talk about. Old age being one of them.

MFKF: Yes, such as was the case with pregnancy. In fact, the only thing every talked about was being young and innocent.

DL: Do you remember a piece you wrote, it's wonderful and very very horrifying, in *Sister Age,* the old woman on the ship who died, essentially in your arms, as you were disembarking.

MFKF: That was straight reporting, didn't change a word except at the beginning. I said, dearest Nonie, I'm going to write you exactly what happened these last few days. Nonie read it and was fascinated by it, said it was a good story and why don't you send it out. So I did. Just cut off the "Dear Nonie," and the "see you soon" at the end. Same thing happened with "The Wind Chill Factor." Straight experience.

DL: Straight experiences somehow very clearly, sharply seen.

MFKF: I sat down, you know, had to, write it while it was hot. All the time, I was thinking I was going to die, but in case I don't, the first thing I'll do was mark this down. Staggered down to the typewriter that morning, and so Nonie came out that noon and said what have you done to it. I said not much. And I said would you please take this in on Monday and give it to Bill Shawn? And oh, she was horrified by it. "Awful, awful." And he said, "Oh my god this is awful." So he took it to his psychiatrist and his psychiatrist said "this is awful." So true you know, just as I wrote it, didn't change a word. Which is good. I don't know, I just wrote it, no sense of form. Just the wind started to blow and it blew and blew, and I recovered and wrote about it. I didn't read it, but it got a lot of psychiatric attention because his psychiatrist was quite famous. All the psychiatrists in New York were buzzing about it. It was good. The reaction to death because nobody believes it. Absolute cold fact. I thought if I lived through it, I would definitely write about it. I did, and I did. Well, now my own experience of age is so frustrating to me.

DL: What about the American concept of retirement? Doesn't that seem like institutionalized boredom to you, a kind of state in which there is no intrinsic concern for the possibilities of experience?

MFKF: Oh yes, American men always die or they get cranky or their wives go mad. But in France, the minute you get a job, you start retiring. Buy a little place in the country and you work like a dog, build paths and do things so that when you retire, you retire there happily. What you've worked for all of your life and there you are. That's a good idea. So people lead can lead double lives or have double troubles. Better than no life. The advertisements I'm listening to now for new convenience foods. They say you can save time. Time for what? You know?

DL: Yes, it's very strange. This comes up for me all the time as a teacher. How alienated people are from their work for one thing. How they seem to be always working to some obscure golden age where all they'll be able to do is not work. To be spending all your life working for the short period when you can kill time.

MFKF: I think the phrase I hate the most in the language is kill time. God, that's one thing you don't want to kill. A lot of people don't know that at all. Well, they say, oh we're just killing time. Maybe they're sort of enjoying themselves but not really. And when you think about it, there's no time to kill, you can't kill time, time kills you. And the minutes should be full. I've always hated it in this country. When I first lived in Europe, I realized I could remember every single thing that happened everyday. Here I have to think, what'd I have for lunch yesterday? Not that I hinge everything on meals, everything is important: what was I thinking as I woke up, what was I dreaming last night? God I hate to waste time.

DL: But to save time, people develop routines and standardized meals and there's less to remember. Don't you think?

MFKF: Yes, but don't they want to remember anything? People say, well you have such a wonderful memory for things, but I don't have a wonderful memory at all. Other people say you live in the past because you remember all those things, you must live in the past. I don't at all. But the past makes the present and the future and everything else.

DL: But in a society that has its eyes so firmly fixed on some obscure target in the future, memory is an inconvenience I think.

MFKF: What is the future though? To make more money I guess. Well, that's another thing that I realize I'm way out of step on. I've never made money, and I want to make money. All I want from money is to keep out of debt. I hate debt. I'm out of debt now, but that's all. We're practically broke. Nobody believes it because I always seem to live so comfortably. I do live comfortably. I have just what I need. But now I've got to change my ways. I've got to talk to Nonie about that.

DL: Cut down expenses?

MFKF: As I become more dependent I keep paying more wages to people. And I'll keep getting more dependent as I get older. Twist of fate, fate keeps stepping in. I never thought much about it before. I didn't expect to live this long you know.

DL: No? Why?

MFKF: I could die any time but I will probably live about another five years. And I can't work all that time, I know. So it's getting harder and harder. This book about Dijon may be the last book I may write. I don't know. No, I've got one more to do. But. . . .

DL: What's the one more?

MFKF: Well, it's called Work-in-Progress and it's just a whole bunch of stuff. I've been working on it for years. It's a very conceived book. I put down little things that I was thinking. And I don't know if it's any good or not, because for instance, the other day, I cheated a bit, I said I've go to do something about San Francisco. Well, so I looked to see if there was anything in this Work-in-Progress, there wasn't a thing. And I've been pulling stuff out of it, you know, somebody wants an article about Christmas. I wrote a diatribe about Christmas once, and I tried to say to the people on the phone that I never want to talk about Christmas because I wrote about Christmas once and oh of course I could go on and on, but I don't want to. Anybody can go on about Christmas, including me. So I don't know, there may be nothing in this book at all, this Work-in-Progress when I get to it. And also I think that I sound rather sententious.

DL: You mean in terms of making pronouncements?

MFKF: Yes, I pronounce now. It's an occupational hazard I have. People sit and wait for me to utter a bit, so I utter a bit. People laugh at things that aren't funny because they think they're going to be funny, so they laugh. Then they realize I've said something that's not funny at all. I'm supposed to be witty and I'm not witty anymore. Well, I don't give a damn about saying things that will make people laugh. I used to rather enjoy it, making them laugh. I could make them laugh well and happily. I enjoyed that. But I don't give a damn anymore about whether they laugh or not. I hate it when they aren't supposed to laugh, and they do because they think that I've said something funny and I haven't at all.

DL: That happens to me too.

MFKF: Do you feel as if you'd cheated them a little bit?

DL: Yes, and you just start feeling as if the whole encounter is just somehow a waste of time. If they're not getting that, what else are they not getting?

MFKF: Will they ever realize it, I don't know? I could despise them, I suppose. Scornfulness: which I hate too.

DL: What do you make of the enormous amount of attention you've been getting the last few years?

MFKF: Well, I don't like it.

DL: Why?

MFKF: Because I don't think I deserve it. I don't think I'm that good. I think people have just fastened on an idea so they're reading about their own ego by making something more of me than I am. I used to feel that all these people had sort of crushes on me. I liked it, but I felt I was a sham all the time. But I despised them for liking me because I thought they liked a sham, they built up an idea which is not me at all. They're worshipping that, making fools of themselves and I should be ashamed of myself for letting them do it, but I'm not worth it, you know. I really do think that. I know now that I have a gift for writing. I've never used it wrongly so that's all I can say.

The Prime of M. F. K. Fisher

Betty Fussell/1989

First published in *Lear's*, July/August, 1989, pp. 67–71. Reprinted by permission of the author and the Watkins/Loomis Agency.

As I drove into the Valley of the Moon at the southeastern end of Sonoma County in California's wine country, I was as apprehensive as I was the day I drove along the coast of Naples to find the cave of the Sibyl of Cumae. I have looked for moon goddesses in many parts of the world, and the one I now sought had begun to work me over from the moment I entered her valley. Although I'd been twice before to the Bouverie Ranch, now, for the life of me, I couldn't find it. When I paused at the crossroads of Glen Ellen to phone for directions, a silver chain fell from my neck and with it the Peruvian cross blessed by a Quechuan woman in Arequipa. I began to panic. When I finally saw the little stuccoed Spanish house, shaded by live oaks and warmed by a hot October sun, I fell on it with the joy that Hansel and Gretel must have felt when they were lost in the forest and came upon a house made of gingerbread and candy. That's the kind of effect that Mary Frances Kennedy Fisher has on me, and there's not a damn thing I can do about it.

She built her house near Glen Ellen 19 years ago. It has three rooms—one for work and sleep, one for food and company, and a dark red one between for luxurious ablutions—and all are heaped with a totemic chaos of books and manuscripts, paintings and geraniums, Indian wall hangings and children's drawings, golden peppers, brass sculptures, ripe tomatoes and plums. In a shaft of sunlight on the porch, by a bowl of orange nasturtiums, lies a sleeping cat. A Spanish arch frames a perfect backdrop of blue mountains that are haunted by the ghost of Jack London, who built his Wolf House near this place from red volcanic rock. It's all too perfect, this lair of M. F. K. Fisher—Scotch-Irish Celt adept at runes, fifth-generation wordsmith, descendant of a great-grandmother she calls "part witch and part empress," and avatar—or so my fear tells me—of that awesome muse called by Robert Graves the White Goddess.

She greets me warmly from her wheelchair, skin and bones and frail from Parkinson's disease, hobbled despite an artificial hip, cursed with eyes so bad now that she can neither read nor type. "I was putting on earrings in your honor," she says in the whispery, little-girl voice that startles because it so contradicts her imperious brow, just as the snub nose contradicts her cool green eyes. She still pencils her eyebrows, '30s-style. and outlines her cupid's bow mouth in red. At the age of 81, in her person as in her prose, she defies time with bravado.

She has dressed with care and elegance—a hot-pink blouse and matching stockings, a black velvet pantsuit (the trousers covering the leg brace she hates), and multicolored combs to pin back her hair. At one moment she is a baby-faced sophisticate, as glamorous as one of her Man Ray or Annie Liebovitz portraits. At the next she is an icon of Sister Age, a subject that haunted her from youth, until she decided she was too old to write about old age, and then did—compellingly. I am very glad to see her but I am afraid to tell her so.

She moves her wheelchair adroitly but impatiently, hating her dependence yet loving her attendants: her nephew Chris, visiting for a few weeks, and her frequent companion, Cathy, a young writer from Sonoma. Fisher insists that we go at once to see the old barn, transformed now into a center for the 400-acre Bouverie Audubon preserve that protects her land—land that her friend David Playdell-Bouverie gave to her when she moved from St. Helena. She laughs as she tells how, to enlarge the preserve, she "conned this old boy, a monstrous old man," out of the land at the top of the ridge. Clearly she enjoyed the con as she enjoys the new life at the ranch, the bustle and stir of young botanists and docents, the busloads of schoolchildren, the tourists who stray from the path, get lost, and succumb to "wildwood panic." It's a fit place for a sorceress, this small, civilized enclosure in a wilderness that is still home to snakes and mountain lions, and boar that are "lean and mean on their dainty little hooves and put their noses down to root through a whole row of anything you have, snarfing it up." She's off and running with her stories, and I'm caught for good.

M. F. K. Fisher nailed me first in the 1960s in London, of all places, in a secondhand bookstore off Piccadilly, where I bought a bargain volume of five of her works in one called *The Art of Eating.* I was an instant captive to this Circe of the stove. That she could write so wittily, learnedly, and sexily about a subject as base as food shocked my Puritan upbringing and threatened my literary snobbery. But as I gobbled up her pages, I saw that food was merely the ruse of this libidinous oyster-eater, wolf-killer, gastronomical storyteller, kitchen allegorist, American humorist, metaphysical wit. She was an American original and a writer of the first order: a Mark Twain with Bloomsbury overtones, a cross between Emily Dickinson and Colette. I laughed aloud at her stories and regretted that I'd not heard of her sooner.

Later I learned how varied were her devotees (they included W. H. Auden and the Marx Brothers) and how effective were her disguises. Lucius Beebe fell madly in love with the M. F. K. he assumed was "a wispy young Oxford don," and he never forgave the "betrayal" of his assumption. Many who were smitten by her prose were hopelessly enslaved when they discovered that she talked, lived, and loved the way she wrote. They were enchanted by the pornographer who confessed to unspeakable rites involving catsup with mashed potatoes and mayonnaise with caviar. By the logician who frankly anatomized a recipe "To Drive a Woman Crazy" thus: "Ingredients: 1 or more nutmegs, ground; 1 left shoe, of 1 woman." Readers adored the healer who counseled women to regain the use of their senses "by touching an egg yolk, smelling a fresh lettuce leaf or berry, tasting . . . a fresh loaf of bread, or a fresh body."

I saw that her strategy was Circean, Little Red Riding Hood in reverse: Lure the wolf through the door, seduce him into the pot, and eat him up as a savory stew. Her erotic seductions masked steely powers of language, combining passion with precision to produce constant electric shocks. The way she could turn eating snails into a curiously pleasurable act of necrophilia: "Then there were snails, the best in the world, green and spitting in their little delicate coffins, each in its own hollow on the metal plates." The way she could turn homicide into Wildean wit: "She ran her kitchens with such skill that in spite of ordinary domestic troubles like flooded basements and soured cream, and even an occasional extraordinary thing like the

double murder and harakiri committed by the head-boy one Good
Friday, our meals were never late and never bad."

The way she could create ideal worlds under the guise of "factual"
memoirs. With a twitch of her linguistic wand, she could evoke the
"noisy personality" of places as distinct and diverse as Marseilles,
Aix-en-Provence, Vevey, Dijon, Tahiti, Whittier. I had lived in
Provence, but in a barren spot compared with the "home" she
invented when she wrote of spending Christmas in a hotel room in
Marseilles with her two girls, eating a strange breakfast of caviar on
hot rolls and *café au lait,* toasting one another with three chocolate
bottles wrapped in foil, while she told them the story of Joseph of
Arimathea and how he wandered to Glastonbury from Jerusalem to
plant his hawthorn staff in the ground, where it burst into leaves in
celebration of Christ's birth. "We felt safe and trusting—" she wrote,
"home."

Like her I was a westerner, born not far from her childhood home
in Whittier, but my home and family were light years from the
pastoral world she created in *Among Friends.* The eccentric characters of her family was far more real than my own—her handsome
father Rex, her Anglomanic mother Edith, formidable Grandmother
Holbrook, delicious Aunt Gwen, Miss Marrow the dope fiend, and
"batty" Cousin Lizzy. In Fisher's pages they welcomed me to a 100-
acre ranch where they grew oranges and blackberries, mirabelles and
guavas, artichokes and dates. Where they kept a pig and a cow and a
horse named Hi-Ho Silver. Where she and her three siblings spent
Sundays in the print room of her father's newspaper. Where her Aunt
Gwen made a ceremony of mashed bananas on toast and her father
went hunting for antelope and wild kid while her mother read books
and birthed babies. Where they celebrated the great summer canning
festivals at nearby Valyermo and rode horseback on the cliffs above
Laguna and held picnics on the beach and slept within a circle of
horsehair lariats to ward off rattlesnakes at night. "It was," as she says
of another time and place, "a good way to live."

It was also a good way to write. "I think the only good thing about
me is that I stayed honest," she says now, adding, "because I'm the
worst liar in the world." This paradox is why she's a great storyteller
and a compulsive writer and reader. "With my own discovery of the
printed word I came into focus," she once wrote, confessing that she
read books "the way alcoholics drink, from dawn until Fall-down

Time, and from left to right on the liquor shelf." The addiction to
writing and reading was in her genes. "We were a very articulate
family and we all read and wrote all the time and it was lots of fun,"
she says, recalling that she put out her own private little paper when
she was 6, wrote a novel when she was 9, and went to work on her
father's paper at 14. Now she is sorting through boxes and boxes of
unpublished manuscripts, notes, and novels, and is working with
Cathy on a new book about landladies. "I haven't said half what I
wanted to, but I can't possibly do half of that," she says. "I'm a
junkie about writing, I have to have it. That is my way of screaming
primally."

Her primal scream has propelled me through all of the nearly 20
volumes she's published since 1937 on the art of living fully. "I
believe in living fully," she once wrote, "as long as we seem to be
meant to live at all." The Dickinsonian sting reminds us that the facts
of life are based on the fact of death and that hunger is the common
condition that links them. Even in her first book, *Serve It Forth,*
written when she was not yet 30, she was wise to the "dark
necessities" of nature—"we must grow old and we must eat." And
we must die. From the very beginning, she compelled us to link our
hungers to our fears in order to tame the brutes. "Central heating,
French rubbergoods, and cookbooks," she wrote, "are three amazing
proofs of man's ingenuity in transforming necessity into art."

Like any white witch, her art is the art of transformation. Her
works are formulae for turning sensual pleasures and pains into acts
of moral elegance, for turning all the acts of brute necessity into
sacred ceremony. Auden understood her fully when he dedicated his
poem "Tonight at Seven-thirty" to her. It details the perfect dinner
party, with six perfect guests—"men / and women who enjoy the
cloop of corks, appreciate / dapatical fare, yet can see in swallowing /
a sign act of reverence . . ." Auden recognized that she had forged
her own language to keep body and soul together and make them
whole, a language of runes and charms like the tree-alphabet of the
White Goddess who created order out of chaos by the work. For
Fisher, writing is a talisman like the "assefeddity" ball worn in vain by
a childhood friend, like the hired-girl's cure for a fever, which
consisted of tea made from dried jackrabbit turds, like all the folk
remedies she collected in *A Cordiall Water.*

Through her stories she has long taught us that the human need and the artist's need is the same—to civilize our innate savagery, to tame the wolf within. But I was slow to realize that this is also the root of her lifelong obsession with power, specifically the power of women and the division of power among women. Although she was "furious" with her first publishers when they required her to use her initials M. F. K. as a subterfuge, "because women, they said, don't write this way," she's always denied that she is a feminist. She was, she says, brought up to believe that men and women are equal. Yet she was happy to write a piece for *Newsweek* on "Why We Need a Women's Party" as a third party, "because the approach of the two sexes to religion, sex, love, art, money, and politics is completely different" and we stand in need of the "special inner language of the female mind to help clear up a few ever-present issues like war and peace, corruption and the price of beans."

Better than any American woman I know, she has written about women not as imitation men but armored in their nurturing and civilizing powers. In *The Gastronomical Me* she titled every other chapter, "The Measure of My Powers," as if taking stock of her place in the dynasty of "dominating, strong-willed women" into which she'd been born.

She measured her powers against her dowager-queen Grandmother Holbrook, who liked her son-in-law, she tells me, better than her own daughter. "Mother and she were at odds but they never, never quarreled," she says as we sit on the porch, she now in her empress guise, eyes hidden by enormous dark glasses, her throne a high-backed rattan chair. "You just didn't quarrel—even in private." Her Campbellite grandmother was the one who referred to the Catholic Church as "the Scarlet Woman of Rome," and who called Queen Victoria "that old hag in Windsor Castle." Possibly that is why her daughter Edith was such an Anglophile.

As the eldest of four, Fisher measured her height as well as her powers against her parents and siblings. At five feet eight inches she was the runt of the litter, overshadowed by a father of six foot seven, a baby brother of six foot six, and a mother and two sisters all six feet or over. From her sister Anne—"she was a real bitch," Fisher says with affection—she learned the strategies of the frail. "At Christmastime she'd put on such a scene! Two days before Christmas she'd have a terrible bilious attack and lie on the couch, this wan little

fairy, and we'd put all her presents around her and open them for
her—with her permission, of course. What a ham she was,"—and
she pauses—"a beautiful, complex, fascinating woman . . . who died
when she was 55. Like a dog."

When Fisher finally measured her powers against age, she wrote
about an obscure woman, Ursula von Ott, whose portrait she had
discovered in a junk shop in Zurich, painted on a piece of leather.
From then on, Ursula's likeness hung over Fisher's bed—and when
not her bed, her desk—as a symbol, half-eaten by silverfish but still
potent as an image of someone "completely alive in a landscape of
death . . . the enigmatic, simian gaze of a woman standing all alone."
From Ursula she had wanted to learn the art of aging, and that is
what I had come to learn from Fisher. For me, Fisher too is an image
of a woman standing alone, a woman who has survived three
husbands and two younger siblings, one of them a suicide. She is
a woman who supported her two girls by the small sums she made
from writing, and who has lived single for nearly 40 years. And all
this time she wrote well and lived fully.

Her specific against mortality is what it's always been and what
forever links the spinner of tales to the nursery and the kitchen slaves
on the Whittier ranch who "with their soapings and their knives and
their hungers for hidden sweets . . . were all women trying to survive
among savages." Through the power of the word she has not only
survived but prevailed, despite the "damn brace," the sleepless
nights, the eyes that can't read. Now, as before, she puts time in its
place by ceremony. The simple ceremony of our lunch—the slices of
ripe tomato from the garden of a friend, her sister Norah's good fresh
butter, the whole-grain bread with sprouted wheat berries and the
nice local white wine "that goes down easy at $2.98 a bottle"—is like
a perfect dinner party for six, like the picnics at Laguna or the fairs
and fetes in Provence. All are "ageless celebrations of life." So too is
the ceremony of her conversation, her hunger to hold Cathy and me
spellbound, to make us cry and make us laugh with stories about
herself and others.

When I take my leave, she speeds me on my way with all the
bottles of good $2.98 wine that I can carry. It's hard to thank her
with the right words for the gift of herself. As I leave the Valley of the
Moon, the shade is lengthening as the last light flames the leaves of

the grapevines red and gold. I remember Fisher's words on our
common mortality with the plants that give us food and drink—"first
freshness, then flavor and ripeness, and then decay." But that is too
autumnal. My ears buzz with the story she has just told about the
cows that used to have the run of the ranch when it was still "a call-
house for cattle." One day they began to lick the white calcium out of
her stuccoed walls and would then throw it up, so that the house
turned pink while the yard turned white. I hear her delight in imitat-
ing the cow sounds, linking man and beast, loving the absurdities,
embellishing her effects. "Hearing the cows snuffing up, slosh, slosh,
throwing up—*wuuuup, wuuuup*—I knew it was something I'd never
forget," she says.

Nor will I; not a single blessed word. I laugh aloud and am no
longer afraid.

✓

M. F. K. Fisher: Essayist

Bill Moyers/1990

Mary Frances Kennedy Fisher long has said that two things came naturally to her: cooking and writing. Now eighty-two, she has written more than twenty books and countless articles for *The New Yorker.* Her subjects are our three basic needs—food, security, and love—and how they intermingle. *Serve It Forth, The Gastronomical Me,* and *With Bold Knife and Fork*—to name but a few—are enduring works that display Fisher's distinctive views on taste and cuisine. Her forays into fiction—my favorite is the acclaimed book of short stories about aging, *Sister Age*—further attest to her literary powers and zest for living. She lives in Sonoma, California, where she is working on a book about the town of Dijon in France.

Moyers: Sister Age has come to live with you. Is she what you thought she'd be?

Fisher: Well, she's still a good friend. Still a sister, I think. There are some things about aging that I don't like, but I think I'd rather be old than young. I can get away with more. Say more what I want to say and less of what I think people want to hear.

Moyers: Here in the afterword of *Sister Age,* you write, "I notice that as I get rid of the protective covering of the middle years, I am more openly amused and incautious and less careful socially, and that all this makes for increasingly pleasant contacts with the world." We do indeed have that "protective covering of the middle years." Why do you suppose that is?

Fisher: I think we hide from a lot of things in the middle years that we're not conscious of hiding from at all until we get older and find that we've been hiding. You have to call on your own when you get older. In the middle years, you take on the protective coloration of your environment. But when you get old, you choose your own environment more and you choose your own friends more.

Moyers: Did you choose this environment of central California? Did you come here because this is where you thought you wanted to grow old?

Fisher: No, I didn't want to grow old anyplace. I never thought of growing old. I don't think I've grown old. I've gotten older, but I've not grown very much. I haven't developed very much.

Moyers: You seem to have thought about aging very early. You wrote even before you were thirty that there are two things we must do. We must grow old, and we must eat.

Fisher: I do believe that. I've always liked older people. I've always been interested in them. I think one of the main troubles about modern life is that the older people do not live with the younger people anymore. When I was a child, we had a big house, and my grandmother lived with us.

Moyers: And that was important to you?

Fisher: She was a very Christian woman. I was not very Christian, ever. And she was a very severe woman. She was a rabid Irish Protestant. I guess they're really all rabid. She never talked to Catholics, she always spoke with horror of Rome. She had terrible prejudices.

Moyers: And yet it was still a good thing to live in the same house with her?

Fisher: Yes, it was very good for us because we had better manners when Grandmother was around. She demanded them and she got them. We had one set of manners for Grandmother, one set when she was gone. We always ate nicely at the table. Grandmother believed children should be seen and not heard, you know, except she heard me all the time reading. She taught me to read. I liked her very much but I wondered why I didn't love her.

Moyers: Have you figured out the answer to that?

Fisher: She wasn't a very lovable person. But she was my protection. I liked her like a tree or something, she was just part of my life like a tree or a bush or something.

I admired her very much, and Mother admired her too, even though she didn't like Mother at all. Mother was an afterthought. In those days of Irish Protestantism and the Victorian Age, women had childbearing years, then they had to give up all that nonsense and they embraced the Church. Grandmother embraced the Church and then, bang, she had Mother many months later. So she resented her very much. Mother had a miserable childhood, I think. She loved her father, but her brothers were older than she. They teased her; so we never teased at home.

Moyers: Was your home a happy place?

Fisher: Oh, very happy. I was very happy. Of course I was miserable about being the patsy for years. I was the oldest child, but I never got any privileges because my next youngest sister was the invalid of the family. She knew how to get all the attention and I didn't get any. So I would cook. I was always the cook on the cook's day off. And then I realized that I was being a patsy to get the admiration—I loved it. I wanted to get something away from my sister. So I would cook meals. I learned how to cook when I was very young.

Moyers: Look what came of it. A lifelong art.

Fisher: Well, people ask me why I wrote about food. I think I wrote about everything all my life. I've always been a writer, but I eventually found I could earn some money by it. I supported the family for years. The only way I made money was from my magazine articles, not my books. I think I was twenty-three when I published the first thing for money.

But I never think of myself as a writer. I'm a journalist, a fifth-generation newspaper person. Father was a newspaper editor, a small-town newspaper editor, but he never thought of himself as a writer either. He wrote two thousand words a day for sixty years of his life, but he never used a byline. So when I used a byline, I hid it from my father for years. I was embarrassed by it.

Moyers: Was it hard to make a living writing in those days? If I remember correctly, one year you made only thirty-seven dollars writing.

Fisher: Yes, I did. I had an agent then who didn't want me to be a best-seller. I could have been, but I would never have amounted to much.

Moyers: Why?

Fisher: Well, I would probably have made a lot of money and then I would have gone back to newspaper work. But as it is, I've been a free-lancer most of my life. I was under contract once to five magazines, for once-a-month stuff. It was when my children were little. At that point I had divorced their father, and I was paying his alimony for two other wives. And I needed money badly. So I went under contract to five magazines at once. I wouldn't ever do that again.

Moyers: But you never stopped writing after that.

Fisher: No, I write naturally. Just have to write.

Moyers: An early compulsion?

Fisher: I think so, but I don't think I'm a real writer because I've not grown any. I think, well, now my books sell. The first books I published sell just as well now as they did then. Better, maybe.

Moyers: Don't tell me this isn't growing. You're talking about moments of wisdom. "Once, I was lying with my head back, listening to a long program of radio music from New York, with Toscanini drawing fine blood from his gang. I was hardly conscious of the sound—with my mind, anyway—and when it ended, my two ears, which I had never thought of as cup-like, were so full of silent tears that as I sat up they drenched and darkened my whole front with little gouts of brine. I felt amazed, beyond my embarrassment in a group of near-friends, for the music I had heard was not the kind I thought I liked, and the salty water had rolled down from my half-closed eyes like October rain, with no sting to it but perhaps promising a good winter."

Fisher: Well, that's good. It's okay. But I don't think that's really writing. I just did it, you know.

Moyers: No, I don't understand.

Fisher: Well, I said it; I didn't write it. I said it to myself. Then I just put it on paper. I've never rewritten it.

Moyers: Even the metaphor of tears just came to you? You didn't have to sit at the desk and make it work for you?

Fisher: No.

Moyers: And this: "Such things are, I repeat to myself, fortunately rare, for they are too mysterious to accept with equanimity. I prefer not to dig too much into their comings, but it is sure that they cannot be evoked or foretold. If anger has a part in time, it is latent, indirect—not an incentive. The helpless weeping and sobbing and retching that sweeps over somebody who inadvertently hears Churchill's voice rallying Englishmen to protect their shores, or Roosevelt telling people not to be afraid of fear, or a civil rights chieftain saying politely that there is such a thing as democracy— those violent, physical reactions are proof of one's being alive and aware. But the slow, large tears that spill from the eye, flowing like unblown rain according to the laws of gravity and desolation— these are the real tears, I think. They are the ones that have been simmered, boiled, sieved, filtered past all anger and into the realm of acceptive serenity."

Fisher: That's true, but I never heard it before. What is that from?

Moyers: It's from "Moments of Wisdom," your opening chapter in *Sister Age.* You don't recognize it?

Fisher: I don't. I never read anything I write after I think it. I write in sentences and paragraphs and even chapters. So maybe I'm crazy, a phenomenon or something.

Moyers: That's what they said of Mozart. He wrote down what he heard, and he often didn't know what he was writing down, or what he had heard. You've never gone back to your own sixteen, seventeen books?

Fisher: No, never. I wouldn't want to; I'd be embarrassed. Once I did get one of my grandsons to read me a chapter from my book *A Cordiall Water.* I think it's the best thing I've written. It's just old recipes and old receipts I found. How to cure warts and stuff like that. I wrote it when I had not read or spoken English for a long time so it's quite pure. But when my grandson read it all I can remember is that within two sentences there was a mistake, one misuse of a word. If I said it now I would not have said it that way. It was perfectly correct, you know, but I didn't like it.

Moyers: You once wrote that women have an inner language that is peculiarly their own. Do you still think that's true?

Fisher: Yes, I do. Often they don't express it, though. They understand it, but they don't express it. Yes, I do think there's an entente between women. There's an entente between men, too, that women never understand. *You* could be with a man and you'd understand something about him that I could never get.

Moyers: I agree with that, and yet I think many of my best friends are women.

Fisher: I like men very much. I think I would rather be with women, though, than men. I think men are less interesting than women in general. They're more limited. They don't feel the same pain. They don't have the same endurance. They don't know the same things women know. I don't think pleasure is real to most men. Do you?

Moyers: I'm afraid we live too much in worlds that have been constructed for us and organizations that we didn't create. I grew up thinking that I had to succeed out there in a world I didn't make.

Fisher: You had to take care of people.

Moyers: Well, men don't necessarily take care of people. They provide for them. I think the women take care of people. I don't somehow think of men as "civilizing"—to use your term.

Fisher: I don't think they are. Unfortunately, women will always kowtow to men.

Moyers: Why?

Fisher: I don't know. I hate it. I hate the subservience of women to men. One reason women are in such a mess now is because of men in politics, for instance, but women are terrible politicians. Most women become strident, you know. They raise their voices. I don't like that.

Now, my mother and father were different. I realize now that we believed in equal rights and fair play and money for both people. Mother just happened to choose to raise us rather than work. Twice she got ready to get a job, I remember. Once Father was going into the First World War, and Mother practiced being editor of his paper. I don't know what it would have done to us, but then Father was turned down for the army. He was horrified, because he always wanted to wear a uniform.

Moyers: Well, that's a difference, you know. Men do feel the empowerment of the uniform, and I don't know many little girls who do.

Fisher: Oh, he would have hated it, you know, he just would have loathed it, but he wanted to wear a uniform. Back during the Spanish-American War he ran away for Theodore Roosevelt. He became a Rough Rider. His father went down and nabbed him off the decks of the ship to Cuba. He lied about his age; he was not yet eighteen, you see. So he never did make it. And his son didn't make it either. His son said he never would wear a uniform. Never. He never did. His only son killed himself. Which was terrible for Father, and Mother, too. He was their last child, you see.

Moyers: Your brother?

Fisher: Yes, my brother, David. He killed himself the night before he was to go into the Army for World War II. He was just passionate about not wearing a uniform for any country, any man. It absolutely ruined my father and mother. So I'm very bitter about it in a way. I don't really blame David because I've always believed in suicide. You know, my second husband Timmy killed himself, and I don't think he was unjustified. But it was unjustified in David's case because you never know what waves will spread out.

Moyers: The unintended victims of a suicide—the survivors—carry the pain.

Fisher: It's terrible. It did awful things to my father and mother because we thought they'd have a wonderful old age together. They had been married almost fifty years and they were mellowing beautifully, and they were more and more compatible, more congenial all the time. They'd gone through lots of thin and thick. Mostly thin, pretty thin times, I'm sure. And so we thought they'd have a wonderful old age together, but it drew them apart instead of together.

Moyers: You said your second husband killed himself justifiably.

Fisher: He had Buerger's disease. He and the King of England were the only people we knew of who had it at the time. There were thirty-seven identified cases in the whole world. it was quite a rare thing, like a cancer of the blood.

Moyers: Did he take his life because he was so ill?

Fisher: Oh yes. He was doomed. He had a wonderful heart, a very strong heart, that kept beating. His mother had it, and he had it. So this heart would have gone on beating until he was a basket case, which he would have been.

Moyers: And he was in pain?

Fisher: Terrible pain.

Moyers: Did you know he was going to take his life?

Fisher: Oh yes, sure.

Moyers: Did you agree to it?

Fisher: Yes, I did. It was still a shock, though. I kept him from killing himself once, and then I said never again, I never would do that to anybody again. I held him back from jumping off a bridge. He couldn't help himself, though, he was insane with pain. So I think there was justification there. But most suicides are basically selfish.

Moyers: How did you appease your grief?

Fisher: I never did, I guess. I just went with it. I didn't show it to anybody much, though. Timmy and I lived on an isolated place out in the desert. Everybody said, "Now, you must go to work, you mustn't stay here alone." And I thought, Why not? I have everything I need here, including my dog. One night about ten o'clock I said to Butch, my dog, "Now, Butch, you please turn off the radio." And I got a job the next day. I realized I'd just gone over the edge. Talked to my dog as though he could turn off the radio.

Moyers: Just from reading your stories I've the sense that Timmy, your second husband, was your only true love.

Fisher: Well, not my only. I've loved many people. Really loved them, too. But he was the real one for me. I fell in love with him the first time I saw him, I think, or the second. I knew then it was hopeless, but it hadn't occurred to me yet to get a divorce or anything.

Moyers: You've lived single for forty years now. Is that by choice?

Fisher: Well, I haven't been single, I've had several good affairs. But I like to be alone. I don't believe in marriage much. I think it's silly.

Moyers: Now, you've got to explain that. Too many of us are married to be silly.

Fisher: The best thing I can think of is to live with somebody and go through thick and thin together and then come out the end and have good years of love and whatever is left.

Moyers: So is marriage just a device? Just a form?

Fisher: Largely, now, I think. It doesn't keep enough people together. It's too easy to get a divorce. But I don't know, I'm a poor one to talk about it, I think. I've had three marriages, three good ones, too. I loved the men dearly. Always loved them dearly.

Moyers: But you left your first husband.

Fisher: Yes, I did, because I fell in love with the second one. You see, I knew I couldn't lie; I had to get a divorce. But I never could do it until I found that Timmy loved me, too. Then I thought, "Well, pooh." I wasn't really in love with Al the way I was with Timmy. My third husband and I should have never married, but I got from him two wonderful children. He didn't want any kids at all. He was horrified at the idea of one child. But he settled for one. And then two—my God, that was shocking. He'd been a single child, you see. His idea of children was the little boy who came in the room and said, *"Bonjour, Maman. Bonjour, Papa."* You'd kiss him on the forehead, and he left and never saw his parents again. He was raised by governesses and nurses and by nannies and tutors.

Moyers: You raised your two daughters by yourself. Would you have liked to have had some help?

Fisher: It was easier to raise them alone than to raise them and a man, too, you know?

Moyers: You wrote once about the seasons of life. What was the finest season of your life?

Fisher: Well, I think when I was with Timmy. I was with him for seven years, though we weren't married for that whole time.

Moyers: What made it so good?

Fisher: Well, he was just right. I don't love unquestioningly, but I do love completely. And I think I learned a lot of that from Timmy Parrish. He taught me how to love because he knew we wouldn't be married very long.

Moyers: When you were married were you aware that he was ill?

Fisher: No. But we learned soon after. And the last few years of his life we knew.

Moyers: You've had so much independence in your life. Has it been hard to give up that independence with the coming of age?

Fisher: Oh well, there's some things I don't like about it. I think giving up driving a car was the worse because I started driving when I was ten years old. By eleven I was taking the whole family to the beach. But driving was different in those days, thank God.

Moyers: What else have you had to stop doing?

Fisher: Well lately, I don't write anymore. I can't write with my hands. I dictate.

Moyers: Somebody once asked de Gaulle if he feared anything. And he said, "I fear only one thing. The shipwreck of old age."

Fisher: Well, he was not shipwrecked. I don't think it's a shipwreck at all.

Moyers: But when I think about having to give up driving, when I think about wheelchairs and failing hearts and arthritic joints and all of that, I think of the southern French wine that you used to write about; it peaked very slowly and then decayed very quickly. And sometimes I wish life were like that. That we peaked slowly and then we were gone instead of waiting around.

Fisher: So do I. I don't think it's worth living, but I do live. So I'm alive. So I make the best of it. I would have died twenty years ago if somebody had shown me this recent picture of me with, you know, pouches and bags, and stuff. I don't like those things. They're not very pretty, but I'm me.

Moyers: You wrote once about an older woman who was "past vanity." Do any of us ever get "past vanity"?

Fisher: Oh yes. Although I don't think I ever was vain, so I didn't need to go past it. I've never really thought of myself as beautiful at all. I never thought one way or another about it until later. I had the kids when I was quite old, you see. And when Anne was almost seventeen, we went to Aix-en-Provence, and there was a young Englishman who was in love with her. One day I was sitting there and he said, "Your mother must have had lovely gams once." And I thought, Lovely gams once, what does that mean? It meant that when I was younger I must have had good legs. Now my legs were pretty much all right then, but they were gone for him forever, because I was too old to have them. I was thinking about that the other day. They're the same old legs. I never thought about it, never thought I had pretty legs, but I guess I did once.

Moyers: You wrote once that our basic needs are food, security, and love. Would you add anything to that now that you're in your eighties?

Fisher: Well, in order to exist, you have to be warm and fed and protected by other people, which means love; and you're also protective to other people, you feed other people first usually and keep them alive. And security is the place where you can hide your head, go to bed with somebody you love. Well, there you are.

Moyers: You write of one of your characters, "She does not need anything that is not already in her." I like that.

Fisher: Yes, I don't think any of us needs more than that. I have just enough, I think. I'm very fortunate, because I've always known more than many people do. Some people were born dumb. I wasn't born dumb.

Moyers: What you seem to have done is to store up almost everything you ever experienced.

Fisher: Well, maybe that's stupid.

Moyers: No, it's paid handsome dividends in terms of the richness of your writing, your memory. I mean, there is joy in your books, even when there is sadness. The tears of wisdom commingling with the joy. In a wonderful scene in *Sister Age,* you're a little girl in the house outside of Whittier, and a Bible salesman comes to the door.

Fisher: Yes, I remember that. That's the first time I cried for anybody but myself, I think. I was eleven or twelve then. The salesman knocked on the door, and he wanted to see Grandmother, who had died just a few days earlier. He stopped at the gate in the tangle, and plucked a rose, and at the moment tears fell—just fell out of my face. I didn't mean to cry at all.

Moyers: What you called "the tears of new wisdom."

Fisher: I think I suddenly knew why he was old and tired and dusty, and I was so stupid, and Grandmother's gone, and I understood about a lot of things.

Moyers: Did you ever try to give your daughters a certain treasure? Did you say to them, this is the right treasure to store?

Fisher: No, I don't think so. I just trusted them to find their own treasures. I'd say, well, I think this is good, or I think that's good, but I didn't say, "You should think that," ever. I don't think anyone should ever say that to anybody.

Moyers: Did you finally do everything you wanted to do in life?

Fisher: I don't know. I think so. I think I never did enough, though.

Moyers: You've traveled, you've loved, you've eaten, you've—

Fisher: Never enough, though.

Moyers: A friend of mine said there's one question I want you to ask Ms. Fisher. What use are good wine and ripe tomatoes in the face of pain and evil in the world?

Fisher: Well, that's a silly question, I think. One has to live, you know. You can't just die from grief or anything. You don't die. You might as well eat well, have a good glass of wine, a good tomato. Better that than no wine and a bad tomato, or no crust of bread. Since we must live, we might as well live well. Don't you think?

M. F. K. Fisher

Katherine Usher Henderson/1990

From A Voice of One's Own: Conversations with American's Writing Women, by Mickey Pearlman and Katherine Usher Henderson (Boston: Houghton Mifflin Company, 1990), pp. 93–102. Copyright 1990 by The University Press of Kentucky, under the title Inter/View: Talks with America's Writing Women. Paperback edition published under the title A Voice of One's Own: Conversations with America's Writing Women by Houghton Mifflin.

On the route from San Francisco to the ranch in Sonoma County where Mary Frances Kennedy Fisher lives, a thin November sun revealed soft purple hills and small vineyards, their stakes entwined with leaves of deep red or pale green. Fisher's home, located just beneath the main house of the Bouverie ranch, is approached by climbing a gentle slope through California brush and bits of volcanic rock from the eruption of Mount St. Helens. My knock was answered by a handsome young man with a shock of dark hair who introduced himself as Chris, "the grandson," and took me to Fisher, a slender, strikingly beautiful woman of eighty-one with silvery hair and high cheekbones, dressed in a black jersey and long red skirt. From the bedroom/study where the interview began we looked out on a hill with a vineyard and a tall red belfry in front of a stone ranchhouse.

Temporarily unable to walk because of a back injury, Fisher sat in a lounge chair and invited me to sit on her right in her leather wheelchair. Her desk, books, and papers filled one end of the room to my left; a large calico cat bounded through the room at regular intervals.

After one phone call for Chris and another in which Fisher rescheduled a lunch date because of a filming crew about to descend upon her house to do a story on her, Chris brought me a cup of tea and Fisher expressed a few reservations about the interview. First, because one writer once claimed that she was born in Nome, Alaska, and another that she was born in Savannah, Georgia, she would like to see a transcript of the interview. (Fisher was in fact born in Michigan, but has lived most of her life in California and in Europe, with twenty-two years in France and Switzerland.) Her second concern—"I'm very indiscreet. I say 'O God' a lot"—was simply stated. Her final concern arose from my statement that we are interested in "configurations of space" in writings by women; she said this sounded "esoteric and weird." When I explained that women writers often define characters in terms of their homes, rooms, and other "spaces," she responded, "Sex and food and shelter, those are the three main things in life. We really can't live without them. Some people try to, but they don't. If you were terribly cold all day you wouldn't want to eat and you wouldn't want to have sex."

To say that sex, food, and shelter are major themes in most of Fisher's sixteen books is true, but crudely put. Fisher is perhaps America's best anthropologist and historian of food and its rituals and attendant pleasures. Food in her writings is always tied to work (fishermen and farmers and vintners) or love, the nurturing love of the parent teaching her child to make gingerbread or the harmony of food shared in friendship. There are recipes in her books, but they are there "like birds in a tree—if there is a comfortable branch" (from the introduction to *Serve It Forth*).

In addition to writing about food, Fisher has written a novel and dozens of short stories, a history of folk medicine, an autobiography of her childhood called *Among Friends,* travel books, a book on winemaking, and a translation of Brillat-Savarin's *The Physiology of Taste.* Her writing has captured the spirit of places as exotic as Paris and Marseilles, as sleepy as Whittier, California, as beautifully serene as Napa; but she always writes not merely about a place, but about her own subtle, observant, richly nuanced relationship to that place. Much harder than citing the themes of Fisher's work would be to discover a theme on which she has *not,* in a lifetime of professional writing, discoursed with grace, intelligence, and wit.

Fisher said that she wrote "from the time I was four. It was my way of screaming and yelling, the primal scream. I wrote like a junkie; I had to have my daily fix. The stuff I wrote fifty years ago is as good or bad as the stuff I am writing now. I became more sure of my craft, but I was a good craftsman from the very beginning. I can't hold a pen or type now, which is one reason I'm rather frustrated. I can and do dictate, but it's not the same. I'm forcing myself to use cassettes, but they're not the same either."

She currently spends her afternoons going over her unpublished journals and fiction. "See that end of the room, all those papers. We dug all those up . . . They are journals and novels and stories. A friend is going through them with me. We've rescued about five books and have more to go. They are really good stuff, I hope. I can read them but I can't read what I've already printed."

Fisher is a "fifth-generation journalist." Her father, the son and grandson of printer-writers, bought the daily paper of Whittier, California, in 1912 and edited it for the rest of his life. Writing in Fisher's family was as natural as breathing. "No one encouraged me—we all wrote." From the age of seven she presented petitions to her parents in writing, the first a plea for an end of dosages of castor oil; the second—signed by her sister, the hired hand, the cook, and even the ice man—a petition against her mother bobbing her hair in imitation of the dancer Irene Castle. The fact that Edith and Rex Kennedy "took our manifestos very seriously" must have helped convince Fisher of the power of the written word.

Fisher's parents emerge in her autobiography as rational, sensitive, and highly principled people. Her mother "went to a ladies' finishing school in Kenyon, Ohio, when it was the hotbed of radical liberal Episcopalian thought. She was mildly suffragettish when she went to London. Her rich relatives wanted her to come out, to be presented at court. Only a few American girls did back then, unless they were to be married into English aristocracy, like Mrs. Astor, or to marry Italian counts. The Italian and English wanted the money and we wanted the titles. Mother didn't want either, [but] she went off to England to be presented to the queen. They got all ready to send back the pictures of this beautiful American girl; the one they sent was of her chained to the iron gates of Buckingham Palace with some leaders of the suffragette movement like Mrs. Pankhurst and Mrs. Sanger. So she lost caste . . . she was not presented at court at all."

Fisher's household consisted of her parents, her maternal grand-mother, and four children, three girls and a boy, of whom she was the oldest. As Anglo-Irish in a predominantly Quaker town, she and her siblings were subjected to much teasing and prejudice, but their stable, loving household enabled them to offset the miseries known to children of any ghetto. "A lot of people think that I liked my father better than my mother and that's not true at all . . . In fact I preferred my mother. Maybe I talk more about Rex than I did about Edith, but I liked them both very much." She told a story about roller-skating on the bumpy sidewalks of Whittier. "Did I talk about how I used to try to collect my skin? I lost so much of my legs on the sidewalks, which were put directly on the roots of trees [which] kept on growing. I went dashing back to mother once, screaming with blood down one knee, and said 'Mother, where's that pillbox?' She said, 'Why?' I said, 'I have to go and get my skin.' I found some of it and tried to put it on, but it wouldn't stick so I came home. She loved having children. It was her best job."

I mentioned my surprise, in reading *Among Friends*, to find how relaxed an attitude toward the human body her parents conveyed to their children. "She and Father were both what we now call broad-minded. We did talk very freely and casually. One time I thought I heard my little brother crying (he slept in my parents' room) and sneaked into the bedroom, and I realized father and mother were making love so I just disappeared. I was kind of embarrassed, but mother said 'That's all right.' Years later my mother asked me whether I realized what they were doing and I said of course I did and it didn't bother me a bit. One night I went into their room stark naked to get a handkerchief, thinking they were asleep. The next day Mother told me that Father had said that I was growing up and my breasts were like half-apples." Yet they were strict about social conventions regarding language. "There was a backyard language and a table language and I erred by saying *turd* at the table."

I asked Fisher about her grandmother's impact on the family. "I like all Victorian middle-class ladies, after she got too old for childbearing, she embraced the church, the Protestant church. . . . You don't love anybody but God. You don't love peanut butter or anything. She wasn't lovable, but she commanded respect and admiration. We had steak and watercress when she went to religious conventions and we gabbled away. She believed children shouldn't speak unless spoken to. I wondered profoundly why I didn't cry when grandmother died."

I asked whether she cried when mother died. "We were taught not to show any emotions much, except Mother did. Stiff-upper-lip

school, terrible, awful—I never raised my kids that way. We bit our
tears back . . . we were stoical. We behaved well, but not too well.
Oh God, I cringe at some of the things I've done." I reminded Fisher
that she is always generous to her family, that she nurtured her
younger siblings and her aging parents in addition to her own two
daughters. (Before her back injury she had planned to take Chris,
who graduated this spring from the University of Oregon, to Marseilles for Christmas). Generous is "what I'd like to be." She remains
close to her two daughters and her three nephews, the sons of her
sister and closest sibling Norah. "We were both single parents so we
raised her three boys and my two girls together. They are all very
dear to me."

Although Fisher wrote from the age of four, she was in her twenties
before she realized that writing might be a source of economic support. "I didn't really earn my living until my first marriage in the
middle of the Depression. That was when I became almost militant
about being poor. We worked as a team, my husband and I, cleaning
houses on Laguna Beach. We lived there all year round. And I got
thirty-five cents an hour and Al got fifty cents because I was a
woman, you see. And he didn't work very much because he was
writing the great American novel. I did all his work and mine, and it
made me so damn mad to get thirty-five cents an hour. I did it all
because it never occurred to me to write."

Fisher became a professional writer in the late thirties, earning
most of her income through writing for magazines. ("The books I
wrote for fun; I never earned any money from them until lately.")
She had a problem with writing for magazines, however, for she felt
compelled to "bend certain ways. I wrote for the *New Yorker,* and
I was very happy *not* to write for the *New Yorker.* When I wouldn't
bend once, I learned to bend. Bill Shawn, the editor, read every word
everyone wrote for the *New Yorker.* He would make a faint pencil
line with a teeny square in the margin with the initials W.S. and a
teeny question mark. And I'd say no or yes. He would question the
position of a word in the sentence, so I would think more before I'd
put a word on paper."

Other magazines required more dramatic forms of "bending."
"Years ago my agent sold a story to the *Ladies Home Journal,* mostly
in the Midwest. The schoolteacher in the story had a glass of sherry

before dinner. They said, 'No, no. A teacher in the Midwest does not drink.' So they changed it to milk. I said, 'Damn, I can't do this. She wouldn't drink milk before dinner.' I needed the money very badly, but I told them absolutely not, I can't do it. My agent said, 'What the hell difference does it make? It's a good story.' So that's a compromise I learned I can make, but I don't like to." She enjoyed writing pieces for the California Automobile Association because they gave her freedom: "When I didn't have to bend, I just said, 'Whee!'"

Fisher's family was not impressed by her prolific writings, nor did they understand why she had a byline when writing for magazines. "Now newspaper editors sign their own stories and editorials, but in father's time they didn't." She remembers a family dinner when "I asked casually, 'How did you like my last book?' It must have been my seventh. Mother said, 'We saw that book, didn't we Rex? It was very nice.' He said, 'Yes, I think it's around somewhere.' I said 'God damn it!' There was a hushed silence and father said, 'You may leave the table.' I slammed the door and began to laugh and then everybody laughed." But "they still didn't remember the book or take it seriously. My father wrote 2,000 words a day for sixty-five years at least—he was working on a paper when he was nine or ten. If there was extra space, Grandma turned out a sonnet. You never signed anything. Then I signed myself. O dear. But I had to earn a living."

Fisher had taken several phone calls ("Not this week, dear. Monday'd be marvelous. Come and have lunch with me. I have to go to work at two.") and received a visitor during our morning interview, a neighbor who stopped in to bring her a bouquet of large yellow mums. Chris then summoned us to lunch, helping his grandmother navigate the wheelchair into the kitchen/living/dining room, a large room with enormous windows that open onto distant mountains on two sides and a descending slope on the third. As Chris served us a light gourmet lunch that began with ginger broth followed by brown bread, cheese, and pasta—and of course wine—Fisher told the story of the building of her house in 1970. "I knew I would live here for the rest of my life. I sold my house in St. Helena for $25,000 and gave the architect [her friend David Bouverie, who invited her to build on his ranch] the check and said, 'Goodbye. I want two rooms and a big bathroom.' When I came back the house was almost built. It's a terribly selfish house because it doesn't have any bedroom for

anybody but me. Have you seen the bathroom?" I had seen the
enormous bathroom with its huge tub, plants, and long counter. "I
don't believe in the American idea that a bathroom should be a nasty
little hole. We spend a lot of time in the bathroom doing our hair and
our nails." I thought of the descriptions in *Among Friends* of Fisher
and her sisters as little girls playing in the bathtub of their Whittier
home while their father stood naked humming and shaving.

As we chatted over lunch Fisher's image of herself as writer
became clearer. Although her short fiction is brilliantly crafted, she
does not think of herself as a fiction writer. She related that during a
period of boredom in school "I started to fabricate stories. I got rid of
all of them so that when I finally had to write a novel I couldn't. My
husband and my publisher said that every writer has one novel in
him or her, but I didn't have a novel in my system, so I invented a
character who's the exact opposite of me, the eternal bitch, destruc-
tive, cruel." (Jennie, the central character of *Not Now But Now* is a
beautiful, elusive woman who travels through time and social class,
seeking selfish, often material satisfactions).

Fisher is puzzled when people describe her as a cookbook writer.
And she is right, for her books are in fact reflections upon the rituals
of eating, essays on the cuisines of various times and places. Asked
if men have written broadly and intelligently about food, she named
two classical writers from ancient Rome before realizing that I had the
present in mind. "Lots of homosexuals now write very well about
food. Elizabeth David writes well, too, although her recipes are
sometimes hard to follow because she assumes everyone knows as
much as she does about the methods and techniques. She's the kind
of intuitive cook who tells you to mix ingredients until it feels right."
I recalled Fisher's own essays on wonderfully vague Elizabethan
recipes. "One of the Elizabethan recipes I loved said in making a
sponge cake you put your elbow in the oven, and if it burns it's time
to put the cake in instead of your elbow."

When I confessed that improvising usually leads me into culinary
disaster, Fisher acknowledged the value of precision in a cookbook.
"Julia Child is a case in point. If you follow her exactly, word for
word, you can't possibly fail. If you know nothing, you can follow her
and produce a beautiful thing. A lot of people say, 'I'll just skip this or
that' and they fail. I can't follow her exactly because she bores me

silly. I now use Mrs. Rombauer's *The Joy of Cooking* and Julia's two books. If I had to have just one book I'd have *Joy*. I have several editions; now they're into microwave and deep freeze." Fisher does not have a microwave because of concerns for safety, but "My daughter, who is a stage manager, uses one because she always has rehearsal or try-outs. She takes off one day a week or every ten days and cooks all day and puts it all in order. She has everything ready, and it's all good food, no preservatives."

As we were finishing lunch with exotic chocolates, Fisher took the fifth phone call since my arrival. "That was Judith Jones in New York. She's going to Provence. *Omni* wants to interview me about the cities of the future. My view is very dim. Judith told me that the *Omni* people were quite prepared for that."

The topic of cities and the upcoming California election with the AIDS disclosure proposition on the ballot led us to contemporary issues. "I have two tickets to the Nutcracker Suite and [the money is] to go to AIDS through the church. The Catholics and the Episcopalians, the stuffiest churches in the world, are doing the best work for AIDS. I was Christian and Episcopalian, but I don't like to be labeled as such. Neither do I have AIDS, but I've been tested for years because I took a batch of bad blood which a woman died from. Nine people got the same batch. That would make an interesting story. Nobody died except this one woman, who was a deaconess in some Pentecostal group. She said, 'I have AIDS' long before anyone had even heard of it. She died in 1984, in the worst possible way, and her church quite properly made a great heroine of her. So we were all tested *every* few months, then every six months. Now we're clear. Most people are unbelievably ignorant about AIDS. Somebody told me the other day to put newspaper on the toilet seats. I said, 'Who are you and where have you been?'"

M.F.K. Fisher knows who she is and where she has been. With a past rich enough to live in, she has chosen to live fully in the present. She was preparing to vote in the upcoming general election, having reached decisions on the complex propositions for which California is famous. "I'm a Democrat and usually vote straight ticket. I'll vote no on [the cigarette tax] because, although I don't smoke, I defend the right to choose. I was not in favor of Prohibition; nobody voted it in."

Her social calendar, kept by her phone, must rival that of Barbara

Bush. And who would not seek out the company of this woman? Her dialogues during phone conversations revealed both wit and courage: "How are you? I have a brace on now. . . . The doctor said it was to remind me so I wouldn't have to go to hospital again, and I said, 'It's very expensive . . . this is the second time around. . . . Why couldn't you put a string around my finger?' He said the more it cost the more I'd remember. I wish you'd come and sit for a while. The 15th? I'll mark that down right now. Let's have lunch together. . . . I don't cook now but my grandson's here." I was reminded of Fisher's own borrowing from Alexander Pope's translation of Homer for the title of one of her books: "Here let us feast, and to the feast be joined discourse, the sweeter banquet of the mind."

table for saying something that he considered obscene. I was, oh, fourteen."

"Do you remember the word?" I asked, sure that no one ever forgets this high point in life, the unexpected escape of the first swearword in the presence of the horrified-speechless parents, the end of innocence, their innocence.

"Oh, yes," she said, one pinkie stuck elegantly into the air as she lifted her wine glass slowly, with real grace. "Turd."

For a moment even I was caught off guard. It was, to put it mildly, not her sort of word. She looked so queenly this day, due in part to the majesty of the surroundings. She took them on, like a chameleon, using them for effect and for fun.

"That was nothing," she was explaining, "compared to this bastard business."

"Bastard?" Obviously she had decided that, in this impeccably proper setting, something a little scabrous would add just the right note: She proceeded blithely from *turd* to *bastard*.

"I was misquoted," she protested, before I even knew what she was referring to. "Nevertheless, everyone in Whittier was scandalized," she went on, smiling.

"In Whittier?" I was confused.

She explained that her childhood hometown had recently held its centennial and that she was invited as one of the towns's eminent *émigrées*. This event struck me as the kind of affair she loves to be invited to so she can say no. But for some reason she accepted. Perhaps it was the fact that her fiftieth publishing anniversary coincided with the one hundredth anniversary of the small Quaker town in which she spent her childhood and about which she wrote *Among Friends*. Or maybe it was the promised accommodations, at the Whittier Hilton.

"The Whittier Hilton," she says, chuckling. "Can you imagine? They don't even realize how funny it is, the idea of a Hilton in Whittier. Rex would have died laughing." She laughed out loud, maybe the way he would have.

"It was a very modern hotel, you know. The very latest buttons to push, everything electronic. Nothing like this place." She waved her right hand up and down, to make sure I was getting her point. The

"Oh, yes, well," she came back quickly, clearing her throat. "Well, someone quoted me as saying that all Quakers were bastards. What I really said was that *some* Quakers are bastards, and *some* are very nice." She fussed a bit more about this inequity, pulling her black fringed shawl about her, muttering the name Cleveland Amory as the culprit responsible for the alleged misquote in his review of *Among Friends*.

Nevertheless, she is the first to admit that in her family it is an honored tradition to get in trouble because of one's ornery words. A fifth-generation writer with Scottish and Irish newspaper people loitering among her heritage, she follows a great-grandfather whose leaflets against Queen Victoria won him a death sentence (he got out, so she says, just in time) and a midwestern grandfather whose provocative editorials impelled him toward a peripatetic life style, to escape the wrath of the offended. Rex's newspaper career also had its pugilistic aspects, though through no fault of his own.

"Rex started out in Chicago as a goon for Colonel McCormick," she said, and I said, "A goon? For Colonel who?"

It seems that Rex went to work for Colonel McCormick at the "other" Chicago newspaper—"the one not owned by William Randolph Hearst," she explained—the *Chicago Tribune*.

"The delivery boys from the Hearst newspaper would beat up the boys who delivered Colonel McCormick's *Trib*. The Hearst forces outnumbered the colonel's boys three to one. Finally Colonel McCormick enlisted the services of two of his reporters, who also happened to be former football players from the University of Chicago—Rex and his brother Walt—to protect the *Trib*'s delivery boys.

"McCormick called them Stagg's men, after their coach's name, Amos Alonzo Stagg.

"Uncle Walt was built like a ton of bricks, broad shoulders," she described, pulling up her shoulders and upper arms to simulate her uncle's quarter ton of billowing hulk but looking more like a baby wren about to fly for the first time. "Whereas Rex," she laughed with an affectionate sigh, "well, he had the broad shoulders, all right, but he was thinner, much thinner; long bones, you know."

I tried to imagine him, remembering some pictures I'd seen.

"He was only on the team at the University of Chicago because he came in after Walt, who was the big star, but the coach wanted Rex on the team, too. Stagg was very powerful, 'the old man of football,' they called him."

Not only did the brothers manage to protect McCormick's newboys from the Hearst "thugs," but they made a big impression on William Randolph himself.

"Hearst always hated Rex from then on. All through his career."

In true Kennedy fashion, her father and uncle did eventually leave town. They moved on to Albion, Michigan, where they bought and ran *The Albion Recorder.* It was the kind of town where the fire department hooked up its hoses and sprayed the Kennedy home to cool it down on the day Mary Frances was born, July 3, 1908.

"It was a sweltering hot day," Mary Frances recounted with all the detail of a reporter assigned to cover the event instead of the infant being born. "It was Rex who got them to do it." About two years later Rex decided to leave this town also and to sever the four-generation thread of newspaperism. He sold his interest in the paper to his brother.

"He decided he wanted to become a geologist." Mary Frances announced in the resigned, airless voice that women use to describe the catacylsmic, tradition-shattering, crackpot schemes of the men they have had to contend with. "And so we went to Puget Sound."

"Oh, Washington?" I said, trying to imagine her in the wilds of the Pacific Northwest. "Did you like it there?"

"I was about two," she informed me, her eyes looking away from mine as if she was trying to think of something else. "I don't remember much of it."

"And did he really work as a geologist up there?"

"No, he was mostly a beachcomber. Mother, too. The whole thing was an attempt to escape the family destiny, journalism. They stayed there till the money ran out."

I was curious about how he was then able to buy the Whittier town paper.

"Grandmother Holbrook bought it for him," she explained. "He ran it, of course."

He must have been more tactful about his opinions than his fore-bears, since the family was never run out of Whittier. They didn't have to be run out, judging from Mary Frances's descriptions of

Quaker attitudes in Whittier; they could stay right where they were and be effectively excluded. Maybe that's what she meant by "bastards." At any rate, Rex's opinions and preferences within their household had lasting effects. Not only did they continue to this day, helping to prevent unruly daughters like Mary Frances from robbing banks, but they were responsible for her very name as a writer: M. F. K. Fisher.

"You see, I'd sold a story to *Westways* magazine for money," she explained, sounding guiltier than any mere bank robber. "I used the byline Fisher because I didn't want my father to know that I had taken money. I got ten dollars for the story, but I got twenty-five for the drawings."

"When was this?" I asked, imagining she must have been a young child but realizing that it had to have been after she married Al Fisher, or she wouldn't have had his name to pin on at the end.

"Oh, about 1934," she said. "I guess I was twenty-five, twenty-six," she added, getting my point.

"Of course, it was silly to think I could avoid my father, since he had helped found the damn thing." Some of his friends had started *Westways* as a kind of house organ for the Southern California Automobile Association.

"That started the whole damn silly business about M. F. K. Fisher," she said. Naturally many people—including, at first, Hamish Hamilton, the publisher of her first book—thought M. F. K. Fisher was a man. "He was astonished to meet me," she said with a selfish-satisfied smirk.

"So I was very 'ambisexual' from the word go, I guess," she said wistfully, enigmatically.

"Do you think things would have worked this way for someone named Mary Kennedy?" I asked with a teasing smile, trying to imagine her decked out in such tame and ordinary nomenclature as these, her maiden names.

"I tried to change it," she said, but once she was becoming known, it was futile. "But I am Mary Frances, not MFK," she asserted. "When people call me that, I know they don't know me at all."

I ask her about her mother's name; was she ever nicknamed EOHK?

"Edith Oliver Holbrook Kennedy," she pronounced, acknowledging that her mother's four-part name might have whetted her own interest in elongated strings of anonymous initials. But she never gives her mother much credit or dwells on Edith for very long. One exception was the story she told next, about how Edith "cornered the market" on the town librarians, getting them to order the books she thought should be available.

"And every Christmas she would give them nightgowns, big, white, expensive. They never saw anything like it. And when Mother died . . ."—she stopped to calculate—"thirty-five or forty years later, one of the librarians wrote me a letter telling me how wonderful those nightgowns were.

"Still, they never would order copies of Krafft-Ebing's *Psychopathia Sexualis* or Radclyffe Halls' *Well of Loneliness* or anything too lesbian, Freudian, or sexual. So she bought them herself."

"Your mother bought books for the library?" I asked.

"No, for our home." She answered curtly but with a provocative incompletion in her voice. I fell into this trap, as always. "And why did she want them?" I asked, unaware that I was about to discover something about the boarding school that Edith shipped her eldest daughter off to in her early teens.

"All the girls fell in love with me," she said flatly with a shrug. "And most of the teachers, too. I was attractive to them, for some reason."

When she came home and told her mother, Edith advised her to read a few of those books. But they didn't have them in the library, so Edith bought them herself.

"Wasn't she upset to discover that she had put you in that situation?" I asked, trying to imagine my own mother accepting with equanimity such a revelation about the bastion of chastity, Sacred Heart Academy, that I attended.

"Oh, no. She *knew*." She said it like that, emphasis on *knew*. She went on to say that she had never really minded going to boarding school, which she attended with her younger sister Annie. It was better than being a mother to the two little ones, Norah and David, whom she felt she had charge of since the day they were born.

"I feel like I became a mother when I was nine years old. After Norah and David were born, Mother took to her bed."

I was not unaware, and neither was she, that statements like these have prompted analyses of her work that approach Freudian proportions. And though she protests that she never reads anything

written about her, favorable or otherwise, somehow she manages
to get all the details and innuendos of any reference to her. Furthermore, she always has ready a saber-sharp reply. One of these probes
into her privately held psychology elicited the response: "I started to
read it; I just howled," followed by her own précis of the author:
"She's the one who should be analyzed . . . like most doctors." So
I said nothing too presumptuous, even when she summed up with
tempting, double-dare-you bait like "I loved my mother, and I—"
And then she stopped and started over: "Well, I didn't love her, but
I thought she was a fascinating woman."

Rex, on the other hand, seems to have been fascinating as well as
loved; he was a force, a presence, from morning till night. Her body
loosened up and her face relaxed when she returned to Rex and how
he "always read three newspapers at the breakfast table." She described how he would sit down and perfunctorily ask how they all
were.

"We would always say fine, fine." She recounted the scene: four
child-sized heads bobbing around the table. Except that one morning
her brother said he wasn't feeling well. This tremendous break in
protocol was so upsetting her father put down the paper and addressed little David directly. From her nuances, not her words, I got
the feeling Rex was more disturbed at the rift in routine than by her
brother's health. At any rate, David dutifully reiterated his sick
feelings, excused himself, and went back up to bed. At that point
everything returned to normal. Balance was reestablished. All was
right with the world, except possibly for David.

The next time they would see each other was at the dinner table.
But the important things happened later, not at dinner but just after.

"Where shall we go tonight?" Rex would ask. Edith would leave
the table to seclude herself in "her little apartment," as Mary Frances
called it, just off the dining room. Then Mary Frances and Rex would
go on their white-wine trips.

"Mother would always retire from these discussions. She called
them arguments."

They seemed to be more like flights of fancy, imaginary excursions
that they would plan around the world or to some specific island in
the Caribbean. Their fantasized itineraries included the chartering of
old freighters and leisurely travels down to the Panama Canal.

"Rex loved going to Mexico," Mary Frances sighed, a small catch in her voice. Eventually one of these white-wine trips turned into a reality.

"We kidnapped Rex once," she chuckled, her not-so-latent outlaw instincts surfacing once again. The whole family was in on it, plus a friend who was the captain of a Swedish freighter. Before Rex knew what was happening, he and Edith were out to sea, heading for the heretofore imaginary canal and, ultimately, Amsterdam and Switzerland.

"That was a white-wine trip that really took off," she laughed, adding a bit sadly, "but they were all very real when they happened."

For a moment I felt as if I might soon be on a white-wine trip of my own as I finished the last crisp drop in my glass and watched her refilling it. The feeling was sufficiently fortifying to allow me to make an analogy that had been lurking. I told her about sitting around the after-dinner table in my family. I would try to engage my father in conversation, not only because it was interesting to talk to him about something—current events, mythology, science—but also because my mother, if I was involved with my father, would eventually decide she might as well do the dishes alone. Most of all, I enjoyed the role reversal: taking my mother's place as a companion at the dinner table, and having her take my place as the washer of the dishes. Mary Frances laughed and shook her head, as if recognizing the similarity of our experiences.

"Yes, I see what you mean," she said, "but that wasn't my situation. For one thing, Father had a rule that we never spoke at table about politics, sex, or religion. And also, Mother was present the whole time, even though she was in the next room."

She would go off to read her book. "She was always reading a book. You know, pretending to read. But she was listening the whole time. We could hear her chuckling in there once in a while."

She never had the sense of monopolizing her father that I did.

"To tell the truth, I once wrote a poem about it," I confessed, narrowing my eyes as I tried to squeeze the words out of my Chardonnayed brain. "Dad ate green grapes. Mom cleared the table, and I started avoiding the dishes by asking my father, 'How come . . . ?'" But that was all I could remember, or wanted to.

"I'll send it to you some time," I offered, half in jest.

"I look forward to reading it, dear," she smiled.

I went back to concentrating on her wine trips. Were they prescient or casual, I wondered for a moment, remembering all the freighters and ships she did travel on as soon as she left home: her first ship, the *Berengaria,* which she took with her new husband, Al Fisher, to Dijon; then back to California on the Cunard line; later the Italian freighter *Feltre;* a Dutch passenger freighter; the *Ile de France,* the *De Grasse*; the *Normandie*—all within a decade or so. Her white-wine trips were like programming; her life, wish fulfillment.

Did she choose to leave the country to live her life for the same reason she would choose to leave the country to rob a bank: so she wouldn't embarrass Rex? Or maybe she had to be truly out of his reach in order to flourish on her own? While I teetered dangerously on these foggy psychoanalytical precipices, Mary Frances began to describe another of Rex's domains: the spanking department.

When he came home from work, her mother would indicate which of the children required paddling, and he would execute the deed. With the girls—and there were three out of four—the paddling stopped, for modesty's sake, at a fairly young age.

"Thus allowing criminal tendencies to flourish unchecked in those of the girls so inclined," I added with a kind of Sherlock Holmes coups de grace.

That was only one of the good things about being a girl of a certain age, it turned out. Shortly afterward Mary Frances went off to boarding school and decided to write her father a letter. In it she asked a question she hadn't dared ask in person: could she call him Rex?

"He wrote back and said all his friends call him Rex. And I was his friend. So, yes, why shouldn't I call him Rex?"

She reported this with a look of total satisfaction, bashful and proud. She has been calling him Rex ever since, every chance she gets.

M. F. K. Fisher

Ruth Reichl/1991

From *The Los Angeles Times*, 6 June 1991, in the Home Edition, Food Section, pg. 1+. © 1991 *The Los Angeles Times*.

". . . the most interesting philosopher of food now practicing in our country."

—Clifton Fadiman

"She writes about fleeting tastes and feasts vividly, excitingly, sensuously, exquisitely."

—James Beard

"M.F.K. Fisher is our greatest food writer because she puts food in the mouth, the mind and the imagination all at the same time."

—Shana Alexander

"I do not consider myself a food writer."

—M. F. K. Fisher

Mary Frances Kennedy Fisher lies in her bed, propped up on pillows, eating oysters.

At 84, it is one of the few sensual pleasures left to the woman whose impeccable prose introduced two generations of Americans to what she called the "Art of Eating." Her genius has been her absolute insistence that life's small moments are the important ones. "People ask me," she wrote, in the most-quoted passage from her 30 books, "why do you write about food, and eating and drinking?" The answer: "There is a communion of more than our bodies when bread is broken and wine drunk."

Fisher's own body has, at this moment, betrayed her. Her voice has been reduced to an almost inaudible whisper, her hands cannot write much more than a signature, and her eyes no longer permit her to read. Movement is difficult. If any of this bothers her, she would not deign to show it; she is as imposing now as she was when I interviewed her for the first time 15 years ago.

"But how will you talk to her?" people have asked with alarm. These days her many visitors (Cyra McFadden was here yesterday; Alice Waters will be here the day after tomorrow) tend to come in packs and, in entertaining one another, entertain their hostess. What

198

I found is that conversation is no problem: M. F. K. Fisher is still so intense that she virtually wills you to understand her whispers.

"Please don't whisper" is almost the first thing she says. Visitors unconsciously lower their own voices until they are no louder than hers. But Fisher will not suffer condescension. The sounds are soft on her Sonoma ranch: occasionally a beeper gives out a peremptory honk, and there is the swish of cars moving on the road below, but the loudest noises are the quiet murmur of the television in the nurse's bedroom next door, the radio's gay, if slightly incongruous, tinkle in the living room and the thunk of the cats as they land on Fisher's bed. Into this silence her whispered command has the effect of a shout.

Things are awkward at first. She begins by putting down the oyster, sipping on a mysterious pink drink and talking—if these all-but-inaudible mouthings can be called talk—about the two new books she has just published. These are *The Boss Dog,* stories about life in Aix-en-Provence in the '50s with her two young daughters that make you wish, with all your heart, that you could have been there with her, and *Long Ago in France,* a compilation of stories from the '30s when Fisher was young, in love and living in Dijon.

She accepts congratulations for her election—just announced—to the American Academy of Arts and Letters. She says—as she always does to people who ask—that she does not consider herself a writer. (Asked which of her own books is her favorite, she has always taken the most modest route and chosen *The Physiology of Taste*: "I didn't write that, you know. Brillat-Savarin did. I just translated it," she says for what must be the hundredth time.)

Fisher goes on to say that she is working on three new books, dictating every morning when her voice is strongest. "Writing is just like dope," she says. "I have to get my fix every day." She gestures off toward the corner of the room, where there are stacks of boxes, overflowing with papers. "There are thousands of pages. It's impossible to put into order," she says with a little sniff of disdain, as if this were something of which she were vaguely ashamed.

"I've always written naturally," she says now, as if that minimized her accomplishment. "It was just something I did." She insists that writing is so much a part of her that even her children Anne and

Kennedy, to whom she refers as "nice girls," never thought of her as a writer.

Can this be true? I wonder, leaving Fisher's bedroom to allow her to rest for a while. I wander around the living room/kitchen—looking at the art. On the door is a 1953 poster of Aix-en-Provence and on the wall by the refrigerator some canvases done by Fisher's second husband, unframed. There are lots of books—art books, a life of Isabella d'Este, *Little Women,* some Sylvia Plath, a copy of *Mrs. Bridge.* There are a few cookbooks, too—signed from James and Julia and Craig. The only copies of her own books I can find are the ones in fancy bindings that publishers bestow upon their authors at Christmas. I find a copy of *The Gastronomical Me,* and as I sit down to read it, the smaller of the two calicos jumps onto my lap.

Fisher's prose is so good, so strong, that in seconds I am with her in France—just married and falling in love with food. Later I will ask, "Why did you marry so young?" and she will reply, "To get the hell away from home."

Fisher's books are mostly autobiographical; her millions of readers know that she was brought up in Whittier, and that her father, Rex Kennedy, ran a newspaper. They know that she married a man named Al Fisher (who later became the dean of English at Smith College) and went with him to study in France. And that from 1929 to 1939 she seemed to bounce back and forth between France and California and cook and eat and drink a lot of really wonderful food and wine and somehow get divorced and married again. But let her tell it.

"Paris was everything that I had dreamed, the late September when we first went there. It should always be seen, the first time, with the eyes of childhood, or of love. I was almost 21, but much younger than girls are now, I think. And I was wrapped in a passionate mist."

And in *The Gastronomical Me* this is now she described her first serious meal in France:

"We ate the biggest as well as the most exciting meal that either of us had ever had. As I remember, it was not difficult to keep on, to feel a steady avid curiosity. Everything that was brought to the table was so new, so wonderfully cooked, that what might have been with sated palates a gluttonous orgy was, for our fresh ignorance, a constant refreshment. I know that never since have I eaten so much.

But that night the kind ghosts of Lucullus and Brillat-Savarin as well as Rabelais and a hundred others stepped in to ease our adventurous bellies, and soothe our tongues. We were immune, safe in a charmed gastronomical circle."

Back in the bedroom, inadvertently whispering again, I show Fisher the book. She looks at the photo on the jacket—a head shot with eyes almost closed and long hair thrown back—she says, "That's rare, you know. They pulled that jacket after the first edition. The picture was considered too sexy."

No wonder, I say, and read her the passage underneath: "He had hung all my favorite pictures, and there was a present for me on the low table, the prettiest Easter present I have ever seen. It was a big tin of Beluga caviar, in the center of a huge pale-yellow plate, the kind sold in the market on saints' days in Vevey, and all around the tin and then the edge of the plate were apple blossoms. I think apple blossoms are perhaps the loveliest flowers in the world, because of their clarity and the mysterious way they spring so delicately from the sturdy darkness of the carved stems, with the tender little green leaves close around them. At least they were the loveliest that night, in the candlelight, in the odd-shaped room so full of things important to me."

"Oh pooh," she snorts, "that's not sexy." She says it as if there must be some unfathomable generational divide between us, if I could find sexiness in a passage such as this. "They put another picture by George Hurell on the cover after that," she muses. "He was a friend. He's been taking pictures of me all my life. He used to come to Laguna Beach and eat with us and take pictures of us because he didn't have any money to pay models. He was a darling little Jewish boy. He lives quite near here now; he came two or three years ago and took a lot more pictures of me."

Fisher stares at the photo for a while, then says, "That wasn't my first book, you know."

Her first book was *Serve It Forth* ("a book about eating, and about what to eat and about people who eat"). Fisher wrote it in one of those times when she was between jaunts to France. "After Al got his doctorate," she reminisces now, "we came back from Dijon and lived in my family's beach shack at Laguna Beach. Today we would have been called far-out hippies, I think, but then we were just victims of the Depression. I was always writing, but I never sold anything. Al was writing the Great American Novel. Then Al got a job in Occidental College. He was earning $650 a year. I got a job in a postcard shop in the afternoon, but every morning I went to the library and worked on the book."

Afterwards, she says, she'd come home and show what she'd written to her husband. "I have to write towards somebody I love. Express myself as that person I love would want me to be. I've never written just for myself. That's like kissing yourself, don't you think?"

Her husband, in turn, showed it to author/painter Dillwyn Parrish, who lived next door. "He picked up little pieces and sent them to his sister Anne, who was a famous writer. She was the one who sent it to a publisher. I didn't even know it had been published until Mother and Father came to Europe in '37 and told me."

This is, of course, more of Fisher's slightly unbelievable modesty. She must, after all, have signed a contract for the book before it was published? "I guess I did," she says dismissively, "I don't remember."

What she does remember is that by the time the book was published she was living with Dillwyn Parrish, who became her second husband. Parrish was the great love of her life, and her most wonderful stories are about being with him in Europe. Fisher unhesitatingly says that of all the times in her life, "I liked being with Timmie (Parrish) the most."

Fisher wrote her third book, Consider the Oyster, "to amuse Timmie." She pauses. "He died just before I finished it," she whispers. And then asks me to leave so she can rest again.

This time I poke into her cookbooks. ("Food still tastes good, but I don't get much of it," she has just said. "I eat to live now. It doesn't matter much.")

The books are all well used and carefully annotated in her small, precise handwriting. Actually, the meals I remember sharing with Fisher have all been simple ones. Once she made me split pea soup and served it with sourdough bread with sweet butter and fruit compote and two kinds of shortbread cookies. A couple of times there have been salads. Once I brought her some caviar, and I could tell from her comments about liking to eat it best with a spoon that there wasn't enough to please her. Always there has been wine.

Fisher is as unpretentious about wine as she is about food. "Nobody with any humility would consider himself a connoisseur," she once told me. "I know red from white and I think I know good from bad and I know the phonies from the real, and that's about it."

But wine has always been one of her real pleasures. Now Fisher sends the nurse out to press some wine on me. "Mary Frances wants you to know that it's in the refrigerator," she says. And indeed it is—four different kinds of white wine, all local.

"I have almost always lived near vineyards," says Fisher when I go back into the bedroom, wine glass in hand. "That's where I have been happiest."

Where she has been unhappiest is in Los Angeles. "I was horrified when I discovered that you were moving down there," she whispers. "I myself had to get out."

Fisher's Hollywood period was in the mid-'40s, during her third marriage (to publisher Donald Friede). "It was a short, dumb but good marriage," she begins. "We were living in Hollywood mostly, and commuting to the house in Hemet 120 miles away. We had two kids, two houses and a very social life. Life was too hectic." Before long Fisher is painting a picture of herself frantically trying to keep up—and not doing a very good job.

"Then Donald got me into the translation of *Physiology of Taste*. I did it," she says firmly, "under duress."

Fisher admits—has always admitted—that she is pleased with the translation. Even before she did it she wrote, "There are two kinds of books about eating: those that try to imitate Brillat-Savarin's and those that try not to." But although the book was immediately acclaimed, Friede was not satisfied; what he really wanted his wife to do was write a novel.

"He thought every writer had one novel in him, but God, no, I'm not a novelist." She grimaces a little. "I wrote my first novel when I was 9. I wrote a chapter a day, and I would tell it to my family after lunch. It was about love, with a nurse, a sailor—all things I didn't know about. They laughed. Finally I realized that they were really laughing at me—and that I was not a novelist."

Pressed into fiction once again, Fisher "tried to choose a woman who was the opposite of me—to be everything I wasn't. It really is just short stories nailed together."

The book, *Not Now But Now,* was published in 1947. It didn't sell.

The same year, Fisher divorced Friede. "I didn't contest anything. I just wanted the kids. He was delighted."

The two remained friends, and it was Friede ("finally accepting that I could never be a novelist") who came up with the idea of reprinting five of Fisher's books as one volume: *The Art of Eating.* "In 1954," says Fisher, with just an edge of bitterness, "he decided that I was through. He wanted me to be a bestseller and I wasn't. So he issued the book. He's very pleased; it's never been out of print."

It's hard now to imagine how Fisher, a single mother with two children and not much money, managed to live on what a free-lance writer makes. She wrote for dozens of publications—*Vanity Fair, House Beautiful, Gourmet*—articles for which she was never particularly well paid, and for which she never once received an expense check. "They just didn't do it in those days," she says. She wrote for the *New Yorker,* too—their vaunted generosity amounted to a retainer of $50 a year.

For a while Fisher worked for her father at the newspaper. "When Rex died, he left us some money, and then Donald's mother died and left the kids $200 a month and in 1958 we went to Europe for four years. The money went far in Europe—and I wanted my girls to learn other ways and other languages."

Lots of wonderful books have subsequently come out of those years. But during the '50s themselves, Fisher was so busy writing for magazines that she published no new books. Even in 1961, when she wrote *A Cordiall Water,* a book about folk medicine, it was just to fill a pressing financial need: "Anne wanted to go to a party and she needed a dress, so I sent the book off to Little, Brown."

The next year Fisher came back to California, to a big house in St. Helena. But her children were ready to move away—and Fisher soon embarked on the one period of her life that she has never written about.

"Tell me about Mississippi," I plead.

"Let me rest awhile," she replies.

I wander onto the sun porch, a comfortably shabby sort of room filled with weathered furniture and books with curling covers. The cat nuzzles at my ankles, demanding that I sit down and make a lap. She looks sleek and well fed; no wonder. "I wouldn't feed them anything I wouldn't eat myself," Fisher had said earlier.

I grab the copy of *The Gastronomical Me* and begin to read my favorite of her stories. It is the one called "Define This Word," about wandering into a restaurant in a remote French village and falling into the clutches of a waitress so passionate about her work that Fisher fears she is never going to be allowed to leave the restaurant. I reach the part where the chef sends out the dessert: "With a stuffed careful smile on my face and a clear nightmare in my head of trussed wanderers prepared for the altar by this hermit-priest of gastonomy, I listened to the girl's passionate plea for fresh dough. 'You cannot serve old pastry!' the waitress is crying"—when the nurse comes to call me back into the room.

"Mississippi?" I ask. Fisher sighs. "In 1964 the kids were all gone and I thought I'd find out if the South was as bad as I thought. So I went to teach at the Piney Woods School."

Piney Woods was a school for black students; the faculty, says Fisher, was half black and half white. She taught English. "The South was worse than I expected. I didn't go to town at all while I was there."

But why did she go in the first place? Did she plan to write a book, to fight a fight? She looks slightly horrified. "God, no, I wasn't planning on writing anything about it. And I didn't go there to fight anything. I just went."

Fisher smiles a little, remembering. "I found it took six months before the kids would eyeball me. But after six months I was without color, and so were they." She smiles. "I was not invited back," she adds with a certain amount of pride, "because I was a trouble maker." She seems pleased by this, and then abruptly stops talking.

"Did you write anything?" I prod. She nods towards the boxes. Of course, she wrote something; she has written all her life. "It's in there," she says. "Marsha Moran (the woman to whom she dictates her work every day) has all that stuff—she can do what she wants with it. I don't like to talk about it." Clearly the subject is closed.

The nurse walks in just then; she is carrying more oysters. They have been baked with a spinach topping, a sort of Rockefeller preparation. "Eating is difficult for her," she told me earlier, "but anything with oysters, she has no trouble at all."

The nurse puts down the tray. Mary Frances Fisher looks at the oysters with both longing and distaste; they are very large. She smiles

up at me and whispers, knowing that the nurse can't hear her: "You
know, it's a shame. Most people can't cook very well."

I look at Fisher. I look at the oysters. Suddenly a line from one of
Fisher's books flashes through my head. "Oysters," I find myself
thinking, "are very unsatisfactory food for labouring men, but will do
for the sedentary, and for a supper to sleep on."

Index